The Radical Imagination
and the Liberal Tradition
Interviews with English and American Novelists

The Radical Imagination and the Liberal Tradition

Interviews with English and American Novelists

Edited by Heide Ziegler
and Christopher Bigsby

JUNCTION BOOKS   LONDON

First published in Great Britain by
Junction Books Ltd
15 St John's Hill
London SW11

ISBN 0 86245 052 7 (hard)
    0 86245 053 5 (paper)

The assistance of ACLS and USICA in the compilation of this book is
gratefully acknowledged.

The extract from 'The Man with the Blue Guitar' by Wallace Stevens is
reproduced from *Selected Poems of Wallace Stevens* by permission of
Faber and Faber Ltd, and from *The Collected Poems of Wallace Stevens*
by permission of Alfred A. Knopf, Inc.

Typeset by Photo-Graphics, Yarcombe, Devon, England.
Printed and bound in Great Britain at
The Camelot Press Ltd, Southampton

Contents

Preface

The last few years have seen an active debate about the changing nature of the novel, its function, its concerns, its relationship to the world which lies beyond the page. It is, of course, an issue whose basic terms reach at least as far back as Plato's condemnation of the artist, an issue that has been reformulated by every age: the problematic ethical status of the aesthetic. The contemporary version of the argument has become particularly vehement, however, thanks in part to the American novelist John Gardner, who sees a retreat from the moral function of art and a disengagement from the real — a substitution, in effect, of a radical imagination for a liberal tradition. And he names names: John Barth, Donald Barthelme, Robert Coover, Stanley Elkin, William Gass, John Hawkes. It is a view that has been endorsed by a number of critics, perhaps most notably by Gerald Graff. But, for the most part, the writers themselves have remained silent. And this was the starting point for this book, for we chose to interview precisely these writers (together with Gardner, whose work is much more equivocally located than he likes to imply). The intention, of course, was not simply to ask them to address themselves to this particular issue, but to solicit their own views on their work and on the craft of writing.

One curious thing about the contemporary debate has been its near obsession with American writers. Few critics have shown any interest in contemporary English writing, and yet such writers are surely relevant to any consideration of cultural change, of transformations in the literary sensibility. Accordingly, we decided to include a series of interviews with major English novelists —writers who might perhaps be thought more likely to lay claim to a liberal tradition but who have also manifestly responded to the same pressures, the same destabilizing insights, the same imaginative energies which characterize their American counterparts.

The interviews were conducted under widely different circumstances. Some were recorded and edited over a considerable period of time and involve a detailed response to individual texts. Others were recorded on the wing. One, at the request of the subject, was conducted by mail. In this context we would wish to thank the writers interviewed in this book for the patience and tolerance with which they responded to our questions, which on occasion may have been overly theoretical or hesitant. For us, conducting these interviews became an absorbing experience, and we hope that at least some of the fascination and immediacy will become evident in the reading.

Introduction

...since the one who writes recognizes, by the very fact that he takes the trouble to write, the freedom of his readers, and since the one who reads, by the mere fact of his opening the book, recognizes the freedom of the writer, the work of art, from whichever side you approach it, is an act of confidence in the freedom of men.

Jean-Paul Sartre, *What Is Literature?*

Poetry is the subject of the poem,
From this the poem issues and

To this returns. Between the two,
Between issue and return, there is

An absence in reality,
Things as they are. Or so we say.

Wallace Stevens, *The Man With the Blue Guitar*

In 1978 the novelist John Gardner published *On Moral Fiction*. It was, at base, an attack on postmodern literature and an assertion of the moral function of art:

In a world where nearly everything that passes for art is tinny and commercial and often, in addition, hollow and academic, I argue — by reason and by banging the table — for an old-fashioned view of what art is and does and what the fundamental business of critics ought therefore to be ... The traditional view is that true art is moral: it seeks to improve life, not debase it ... That art which tends towards destruction, the art of nihilists, cynics, and merdistes, is not properly art at all. Art is essentially serious and beneficial, a game played against chaos and death, against entropy.

On Moral Fiction is a polemical book which, at first glance, appears to be offered rather less as a reaction to the writers whom Gardner attacks (many of whom are interviewed in the following pages) than as a reaction against the critical orthodoxies of the 1970s, which seemed to his mind to overrate the anti-mimetic, the autotelic artifact whose primary virtue lay in its exemplification of theories which were amoral in themselves but immoral in their effect. His target was the 'structuralists, formalists, linguistic philosophers who tell us that works of art are like trees — simply objects for perception' and whose concern was only with 'definition, morality reduced to the positivist ideal of clarity'. To some degree the writers seem merely to have got in the way of the salvoes Gardner wished to fire at these critics, whose prescriptions were distorting the book market no less than morality.

But as the book proceeds, it becomes apparent that the writers, too, are on the firing line. Thus, William Gass is attacked for abandoning his attempts to 'revitalize the reader's consciousness' in favour of 'mere language — puns, rhymes, tortuously constructed barrages of verbiage with the words so crushed together that they do indeed become opaque as stones, not windows that allow us to see thoughts or events but walls where windows ought to be'. Coover is denounced for his supposed nihilism, Barthelme for his inability to penetrate beyond images of despair and loss, for caring more about ideas than people (an echo of Sartre's attack on Camus), which Gardner sees as less a failure of moral vision than as a species of romantic indulgence. With reservations he makes much the same point about Stanley Elkin, about the 'godless terror' of John Hawkes, and the irony of John Barth, who appears 'tangled hopelessly in his own writing'.

The premises of *On Moral Fiction* constantly change. Thus, the enemy is first seen as a soulless positivism, then as a decadent romanticism; literature is denounced for its nihilistic conception of the real, though it is precisely Gardner's own sense of the essential reductivism of contemporary existence which leads him to make his desperate plea for moral fiction. His own position is that art imitates process rather than fact and that it 'discovers *by its process* what it can say'; yet this defers to a vision of the real and the good as unproblematic. It would seem as though Gardner had never written the brilliant *Grendel*, which engages the mythopoeic world he suspects in Barth, which draws attention to its own fictive fragility, as does Coover's work, which confesses to the process whereby reality is linguistically constructed, much as does Gass, which acknowledges the entropic nature of existence, as does Barthelme, and which sees character and plot as contingent in the same way as Hawkes.

Why, then, take such a critique so seriously? After all, one of John Gardner's more endearing qualities has always been the obvious delight he takes in finding legitimate reasons for removing from the ring those he sees as his opponents until only he is left standing — a kind of bemused and reluctant hero of his own game, much like Hemingway and Mailer made gentle by his own obvious championship of the good and the beautiful. The answer is because he reveals an exposed nerve: he registers a widespread sense of unease. Modernist art had proposed its own coherences as a defence against anarchy — not confidently, it must be said, but with a desperate, stubborn conviction concerning the need for consonance. For the postmodernist, it seems, even this desperation has been surrendered. The imagination, it is implied, no longer presses back against the real, since reality has been exposed as no more than a series of competing fictions, experiences shaped by language and perceived through prismatic roles.

For Gardner it was necessary to assert the power and substance of another stance, that adopted by 'writers of the "liberal tradition", that is, writers concerned with discovering and passing on the values of a free society'. Though he is sparing with his definitions and even more sparing with his praise of other writers, it seems clear that by this formulation he means writers who continue to acknowledge their duty to confront man with an image of his moral choices, who regard the individual as more than an ironic possibility, and the notion of the other, to whom an ultimate responsibility is owed, as a necessary proposition, not a convenient fiction.

The question is whether there is any legitimacy to this division of ethics and aesthetics, dependent, as it is, on a series of assumptions about the nature and substance of freedom, on the degree to which Gardner's own analysis is immune to the very positivism which he attacks and to the romanticism of his own stance; whether the innovations of the radical imagination are indeed at odds with a liberal tradition. Certainly Gardner chooses to deny any force to the simple paradox whereby a realist text may itself be authoritarian in so far as it chooses to offer a confident model of the real, a model with genuine coercive power, while the postmodern text may be liberal in its narrative strategies, in its acknowledgement of a pluralism of realisms, in its recognition of the possibility of radical disruptions at the imaginative and perhaps subsequently at other levels.

Gore Vidal has a simple answer to this paradox. Though he did not use the word 'postmodernism', he argued, in an essay provocatively called 'The Hacks of Academe' which appeared in his book *Matters of Fact and of Fiction* (1977), that this kind of literature was the product of an unhealthy symbiosis between writer and critic, an offshoot of the professionalization of the study of literature. In a desire to justify their status and their subject, professors of literature, he suggested, favoured complexity much as fleas might vote for dogs. They displayed, in effect, a positivist bias, longing for a scientific methodology which could grant legitimacy to their work. He saw the pronouncements of American academic critics as simply parroting French theoreticians whose work they frequently misconstrued.* Thus, John Halperin's observation that 'modern theoretical novel-criticism ... is occupied less with the novel as a mimetic and moral performance than with the novel as an autonomous creation independent of or at least not wholly dependent upon the real world', accurate or not, is dismissed as a consequence of an insufficiently fastidious ontology and altogether too vigorous a flirtation with the harlotry of French intellectualism. But the worst sin was that such pronouncements tended to feed back into the novel like a snake swallowing its own tail.

Such assaults are easily dismissed, and certainly Vidal was defending his own aesthetic conservatism. Committed to the historical novel, he could hardly capitulate to an attack on mimesis or to theories of the self-sufficiency of the imagination. But though both Vidal's and Gardner's accounts derive much of their energy from a sense of pique, recast as moral affront or plain common sense, they do acknowledge a submerged debate about the nature of the real and about fiction's relation to it. Both argued that structuralist and poststructuralist critics, and even more so the academics who borrowed their language but not always their intellectual rigour, were altogether too confident in their analysis of a fictive universe of which art is merely one facet. They questioned where these critics derived their sense of authority and authenticity from if they had to present parody and a metafictive

---

*George Steiner has recently indicted what he calls 'the terrorism of jargon' in the work of poststructuralists and their Anglo-Saxon followers; the attempt to generate a set of critical hieroglyphs to usurp the status of the hieroglyphs of fiction and to deny the humanizing role of art.

reflexiveness as an honest confession of the fictive nature of experience and the fragility of art. And this was a question posed, with rather greater sophistication, by the critic Gerald Graff.

Graff, in *Literature Against Itself* (1979), does not reject structuralist and poststructuralist emphasis on textuality but insists that

> the fact that literature possesses an internal grammar of forms does not mean that this grammar cannot or ought not to be answerable to anything outside itself. The fact that meanings in general are products of artificial systems of signs does not necessarily discredit the enterprise of enquiring into the reference of these meanings to nonlinguistic states of affairs. And the fact that a critic does not have to be concerned with the truth-claims made by a literary work in order to proceed with his analysis — and produce a certain kind of critical article —does not necessarily mean that these truth-claims can be dismissed or turned into non-claims.

Once again, the argument, at this stage, seems to be more about criticism than the novel. And it certainly is a genuine question whether this form of criticism emerges as a response to changes in art, or whether we view this art in the way that we do because of the limited range of tools with which we set out to perform our analyses. As Graff points out, an increasing number of articles are being written which demonstrate that supposedly realist writers were themselves concerned with deconstructive processes, with casting doubt on their own premises, and with making assertions about the autonomous sphere of art. Many of these are, indeed, convincing. But, in so far as they are, they tend to diminish our sense of the innovative quality of recent fiction. Indeed the very idea of postmodern literature as innovative, in its self-referentiality, in its conscious retreat from mimesis, in its deconstruction of the traditional role of character, its view of the real as a series of competing fictions, is undermined by a postmodern criticism which implies that these have in a sense always been essential qualities of art.

Though Graff's analysis is more clearly argued and incisive than Gardner's, it is plain that at base it too rests on a moral objection. And by way of defence he suggests that the proponents of a fictionalist or linguistic approach to literature are themselves disguising moralism as intellectual rigour. For example, Graff takes Edward Said to task for identifying realism with conformity, and the non-mimetic with freedom and excitement. And certainly a number of such critics, and some of the novelists whose work they admire, could be accused of failing to enquire too far into the constraints which limit and define the freedoms claimed by fictions which ironize, but which do not thereby escape, the subtle tyrannies of the words they use. After all, the language they inherit bears the imprint of history and of ideological power as well as the possibilities of intertextual irony and wilful playfulness. It could be argued that Gass assembles words in such combinations as to try to sever their links with their own past. Yet he knows the pressure is always there for them to reassert their former shape; indeed, to some degree, this pressure is necessary for the work to create its innovative effect. The traditional import of words is indispensable to the willful act whereby their arbitrariness is exposed. Coover acknowledged no less in *A Public Burning*.

For Graff postmodernism finally comes to mean 'the movement within contemporary literature and criticism that calls into question the traditional claims of literature and art to truth and human value'. Moreover, postmodernism, or, rather, the criticism which it has provoked, expresses a bias against 'meaning', that gap between appearance and reality from which high art, as opposed to popular culture, was presumed to proceed. It has destroyed the ground upon which a moral order can be constructed. Thus, for Richard Poirier 'writing is a form of energy not accountable to the orderings anyone makes of it and specifically not accountable to the liberal humanitarian values most readers want to find there'; its only responsibility is to be compelling about its own inventions. Jorge Luis Borges conjectures that we indeed dream the world, while the novelist-critic Raymond Federman claims that 'fiction can no longer be reality, or a representation of reality, or an imitation, or even a recreation of reality; it can only be a REALITY — an autonomous reality whose only relation with the real world is to improve that world'.

Graff appears to fear a total relativism which, instead of validating possibilities, reduces a pluralism of perspectives to a mere anarchy of fictions, none of which can claim any authority in terms of human needs or values since these, too, are fictions with no status beyond themselves. In particular he has attacked those critics, and especially such figures as Susan Sontag, Leon Bersani and Richard Poirier, who presume that 'the psychic experimentalism of modern art is incompatible with the collective

goals of humanitarian social reform, whether liberal or socialist', and this, he implies, is some kind of final betrayal. But,
recently, the novelist critic Ronald Sukenick has challenged the
very premises of Graff's stance. Hinting at the historic failure
of liberal humanism to resist the totalitarian impulse he asks:

> Is it radical esthetics that encourages a mindless consumer
> society, or is it that conventional mimetic realism? ... Is the
> 'politics of the self' a way of reducing history to psycho-
> drama, or is it a quixotic attempt, in the absence of a viable
> politics, to salvage individual experience from the assaults of
> consumerist manipulation? Is it not all the more urgent,
> given the pressures of that manipulation, to present the
> reader with a literature that gives him models for a creative
> truth of 'construction' rather than a passive truth of 'corres-
> pondence'?

In other words, he accepts Graff's moral concern, but
suggests that it attaches itself to the wrong mode.

It is not a new debate. It is reminiscent of the Marxist
critic's struggle with modernism. Sartre and Adorno worked to
reconcile the notion of an autonomous literature with a moral
and political commitment by insisting on the realist bias of all
art. Thus Sartre, agreeing with Kant, observed that 'the work
of art ... *does not have* an end', insisting that 'it *is* an end' in
itself, but only in the sense that the Kantian formula does not
account 'for the appeal which issues from every painting, every
statue, every book'. On one level this was perhaps no more
than an assertion of the incorrigibly ideological nature of all
art, but there are hints here of a pressure for reconciliation
which goes even further in Adorno. Thus Adorno, too, insists
that

> the imagination of the artist is not a creation *ex nihilo*; only
> dilettanti and aesthetes believe it to be so. Works of art that
> react against empirical reality obey the forces of that reality,
> which reject intellectual creations and throw them back on
> themselves. There is no material content, no formal category
> of artistic creation, however mysteriously transmitted and
> itself unaware of the process, which did not originate in the
> empirical reality from which it breaks free.

But, in a surprising attempt to reconcile the postmodern impulse to a political stance, he balances this position against a view of Beckett, for example, which transcends the realism he seems to advocate. Thus:

> Philosophical apologists may laud his works as sketches from an anthropology. But they deal with a highly concrete historical reality: the abdication of the subject. Beckett's *Ecce Homo* is what human beings have become. As though with eyes drained of tears, they stare silently out of his sentences. The spell they cast, which also binds them, is lifted by being reflected in them. However, the minimal promise of happiness they contain, which refuses to be traded for comfort, cannot be had for a price less than total dislocation, to the point of worldlessness.

For Adorno, the power of Beckett or Kafka derives from the fact that they work precisely by dismantling appearance, by penetrating the carapace of objectivism, and hence exploding from within 'the art which committed proclamation subjugates from without, and hence only in appearance'. And so, 'he over whom Kafka's wheels have passed, has lost for ever any peace with the world'. It is, if you like, an aesthetic of absence. It is precisely those values rigorously excluded from the novel which create the pressure under which we read the novel. And perhaps this is the root of the anxiety in contemporary criticism. There is, as yet, no adequate way of describing or legitimizing such absences. Adorno's observation on Beckett's works that 'everyone shudders at them, and yet no one can persuade himself that these eccentric plays and novels are not about what everyone knows but no one will admit' surely rings a bell, but its very assurance is the root of a certain suspicion or alarm. Thus John Gardner takes absence for neglect, while Malcolm Bradbury suggests that it is precisely the moral vacuum of the text which creates the necessity for the reader to fill it. And certainly even the most programmatically irrealist text relies on plausible and reasonably authoritative versions of the real for its definition of irrealism. But the a-realist text surrenders control over the definition of that real and hence places a pressure on critic and reader which destabilizes what, perhaps erroneously, was thought to be a relatively stable relationship. And out of that instability has derived the debate — in some senses a displacement of other concerns about the shape and form of contemporary experience, the plight of the self, the nature of the real — with which this book is in part concerned.

In a sense, then, the argument reflects the more general tensions that have always been present in the novel, between a dense, socially engaged mimetic mode, on the one hand, and a consciously reflexive and complex autotelic linguistic product on the other. At times, and with different writers, a centrifugal force seems to urge these elements further apart. An apocalyptic reading of experience, a sense of a radical shift in the processes of perception, precipitates a desire to forge a style, define an approach, locate a mode which can constitute an adequate response to such a conviction.

The argument,* then, has been about the purpose and function of art, about the relationship between innovative techniques and values, about a sense of liberal crisis. It has been a discussion between critics rather than writers, but where actual novels have been invoked they have tended to be American, or, occasionally, French or South American. The English novel has seemingly been invisible. It is certainly not referred to by most of the critics named above, and for that reason perhaps it is necessary to suggest that the English novel has for too long been regarded as a cosily provincial, deeply conservative, anti-experimental enterprise, resistant to innovation, rooted in mimesis, and dedicated to the preservation of a tradition of realism casually related to that of the nineteenth century. It is a view especially popular outside England, particularly in Eastern Europe, which has a vested interest in the 1950s, and in the United States. But it is a view which is also encountered in England itself. Even John Fowles has suggested (in the interview contained in this book) that 'a lot of contemporary English fiction is abysmally parochial and of no conceivable interest to anyone who is not English and middle class', while the novel itself is easily 'the most despised of the contemporary major art forms in this country'.

As Malcolm Bradbury has pointed out, most recently in *The Contemporary English Novel* (1979), whether or not this paradigm would be applicable to the hinterland of the English novel it would have a hard time accommodating Beckett (if he can be claimed for the English novel), Lowry, or, later, Golding, Lessing, Wilson, Burgess or Fowles himself, not to mention B.S. Johnson, Alan Burns, Christine Brooke-Rose, Ian McEwan or Angela Carter.

In part this model is, indeed, the product of simple disregard or critical myopia. It offers a version of the novel as it appeared to be twenty years ago when the English writer discovered the midlands

---

*which has continued in various ways, in such works as Christopher Lasch's *The Culture of Narcissm* (W. W. Norton, 1978) and Christopher Butler's *After the Wake: An Essay on the Contemporary Avant-Garde* (Clarendon, 1980).

and the north of England and when Doris Lessing, Angus Wilson, John Fowles, Malcolm Bradbury himself, and to some degree Iris Murdoch, seemed more unambiguously committed to realism than their subsequent careers have revealed. The truth is that the English novel, at least as represented by those who appear in this book, occupies an interesting middle ground; that it does respond in some degree to a sense of a fundamental shift in our perception of the real but that it reflects above all a sense of disturbance, of cultural dislocation, which leaves it negotiating some kind of *rapprochement* between humanist commitments and an increasing sense of relativism.

If all five of the English writers included in this volume remain in some sense realists, theirs is by no means an innocent realism. It is an enterprise suffused with an awareness of the suspect nature of language, the manipulative power of art, the fragility of character, and the relativity of value and perception. It incorporates the parodic, shifting tenses, multiple narrative possibilities and fictive games, but does so in the context of an art nevertheless drawn to moral imperatives and committed to an assertion of the significance, if no longer quite the centrality, of the individual located against a history whose logic cannot be easily evaded. The real which they engage has expanded to acknowledge a spiritual dimension (Murdoch and Lessing), the significance of fantasy (Wilson) or the compulsive and coercive fictionalizing of the private and public world (Bradbury). But the freedom which these writers assert is not limited to the imagination or the spinning of fictions. There are other urgencies, which may be political as well as social, and which link them to writers like Bellow or to some other American writers who also inhabit this border territory. Perhaps, indeed, this border territory is wider than critics have been willing to concede.

If no longer central and certainly not definitional, the concept of value is clearly not defunct — though it may increasingly be located outside the context of a liberal humanist ideology. In the interviews which follow, William Gass purports to find a 'positive quality in art itself' and John Hawkes insists that his work is 'affirmative from beginning to end' (while characteristically asserting that '"the dark constants" are evident in my work from first to last'). Coover sees self-conscious fiction as 'a moral act'. The question is what those values are, how they operate and where they derive from. If fiction is, as Coover says, a 'self-revealing model ... for the universal fiction-making process', some fictions are evidently seen as being more deadly than others. But how is a meaningful distinction between 'exemplary' and 'deadly' fiction to be made? Or is it a distinction that is useful in such a polarized formulation?

The ethical issues involved in such discussions invariably centre around the problematic nature of language, and, more particularly, the troublesome status of fictional language. It might even be fair to say that such a concern with language is the chief characteristic of Western culture in the late twentieth century. Most commentators agree (though they react to their insight with far less uniformity) that there has been a change of attitude towards language: from being regarded purely as a vehicle, it tends to be seen as an end in itself. While this shift in emphasis has greatly broadened our conception of language, it has at the same time revealed new and hitherto unforeseen problems. Marshall McLuhan's proclamation that the medium has become the message indeed pinpoints the fact that the hazards implicit in the language of the past have developed into explicit actuality: by becoming virtually omnireferential, language threatens to lose its metaphoric character. Words and things stand farther apart; and as things seem to elude our sense of order, words tend to become more and more powerfully self-sufficient.

There seems to be no remedy for this dilemma unless we adopt either an ironic or a utopian attitude: we either have to adjust to the notion that language can become an end in itself, and that we can treat words, phrases, sentences, and texts as so many things that we chance upon in our personal environment, while at the same time regarding them as a potential treasure, or we have to try to transcend that notion and, by a leap of faith, arrive at the conclusion that any expansion of the function of language will be qualitative as well as quantitative, an increase in responsibility as well as in range.

If they are exercised conscientiously, both attitudes may eventually contribute to a redefinition, if not of liberalism then of liberal value. At this point the artist, as the deliberate originator and manipulator of language, assumes a representative function. The ironic, self-reflexive, and innovative artist spontaneously avails himself of his creative imagination; yet the phase of artistic conception is followed by conscious restraint, an act of renunciation in which, paradoxically, the artist asserts his freedom. 'His ability to detach himself from any single creative insight keeps him in the "liberal" state of receptivity to new ones', says Raymond

Immerwahr of the ironic artist in the Romantic tradition. Because the freedom of the ironic artist has to be bought with self-denial, his 'liberalism' does not mean an attitude of passive tolerance, but one of active susceptibility to new ideas.

The utopian or moral artist's attitude towards language is dependent not so much on a present precarious balance as on a tentative concurrence of past and future values. His critical analysis of present-day values leads him into a reconsideration of what he believes were their uncontaminated origins, which he then attempts to project into the future. Thus his attitude is at once conservative and radical and, in contrast to the 'liberalism' of the ironic artist, always eminently political.

However, seen from a different perspective, both the ironic and the utopian artists are radical. For their representative function derives from their tacit belief in the prevailing influence, if not omnipotence, of the imagination. For them, the demands of the imagination are inexorable, its pressure can be alleviated only through conscious playfulness or through the self-imposed task of constituting new values. However, if we thus declare the primacy of the imagination, the question must arise as to whether we are trying unjustifiably to repress a seemingly strict opposition between narcissistic and socially engaged literature. One answer to this question would be that the ironic author, because of his self-reflection, will always know that his fiction is metonymically related to the world, that it derives meaning only from its place within the context of experience. The utopian author, on the other hand, must always doubt the ultimate efficacy of language. He must acknowledge its helplessness in the face of brute power and realize that language will serve as much to reinforce convention, prejudice, and sentimentality as it succeeds in questioning them.

However, the most satisfying answer is that both ironic and utopian artists are idealists. Thus, even for the contemporary or the postmodern writer fictional language creates something valid and tangible, not according to the 'art follows life' or 'life follows art' formula, but in the sense that fiction ought to be taken into account as something that might — but never must — make us want to change our lives. In postmodern fiction aesthetic value assumes an ethical dimension: instead of advocating the disinterestedness of art it seems to aim at a constant transcendence of purpose. Its object, in being defined, will begin to become the means to another end: the process of definition as such. Thus, even when he confesses to a liberal political or aesthetic stance the postmodern writer is ultimately motivated by a radical impulse: his belief in the creative power of the imagination.

The interviews which follow are, in part at least, an attempt to solicit the views of a wide range of leading English and American novelists on some of the issues raised by the nature and the status of the contemporary novel. They involve an effort to press some of the apparent paradoxes implicit, on the one hand, in an art which declares autonomy from the world in which it is made and to which it is nevertheless offered in a historically and culturally determined language, and, on the other hand, in an art which asserts its moral function while creating contingent events, elaborating falsehoods, and imaginatively deforming the world it ostensibly describes. But, naturally, the primary purpose in conducting these interviews was to invite writers to discuss their work and to examine the nature of their ideas about writing, their aesthetic strategies, and fictional concerns.

HZ
CB

John Barth

John Simmons Barth, Jr, was born on 27 May 1930 in Cambridge, Maryland. His grandfather, a stone-carver by trade, also dealt in real estate, selling marshland to his fellow German immigrants. His father was the proprietor of a candy store-cum-restaurant and, in addition, he was chief judge of the Orphan's Court in Cambridge. Barth has remained deeply rooted in the traditions of this rural southern corner of the Old Line State, and the familiar Tidewater Maryland setting provides the background for most of his novels. He attended Cambridge High School and in the summer of 1947 he entered Juilliard School of Music in New York City, where he studied harmony and orchestration for a few months. In 1947 he entered Johns Hopkins University in Baltimore where he took a BA in 1951 and an MA in 1952. His master's thesis was a — hitherto unpublished — novel titled 'Shirt of Nessus'. From 1953-1972 Barth taught at Pennsylvania State University, the State University of New York at Buffalo, and at Boston University. In 1973 he accepted the post of professor in the graduate writing seminars at Johns Hopkins and returned to Maryland. His awards include a Rockefeller grant in 1965; the National Institute of Arts and Letters Award for *Giles Goat-Boy* in 1966; the National Book Award for *Chimera* in 1973; and election to both the National Institute of Arts and Letters and the American Academy of Arts and Sciences in 1974.

John Barth could be called an experimental traditionalist. This appears to be a dubious description of an author who generally, after the publication of his first two novels, *The Floating Opera* and *The End of the Road*, both written in 1955, has been considered to be an existential nihilist. Todd Andrews, in *The Floating Opera*, believes that 'nothing has intrinsic value'; and the modification of this notion in *LETTERS*, Barth's latest novel, where the same character reappears and argues that 'nothing *has* intrinsic value' seems but slight. However, the formulation of this, in fact, radical change of accent might be said to represent an ironic counterpoint to the all but breathtaking development and expansion of Barth's fictional scope since the publication of the first two novels.

Barth's third novel, *The Sot-Weed Factor* (1960), introduces the wide range of historical possibility into his writings by pretending to describe the life of the historic Ebenezer Cooke, poet laureate of Maryland, and to expand Cooke's satiric poem, published in England in 1708 under the same title as Barth's novel. However, by treating history in the manner of parody, Barth's *The Sot-Weed Factor* intentionally jeopardizes objective truth while affirming the author's role in the creative interplay of fact and fiction. *Giles Goat-Boy or, The Revised New Syllabus* (1966) then sheds light, through the description of the life and teachings of George Giles, the Grand Tutor, on the forms of religion and myth in Barth's pantheon of ideas. But again the author undercuts the dangers of cliché by using comedy and farce, and he avoids the trap of mysticism by resorting to the structuring device of allegory. Barth's next work, the 'series' *Lost in the Funhouse* (1968), subtitled *Fiction for Print, Tape, Live Voice*, while apparently centring on the development of the artist and the form of the *Künstlerroman*, is simultaneously an ironic foray into the world of multimedia, which threatens the role of the traditional narrator and forces the artist to double back on himself in self-reflexion. *Chimera* (1972), a volume composed of three novellas, is lodged in the realm of myth. But the timelessness of myth is called into question in the pattern of re-enactment which besets each hero, making him conscious of the hazards and perils of the second part or cycle of his life, modifying his success and qualifying even his eventual immortality. *LETTERS* (1979), Barth's most recent novel, of which *Chimera* was the 'core', centres on the theme of re-enactment and expands it into a parody of *Weltanschauung*. *LETTERS* is a multi-levelled orchestration of the theme of second cycle: on the level of character within the novel, on the level of author, on the level of American history, and on the level of literature. The letters written to one another by 'seven fictitious drolls and dreamers', among them the author himself, are cast backwards and forwards in time: they contain information complexes that can never become means of present communication. They are a convoluted tangle of 'scarlet, fatal, forged, misdirected, amatory, doctored, concealed, crossed, purloined' letters, and their potential documentary value is constantly diminished under the fictionalizing pressure of their respective writers' idealisms.

Their eventual meaning becomes dependent not on any one character — least of all on the author — but on the plot which they jointly constitute.

Thus Barth has experimented in many a tradition, but the essential reason for calling him an experimental traditionalist relates to the fact that he has created his own tradition through his series of fictions. Forged, as it were, from his vast, almost encyclopedic interests and — seemingly in opposition to these —from his ironic self-reflexiveness, this tradition increasingly forces him to take on more such interests as so many tasks. It is no mere coincidence that the figure of the ambivalent hero should prevail in all of Barth's writings. The hero's exceptional single-mindedness as well as his endeavour to do real work in the world can serve as an emblem for the author; yet precisely because of his persistence, the hero is subjected to ridicule whenever the gods or the outer world fail to comply with his desires. And the pattern in which the hero finds himself tends to develop in accordance with its own inherent structure, leaving the hero behind and wondering how to catch up with the process moving towards his own destination. Thus for Barth the figure of the hero can assume an exorcizing function: he becomes the ever-struggling, ever-failing *persona* behind which the author hides in order to gain the freedom necessary for further fictional development.

Interviews with John Barth

Baltimore, 9 November 1977

HZ   The book of interviews Chris Bigsby and I are planning is to be called *The Radical Imagination and the Liberal Tradition*. Now, while in your novels you seem to show little interest in liberalism as a social and political concept, it seems to me that by allowing for shifts of masks in your characters or the possibility of varying points of view as, for instance, in *The Sot-Weed Factor* or in *Lost in the Funhouse*, you do seem to employ liberalism as a kind of narrative mood.

JB   Before I ask you more precisely about what you mean by 'liberalism as a narrative mood', it would probably be appropriate to confess about myself that I am a perfectly stock bourgeois liberal humanist with the addition of what I think of as some version of the tragic view. That is, a sense from my experience and the experience of my characters that well-intentioned ideologies and political stances — in fact even well-intentioned life programs generally — don't finally work. At best they usually fail to live up to the best version of their aspirations, in the way that most people fail to do the same thing. But to proceed, with a kind of experienced sense of that probability, almost certainty, of failure — if that can be called a tragic view, it would certainly be my own political stance in so far as I have any. It is an attitude close to the ground of some of the novels, at least when it is transferred out of the political arena to such things as the actuarial paradigm of mythic heroism, for example. The mythic heroes in my fiction usually don't attain, in any unqualified way, the final fate of mythic heroes. If they arrive at any kind of apotheosis at the end of their mythic adventures, it is usually a severely qualified one. Now *mutatis mutandis* that is what I feel about political programs. I share the inability of most of us to reconcile a socialist head, an anarchist heart and capitalist appetites. Could I ask you now what you mean by 'liberalism as a narrative mood?'

HZ   What I meant by 'liberalism as a narrative mood' is a mood in which narrative concepts constantly intersect and in which particularly the concept of character is deconstructed. For example, a radically liberal character like Spielman in *Giles Goat-Boy* is put into a relative perspective by the floundering honesty of the hero.

JB   I think I agree with this characterization of my *dramatis personae* — a qualification of attitudes so that attitudes have their counter-attitudes. In the working out of the plot, chances are that the character who could be said to represent most nearly and sympathetically something like a tentative but qualified and honorable political liberalism, let's say, is likely to come a cropper. The novel, as the plot works out, is not likely to be an unqualified triumph for that character. On the other hand, I don't think the plots of the novels go out of their way to crucify and punish such characters. (Sometimes they do, as in the case of Joseph Morgan in *The End of the Road*.) I guess that in more complex or complicated ways, when we are talking no longer so much about political liberalism as about mythic aspirations qualified by self-irony and the rest — which is something like the psychology of liberals, if you can imagine it foisted upon people like Perseus or Giles Goat-Boy — yes, then I think you are right.

HZ   All of your novels (except maybe for the first two, which have, in hindsight at least, been described as 'witty' and 'brilliant') belong more or less to the comic genre. Now the question is: isn't the comic (along with its related or subgenres, like satire, parody, or farce) the most liberal and, at the same time, most socially oriented of genres, because it relies upon a generally maintained set of values against which it is played off? On the other hand, in *The Sot-Weed Factor* and *Giles Goat-Boy*, it seems to me that you try to parody this underlying set of social values and thereby turn comedy against itself. Or do you take seriously the notion of the comic hero trying to assert himself against society and thereby ultimately affirming society's power or even its demands?

JB   Let's take the novels separately and let me speak briefly to each of them in terms of your question. Society's power, society's demands, the hero trying to assert himself against society — 'society' is the term that makes me a little uneasy. My notion of the theme of *The Sot-Weed Factor*, for example, is that it dramatizes a kind of tragic view of innocence. What the hero of that novel, Ebenezer Cooke, learns, surely, is that innocence, as he conceives the term (he may conceive innocence innocently) is, if not actually guilty, a kind of vice, at least untenable and must come down. Which is not to say that he therefore affirms, as his over-worldly mentor affirms, worldliness as a virtue. No, what Ebenezer Cooke finds, having rejected whatever it is that his tutor and mentor Henry Burlingame represents, is that his counter value — the innocence that he had innocently been affirming as a kind of ontological handle — is also impossible and is actually harmful to other people as well as to himself. Cooke's progress through the novel — his loss of his estate and his regaining it by contracting a social disease — is meant to dramatize, in a comic way, the ambivalence of innocence. From my then youthful point of view, this seemed, to me, to be the tragic view of innocence. One could dramatize the tragic view of experience as well! The affirmation of either as a value is at best a paradoxical and tenuous enterprise. Now, I don't know where society comes into that, except that, of course, among the targets of the comedy is any kind of naïve view of history as being an intelligible record of the past, not to mention being an honorable or objective and accurate record of the past.

HZ   To me the concept of self in *The Sot-Weed Factor* complicates the issue. Because, on the one hand, there is Ebenezer Cooke — and he seems to have an undisturbed sense of self until he loses his innocence and finds out that, as you say, he had to lose it, that clinging to his virginity was his vital sin. But, on the other hand, Burlingame finds a kind of self by exploiting history and people's traditional expectations.

JB   As a matter of fact, he turns to a kind of innocence.

HZ But how can experience abandon itself and become innocence once more, unless a new societal context is established in which former experience can now indeed function as innocence?

JB The sense of self that Ebenezer begins with when he affirms innocence, and specifically physical virginity, as somehow being his essence, is very precarious. In terms of systems analysis, Cooke represents a highly unstable self-regulating homeostatic field, let's say, which, because of its very instability, permits comedy, and, for that matter, dramatic action to be precipitated out of it. He leaves England and comes to America declaring that he is a poet and a virgin, when in fact he is not the one and barely the other. It is a conspicuously fragile and vulnerable self-asser-tion. Cooke's ontology is a declaration of himself more than a sense of himself — otherwise, of course, there could be no comedy and no drama. Burlingame is just the opposite, and their reversal — where the complex man discovers his innocence and the innocent man discovers his complexity or his complicity — has got to be as old as comedy.

Now *Giles* is another story: the sophomoric allegorical transfor-mation of society into the universal university. This, of course, puts society much more in the foreground of the action, as Giles's adversary, than is the case with American colonial society, let's say, or British society in the American colonial period, in *Sot-weed*. Though, in both cases, those are simply the *milieu* in which the action takes place and neither of them, to my mind, is really central to my concern. My interest in colonial history is real but not paramount. My interest in the social divisions of the Cold War — the divisions of politics and society in the mid-1950s when I was thinking of the novel *Giles*, and the early 1960s when I wrote it — are, like the allegory itself, really just a manner of speaking or a *milieu* to speak in and to, rather than the heart of my concerns in the novel. If *The Sot-Weed Factor* is the comic dramatization of some kind of tragic view of innocence, then *Giles Goat-Boy*, by my lights, is the comic rendition of a sort of tragic view of a certain kind of experience — specifically, towards the end of the novel, something like mystical or at least transcendental experience, about which also I have mixed feelings.

You wondered whether the techniques or conventions of comedy are deployed in *Giles* to do what comedy typically does as you describe it in your question, to undercut that conventional activity of comedy. I don't know what I feel about that question except that one thing that's being both affirmed and undercut (or affirmed and qualified) is the conventional view of mystic experience. It is a phenomenon that I was curious about at the time, as I have been curious about, and to some extent tentatively involved in, political liberalism, for example. I take mystical experience seriously, but my feeling about it is like William James's. I believe it's real; I could wish that I had experienced it, but I never have; my closest analogue to it (but it's a fairly close analogue) is whatever passes for grace or the unitary experience for artists. I know what religious people mean when they speak of grace, for example, because one knows, whether as an athlete or a musician or a writer, those moments when somebody else seems to be swinging the tennis racket. I think artists and good athletes and ordinary people, too, if they do anything expertly, know what I mean when I speak of the analogues of grace or the analogues of mystical experience. This is what *Giles* sets about (always comically) to dramatize. The strategy of *Giles* was to begin with farce and even travesty and then to attempt to escalate to something which is not *simply* farce. I had become concerned with the *Urmitte*, and had been reading, by that time, Raglan and Campbell and Jung and so forth — and was interested in the actuarial paradigm of both mystics and mythic heroes. Those two actuarial paradigms are, I think, isomorphic. So much so, that each could easily be used as a metaphor of the other. The figure of Giles —half human, half goat — is, of course, essentially a comic figure. But what I hope the ending of the novel dramatizes is a rather serious, though comically qualified, sense of the tragic view of the mystical experience.

From reading the biographies and writings of the mystics as well as looking at the paradigm of mythic heroism, I gather that that first half of the cycle — the descent through the first two quadrants down to the *axis mundi* where the mystical coming together of opposites occurs — is mystical in nature. The hero sheds things, gets beyond categories, including categories of sexuality, of ego trappings, anything that classifies us in our ordinary non-transcendent experience, and then arrives, with some special luck and special dispensation, at a state where, let's say, 'East and West mean nothing.' But the second two quadrants of the cycle — the attempt to come back to the world and to transmit and implement the essentially ineffable experience that the wandering hero or the mystic brings back to society — that has a tragic aspect to it. So what I added to the paradigm was that the first half of the journey seems to me to be essentially mystical and the second half of the journey essentially tragic: the literal inability of the mystic to implement what he has seen without betraying it. For James, as you know, one of the hallmarks of the genuinely numinous experience — James being a pragmatist — was that it effects real work in the everyday world. What I am interested in is the fact that mystics, like mythic heroes, who come back and are supposed to establish the laws and build the cities, etc., do it, but they usually betray their vision while implementing it. That is, the translation of the experience into language or ordinances or cities and societies leads finally to that last point of the mythic cycle: the hero's fall from the favor of the gods and his fellow men, his exile from the city he himself has built, and then his mysterious evaporation or whatever. This is analogous to the entropy that one observes when religious experience gets institutionalized into religion, or inspiration gets turned into sentences and chapters; it is a necessary betrayal of the experience itself and has, if not a tragic, at least a pathetic aspect to it. The end of the mythic hero, if not a pathetic ending, at least certainly is not a happy one. The end of the mystic is generally similar, and the biographies of writers and artists whom we admire frequently have something like that same characteristic. One thinks of Ezra Pound saying, at the end of his life, that literature is a bad job; that he wished he hadn't undertaken it in the first place. It is a refrain that one has heard much before in the biographies of artists one has loved and admired. At the end of *Giles Goat-Boy* the hero-narrator's experience is betrayed, qualified, postscripted, requalified, etc. It's done comically because I can't do things any other way. But it's the comic rendition of something I take quite seriously. To sum up: society is not at the forefront of my literary concerns, but it's the *milieu* in which the mystic or the hero has to implement the ineffable and which will inevitably falsify, to some necessary degree, the thing he is trying to transmit. Society is the noise in the hero's signal.

HZ   Is it really only noise — an external complication unrelated to the ideal signal — or is it not something like a ground which the mythic hero leaves and to which he has to return? Because the mythical experience, though always apparently absolute and self-evident, is finally subjective. Perhaps the role of the wandering hero could, in a sense, be compared to the role Socrates ascribes to the philosopher: that he who has alone seen the sun of truth has the duty to go and enlighten his fellow men.

JB   Now, Socrates is very optimistic about that project (in fact, we don't know whether it's Socrates or Plato, I guess, who was very optimistic about the project), but I think even a pessimistic mystic would affirm that that is a necessary enterprise. Otherwise the mystical experience is completely self-centered and doesn't go beyond the mystic him- or herself, and so we may legitimately be not interested in it except as a peculiarity. But for the mystic who embarks on that Socratic enterprise, I would understand it to be doomed, if not to failure, at least to a heavily qualified success —perhaps a success so qualified that the difference between it and failure might be almost negligible. This is what gives the mystical-pedagogical enterprise a kind of tragic aspect. That's a paradox, and of course paradox is the mystic's stock in trade.

The term paradox is a very important term. When I speak of 'having things both ways', the paradox is that really delicate line between some kind of hypocrisy and some kind of contradiction. The difference between a contradiction and a paradox, at least as I hope it works out in my fiction, is simply the difference between something inhibitory and fruitless (contradiction) or morally repugnant (hypocrisy) and something which, however hard to lay hold of, is fruitful. It does real work, accomplishes real things in the real world. And that is paradox. Perhaps 'tragic view' is too elevated a term for the kind of thing I'm talking about — it's only the paradoxical qualification in the direction of the tragic view of what otherwise would be, for me, too simplistically optimistic, doctrinaire, ideological, or whatever.

HZ And yet the 'Tragic View of Life' is explicitly adopted by some of your protagonists. For example, there is one woman in each of the three novellas that constitute *Chimera* who chooses a heroic attitude of suffering and pity in the face of unrequited love. Of course, it is also true that the shortcomings of such a view are revealed: although they are treated respectfully enough by the respective male characters (and, it seems to me, by the author), these women are doomed to failure, doomed because they are trying to arrest time.

JB There certainly is, in two of the novellas at least, in the *Perseid* and the one about Bellerophon, a woman who attempts to arrest time. The minor figure of Calyxa in the Perseus novella simply wants time not to keep going because this is the moment in Perseus' biography where she occurs, and she knows that the next panel she paints or sculpts is going to be his leaving her and she wishes that weren't so. I don't see anything in there that smacks of the tragic view. At first Perseus, too, doesn't especially have the tragic view of the mythic hero's biography, the mythic hero's actuarial progress at the time he is living it out. Perseus himself acquires a proper tragic view at the end of his biography, when he and Medusa have been estellated: a heavily qualified immortality! At that point Perseus takes a kind of retrospective tragic view of the heroic cycle and of his own autobiography. Calyxa is simply a woman in a very temporary arrangement. It depends on Perseus' not knowing yet that he is still alive with the rest of his mission, as it were, to be completed — a mission that doesn't involve her. Her position is the comic equivalent of Dido's position *vis-à-vis* Aeneas in the second and third books of the *Aeneid*. Not tragic; just pathetic.

Philonoë, Bellerophon's wife, also wishes that time wouldn't go on, because she begins to suspect that it is going to involve separation between her and her husband. As for Bellerophon: he, too, acquires a kind of tragic view of the heroic curriculum; what he acquires in fact is the recognition that he doesn't measure up to that curriculum. So his ending is distinct from Perseus'. I'm not sure how either of those women, however, ... I see how they both attempt to arrest time ...

HZ Perhaps 'pathetic' *would* be the better word to describe their fate. They do, however, talk about taking the "Tragic View of Life" and so does, if I remember it correctly, Shah Zaman's mistress in the *Dunyazadiad*, the one who founded the country of the Amazons.

JB I had forgotten her, and indeed I'm afraid I don't remember what she says very clearly now. But I do remember that she is the mentor. She takes the role of the Diotima who explains things to the Shah. Yes, that's true.

HZ Perhaps it could be said that the pathetic is often erroneously identified with the tragic. What these women really seem to mean when they talk about taking the 'Tragic View of Life' is that they are aware of the futility of clinging to their own values, yet that these values are the only ones they can envision. For them, there are no real choices. Tragic necessity *and* freedom to choose belong rather to mythic heroes who acknowledge — not repress — the progress of time.

JB Now I know what you mean, and I agree with you. It is as if two things were true. It is as if Diotima were in love with (I'm not talking about Musil's Diotima now; I'm talking about Socrates' Diotima), it's as if she were in love with the person that she is trying to elevate up the ladder of love to that final Platonic realization of true essence and knew that, when she got her lover to the highest point on the ladder, she was going to have to be left behind somewhere. It's as if, to put it another way, Beatrice were in Virgil's position and had to lead her lover out of purgatory to heaven — but had to say goodbye to him at the bottom of *that* ladder. A pathetic state of affairs, if not tragic.

And then the second thing: it's as if all that were finally viewed through a comic lens rather than through a straightforwardly tragic lens. But we are leaving out two other important women. One is Scheherazade, who is in the position, *mutatis mutandis*, of the male heroes in the Perseus story and the Bellerophon story. All three come to realize that the only way they are going to terminate their tasks is to exterminate their taskmasters. This is a famous feature of the heroic labors: you are set one impossible task after another until you see that your real task is not fetching the Gorgon's head or the golden fleece, but killing the person who is telling you to do these impossible things. My Scheherazade realizes that the only way she is really going to get out of the bind of the 1001 nights is to kill the Shah; then she will be free — not the way *he* wants to set her free of the narrative burden, by giving her this tenure, or whatever it is, of formal marriage ... And Medusa, whom I at least attempted to turn not into an adversary, foil, or device for Perseus, but a genuine partner in the heroic enterprise. This was something new for me to attempt; I hope it worked.

Baltimore, 16 November 1977

HZ Perhaps the most striking feature of your writing is the importance you give to the past. In *The Sot-Weed Factor* you are concerned with the historical past; in *Lost in the Funhouse* and *Chimera* with the mythic past. But it is the twentieth-century mind that is at work in all of your novels. In which way do you believe that the past relates to the present in your fiction? Is the present constituted by the past? Or is it illuminated by the past? Or does it gain a certain perspective by being set off against the past?

JB The Latin motto of one of the characters in the work in progress [*LETTERS*] — he is an industrialist borrowed from my first novel, *The Floating Opera*, who has expanded his pickle business into chemical fertilizers and freeze-drying — is *Praeteritas futuras stercorat:* the past shits up the present. His PR man changed that to *Praeteritas futuras fecundat:* the past *fertilizes* the present, a proper motto for a chemical fertilizer firm, I suppose. But in that novel — and I think this applies to the other novels as well — any historical or mythic past that haunts, craps up, fertilizes the present is an emblem of our personal past. The theme, certainly of the Perseus story, certainly of the Bellerophon story, and most certainly of the work in progress, is the comic, tragic, or paradoxical re-enactment of the past in the present. Perseus, for example, in the *Chimera*, attempts systematically to re-enact a past which, at the time, was unselfconscious and heroic. At the midpoint of his life, after he has accomplished the heroic paradigm, Perseus recognizes that he has in fact fulfilled the prerequisites of mythic heroism. And then, at a point where he feels himself stagnating, he attempts a program of rejuvenation by re-enacting his heroic past. Of course, one can't do that: he comes a cropper and finally has to arrive at his new equilibrium or transcension by a different route from the one that made him a mythic hero in the first place. Bellerophon attempts to become a mythic hero by perfectly imitating the actuarial program for mythic heroes. Of course, that doesn't work, and he finds that by perfectly imitating the model of mythic heroism, what he becomes is a perfect imitation of a mythic hero — which is not the same thing as a mythic hero. My characters in the new novel will act out, whether they know it or not, Marx's notion that historical events and personages recur, the first time as tragedy and the second time as farce. This is also what happens to Perseus in *Chimera*: his attempts to re-enact his heroic past become farcical, a fiasco. It is only when he reassesses the situation (with the help of Calyxa and eventually of Medusa) that he is able to elevate his re-enactment into something greater: which, if not heroic, is at least more personally successful.

HZ That implies, then, that it is important that the hero character overcomes his past in the end, doesn't it?

JB Indeed, it does.

Try to imagine a chambered nautilus whose prior chambers are accessible: a creature who carries its past on its back but isn't confined strictly to the present room of that past. He can move. freely into past rooms, using what's there to energize and inform the present.

That's the optimistic view. I am reminded, though, of a statement by D'Arcy Thompson, the English biologist who attempted to describe organic growth and form mathematically. He points out that it is only the very lip of the shell of marine mollusks that is alive and generative; the rest of it is dead material. He also remarks that it is not the snail that shapes the shell, but the shell that shapes the snail. I think that applies in an obvious way to ourselves: our thirties are a product of what we were in our twenties and what we were in our teens. But we are not *just* that product. Our past lives a more or less active half-life in us, let's say, but we're continuously reshaping and reinterpreting it, restructuring it: reorchestrating it, if you like.

HZ   Does this mean that we approach the past as something like a game?

JB   Oh, indeed so! Somebody in *The Sot-Weed Factor* — Burlingame, I think — says that the past is a clay that, willy-nilly, we must sculpt. And sculpting is play as well as work.

HZ   We agreed in an earlier discussion that liberalism as an attitude can never really succeed, because it implies the paradox of having to advocate freedom as well as responsibility, and that in your writings the element of freedom is found in the content, the element of responsibility in the form. But now I am not so sure whether this view takes into account the role of play in your fiction.

JB   It doesn't. But, in our earlier conversation, I don't think we said that 'liberalism as an attitude' can never really succeed. What I meant was that it can never *entirely* succeed. But other attitudes can't entirely succeed either. 'Nothing works', in that most optimistic sense of the word — of course not. What's involved is, as you say very intelligently in your question, a paradox and not a futile contradiction. And paradox may be something to be heartened by. I second your uncertainty about what you are calling a liberal attitude toward the medium — that is, responsibility in the form and freedom in the content. I'm not so sure on reflexion whether that doesn't make just as much sense the other way around. We may have on our hands here a second paradox, or it may be that what you mean by 'play' (ruleless activity) is something different from what we mean by 'game'. The very fact that you impose formal constraints on yourself — and in fiction these *are* self-imposed constraints — means not only that you may chafe under those constraints, especially in a six- or seven-year project, but that your attitude toward those constraints, since they are self-imposed, can become playful dialectic or dialogue. I enjoy imposing a rather complicated set of rules on myself and then seeing if I can bring them off with some energy, spirit, and maybe even grace. So far as that's the case, there is no contradiction in your definition of literary liberalism, let's say, and liberalism as a procedure. The other business: improvising, changing, or purposely defeating even the rules that one sets for oneself in this gaming spirit — out of a spirit of play as contrasted with games — I think there is not very much of it in those fictions, but there is some. It's invoked mainly as an apparent throwing away of one's own rule — apparently unfinished stories, for example, like the *Bellerophoniad*, were finished in fact. Stories like *Giles* which seem to contradict and then to contradict the contradiction — obviously those are not real contradictions, just the final workings out of the pattern.

I don't know about that business of 'freedom in the content'. It seems to me that one's limit of choices is about the same in the matter of content as it is in the matter of form. And if the chronology of conception and execution is evidence one way or the other, it just as often happens, for me, that the idea of the content will come first and the formal things be invented second, as the reverse.

HZ Perhaps I could redefine my statement and say that the play element seems to relate more to the content, whereas the game element is more apparent in the form.

JB That's a definition that makes me easier than the first. Certainly there is a good deal more improvisation in the content than there is in the form. In fact, the form becomes more locked in as you go along; there becomes less and less room for improvisation, whereas in the content what I.A. Richards calls 'the incidental felicities' may be improvised even six-sevenths of the way through a project.

HZ Your use of the mythic pattern seems to exemplify this point. The pattern is the form, the given framework, within which, either consciously or unconsciously, your mythic heroes strive to establish their individuality. But perhaps this is just another instance of your trying to 'have things both ways': to assert your protagonists' individuality while at the same time affirming their roles as representatives of mankind and thereby attributing a precarious kind of immortality to them.

JB That would be a noble project, that last one. And I hope it's true. When I wrote *Sot-Weed Factor*, critics mentioned the pattern of mythic heroism, assuming that I was familiar with that pattern and was echoing it in my fiction. So I went and read Jung and Joseph Campbell and became aware of the pattern that I was hitherto either unaware of or very dimly aware of: the Ur-Myth. As a budding formalist, I liked that pattern and the things that the pattern is isomorphic with. Because I had been re-enacting it in the

Sot-Weed Factor novel unconsciously, I thought that the muse must be speaking right through me. But I realized soon afterwards, in planning *Giles*, that in fact there was nothing extraordinary about that coincidence at all; that, on the other hand, it would be quite extraordinary if one tried to write a novel about the vicissitudes of a wandering hero *without* its falling into the pattern, which, after all, is a very general pattern. Its components can be interpreted symbolically with wide latitude, as they are in those various isomorphs: the same model Jung sees as a paradigm of the psychoanalytical experience, somebody else sees as the attempt to account for natural phenomena — Max Müller's old solar thesis and so forth. Others see it as a paradigm for the mystic quest; others as a paradigm for every man's and woman's progress through the rites of passage. Finally it occurred to me, in a wonderful moment of illumination, that among the other isomorphs is this one: the wandering hero re-enacts the history of a spermatozoon from the moment of ejaculation through the fertilization of the egg. And then the famous transcension of categories: spermatozoons are not male animals, and eggs are not female animals, but what has male aspects and what has female aspects come together into a creature that transcends the categories both of the egg and the sperm, and is both and neither. There is a *coincidentia oppositorum* if there ever was one! Then the magic transformation flight in that third quadrant of the mythic cycle (according to Jung, Campbell, Raglan and company) is really just the first law of embryology: ontogeny recapitulating phylogeny. The reascent across the threshold would be birth, etc. In short, my story 'Night-Sea Journey'.

After *Giles* I decided to revisit the oral tradition, and some of the first myth stories I wrote — the ones in *Lost in the Funhouse* — were for tape and live voice. My interest there, of course, was just the orchestrator's interest of going back to the beginnings of things to see how conventions might be reorchestrated for present purposes — something that, I saw in retrospect, I had been doing all along but then wanted to do more consciously, more programatically. I was reaching middle age myself and so, obviously, the particular myths in the *Chimera* book — the one about Perseus and the one about Bellerophon — are about heroes (not that I regard my own biography as heroic in any sense) who have reached the mid-point of their lives, who have a certain chain of accomplishments behind them and have become, in a sense, a hard act for themselves to follow. That is, they don't want simply to repeat what they have done before. It's anybody's problem who imagines the second half or second cycle of his life as something growing from the first half which will be neither a repudiation of what one has done nor a self-parody or slavish repetition of it. That's a delicate point for many people — not just for artists and writers, but for anybody who thinks about the curriculum of his life; that's what the middle-escent crisis is all about.

Now, how successful *Chimera* and/or the new book are in accomplishing that program — the program for the second cycle or the second half — may be a moot point. But at least that's what the program was. My mythic heroes Perseus and Bellerophon — Perseus belatedly and Bellerophon from the beginning — are addressing, *mutatis mutandis*, just that question. Bellerophon doesn't succeed in his attempt to arrive at genuine mythic heroism by perfectly imitating the pattern that he begins with: what he becomes is an imitation of a mythic hero. Perseus is in a better situation because he has already accomplished, unselfconsciously as it were, certain kinds of things. His problem is the mature sentient individual's usual problem in middle life, that is, to carry out the next development of a personality or a profession or a career of which one has become conscious without becoming inhibitively self-conscious about what one is up to.

Of course, that's a kind of emblem of the way we live in the twentieth century. We are aware of the centuries that went before; we are conscious — maybe hyperconscious — of what's going on around and inside us now. That is, an intelligent person is likely to be. The equilibria that we arrive at are always more or less unstable, and the equilibrium that one may re-arrive at or re-attain is also likely to be an uneasy, delicate, temporary equilibrium. Now, I don't regard that as an unhappy state of affairs, but it accounts for the fact that the endings of many novels — certainly of all my fictions — are not happy endings. But they are not unhappy endings either. They are just uneasy endings. My 'mythic' characters carry on uneasy and precarious dialogues with themselves, with their own pasts, with the roles that they assume and play or which are given them (roles; I'm not talking about masks now); roles as teacher, as parent, as son, as colleague, as friend, as lover or as author — these roles that never add up to oneself but certainly are not separate from oneself. In the language of systems analysis, their lives evolve from one unstable equilibrium to a new unstable equilibrium. The myths are a handy kind of shorthand for that procedure, and if my reorchestration of the myths has an element of parody or even travesty in them, it's because while I take that subject very seriously indeed, I don't regard it as being necessarily a tragic or heroic business in our own lives. It also has a comic aspect.

A systems analyst, I suppose, would define dramaturgy as the incremental perturbation of an unstable homeostatic field and its catastrophic restoration to a complexified equilibrium. The incremental perturbation is the rising action of the story, the complications of the conflict. 'Catastrophic' I mean in the sense that the catastrophe theorists use the term. As Marx might have said if he had had the adjective to hand, the incremental quantitative changes can precipitate catastrophic qualitative changes. In conventional dramaturgy, peripeteia and denouement: the complexified new equilibrium. The ground situation is not the same at the end of the story as it was at the beginning. And that complexified equilibrium is, of course, itself an unstable equilibrium which may lead to further perturbation, etc. — so long as our lives persist and we go through those famous 'catastrophes'.

Baltimore, 7 September 1979

HZ   The most astonishing thing, to me, in your recent novel *LETTERS* is what I would like to call your new flirt with realism. A realism, however, which, although it refers to recognizable times and places, even to strictly autobiographical details, is, at the same time, less past-oriented than it is 'mildly prophetic'. Does this 'realism', then, define a special relationship — a dialectic —between the fictional and the factual? In the sense that not only the impact of the factual upon the fictional calls for a response on the part of the fictional but vice versa as well?

JB   It's been a while since I wrote any fiction that has to do with the here and the now, with recognizable places, and with characters characterized in the fashion of traditional bourgeois realism. The other thing, the dialectic — the contamination of the real by the fictitious and of the fictitious by the real — is one of the main lines of the plot. Do you remember, Heide, Borges's remark that among the four characteristics of the fabulous in fiction is the contamination of reality by dream? We just have to change the terms: the contamination of reality by fiction. But Borges himself, I think, sometimes includes in that notion the contamination of exterior reality by the imagined, by fiction, and, as witnesses the story 'Tlön, Uqbar, Orbis Tertius', the reverse process, where the fictitious begins to contaminate the real. Yes: if that convention is not the backbone of the novel, it's certainly part of the armature of the theme and of the action. But, as you have seen, the whole mode of operation of that novel is the reorchestration of old conventions, beginning with the convention of the epistolary novel. The dialectic between the fictitious and the real is a convention that goes way back past the modernists; it's at the heart of *Don Quixote*.

HZ   Would it be appropriate to say that the apparent influence of the fictional on the factual appears as a perilous version of the 'life follows art' formula? Perilous because, as you say in the novel, he whose life is to follow his dreams has to be careful about what he dreams or, perhaps, imagines. Is the dreamer, then, responsible for his dreams? Do we have to dream within the scope of autobiographical possibilities?

JB   One must be careful. I think Ambrose Mensch (or else the author himself in one of his letters) makes that remark: One must take care what one dreams. The remark in the book is made lightly in reference to some things that, in fact, came true after I had written about them or had imagined them: minor details of topographical changes in the geography over there on the Eastern Shore. But it sounds a note that certainly is elaborated further in the novel. When you said earlier that you found an element of the prophetic in the novel, I wondered what you meant.

HZ   I thought it meant that, once written, fiction can, in a sense influence the subsequent life of its author. In this sense, couldn't we say that the relationship between the fiction an author writes and his own life is a precarious version of 'life following art'?

JB   Precarious but real. And while that prophetic aspect is not at the heart of the novel, it certainly spooks around the corners and margins. The theme of *LETTERS* is re-enactment; and re-enactment is a phenomenon at least as full of hazards and perils as of opportunities.

HZ   One of the most interesting aspects, I find, in your re-use of characters from previous novels is that the characters seem to constitute the author. In a way, he exists *for* them, as the centre for their lives and the information they impart. The characters may, as you seem to imply, exorcize the possible hazards and perils of their author's life through their vicarious — but independent, almost antecedent — personalities. What struck me, though — and what must strike most of your readers — is the question of your *own* relationship to these characters, whom you have, over the years, created, and who, over the years, seem to be influencing you — the greatest manifestation of which is *LETTERS* itself.

JB   Obviously the things we do, either as artists or as human beings, change and affect us. The dreams we dream as novels, novels that occupy years of our imaginative energy, obviously work changes in us. That old convention of earlier modernism — of the dialogue between the author and his characters, the assumption of an independent life by those characters, even the mutiny of the characters against the author — that's simply a metaphor for the way things actually are. I'm not very romantic about writing, and it always makes me uncomfortable when I hear an old-fashioned writer talk about the way his or her characters assume a life of their own: 'I wanted this character to be such and such. But, no, she insisted on ...' This is the kind of hogwash you hear from a certain kind of writer who talks in a romantic way about art. But on the level of simple fact, I think it's undeniable that the work we do changes us; the dreams we dream change us. Everything we do in art is likely to turn out to be either prophecy or exorcism, whatever its other intentions.

HZ   But I think it should be stressed that you make use of this fact in a particular way. I assume that every author knows that his own characters will influence him and that he has to live with them after he has created them. But, in *LETTERS*, the characters literally constitute their own author: he exists on the fictitious level for his other characters in the same way that they seem to exist on a kind of 'real' level for him.

JB   Is that a reversal of Flaubert's famous remark about Madame Bovary: '*C'est moi?*' Not only is Madame Bovary Flaubert, but Flaubert is Madame Bovary. That's certainly true in the case of my characters.

You will find, and I think you have probably found already, that the author of the letters from the author in *LETTERS* is the least characterized character. Not only does the author very properly not engage in the action — he doesn't affect the plot or become at all involved in it. But also he is the one who, if you were trying to draw little character sketches of the characters in the novel, you would have the least handle on, I believe. No doubt that's because, for the purposes of the novel at least (and it's not just a modernist game that's being played), his character is simply a kind of emptying-out — a *kénosis*, as the theologians say.

In a mild way, every author who's involved, especially in realistic fictions, in drawing characters absolutely from the whole cloth, as these characters are drawn — who have no counterparts in real life — is doing just that. No future PhD investigator is ever going to find anybody now living who could be said to be the real-life models for Lady Amherst or Ambrose Mensch or Todd Andrews. That amuses me because most actual realistic writers have not historically worked in that fashion. They do draw from life; and, of course, people from the period of Germaine de Staël boasted of the fact that their novels were drawn literally from their lives and that they were all *romans à clef*. These are not, and I think that this emptying-out of the characteristics of the author into the characteristics of his characters is most likely to happen when you try to write something that will pass for verisimilitude in characterization, but is, in fact, not drawn from life.

Hazlitt made a wonderful remark about Richardson that I came across when I was doing a little homework on Richardson. He said that, for all of Richardson's much touted realism, he, Hazlitt, suspected that Richardson's characters weren't drawn from life at all. Hazlitt's phrase was that Richardson simply spun them out of his own head. I'm sure that's true. Hazlitt meant it as a criticism, but I regard it as a marvellous truth. And I'm sure that, as soon as you have heard that remark, you cannot read through any of *Pamela* or *Clarissa* and for a moment believe in the reality of those characters in the sense that Mr B. is carefully modeled after so and so, etc. They are as absolutely make-believe characters as ever came down the pages of literature, I'm sure. I would regard it as a tribute if somebody made that Hazlitt kind of remark about *LETTERS*. I would be delighted.

HZ   Could this notion of character be related to your concept of history in the novel? That is, if history appears to consist less of factual events than of the interpretation of these events, would it be fair to say, analogously, that the novel consists less of a factual authorial voice than of the constitution of that voice by the novel's characters?

JB   That's wonderful! I agree, I agree, I agree!

HZ   In that case I would like to ask you: does the author, through those characters in the novel who attempt to change the course of historical events (the Cookes and the Burlingames), try to get a secret hold on American history? Because although the author is unable to change the past, he is able to show how this change could have been brought about. The appearance of the author as a Rip Van Winkle figure in one of his own letters seems to me to serve as a metaphor for this possibility.

JB   It sounds like a feasible notion, Heide, but it brings us back to the dialectic that opened our conversation. I don't know myself, confidently, whether the novel's preoccupation with the events of American history comes out of the general theme of re-enactments, their hazards and opportunities, or vice versa. That is, whether I began with a preoccupation with certain re-enactments in history, famously the two Indian uprisings which marked American history (and the second of which, Tecumseh's, was a very conscious parallel to his predecessor Pontiac's uprising), or the war of 1812, which was a very conscious replay, in the minds of some statesmen, of the original American Revolution — whether the theme of re-enactment grew out of my interest in those famous re-enactments or whether it was the other way around. No more than I can, in some respects, say whether the author is shaping the characters or the characters are shaping the author. The themes are parallel indeed, but whether one has a priority over the other, I don't know.

HZ   My next question takes up what we have been talking about on the level of form. In *LETTERS* as well as in *Chimera*, Jerome Bray is trying to create the perfect novel with the aid of the computer LILYVAC II. He wants to create a novel that will of necessity 'contain *nothing original whatever*, but be the quintessence, the absolute type, as it were the Platonic Form expressed'.

JB   I'm sure *LETTERS* doesn't so much aspire to as stumble towards it. It's certainly not 'the Platonic Form expressed', but it certainly participates in the Platonic idea that Bray is speaking of. Clearly this is a novel in which, on one level, there is nothing original whatsoever; that is, it is a novel which is conspicuously assembled out of old literary conventions. On the other hand, I regard it as a very original novel. Bray's serious role in the novel is to be a kind of mad, limiting case of preoccupations which are also my preoccupations. The difference is that Bray takes them dead seriously and, of course, he is going to refine and escalate his aspirations as he goes along until, finally, not even literature will do. No novel made out of mere words, mere language, could ever arrive at Bray's notions of formal perfection and purity.

I look at the activities of the old and new formalists with a kind of fascination: there *is* a kind of madness in the speculations of Propp and Klebnikhov. But they are perfectly fascinating as limiting cases.

However, you are not to regard *LETTERS* as a kind of *Remembrance of Things Past,* where at the end you realize that you are holding in your hand the artifact which demonstrates the author's preoccupations about time: I mean that wonderful climax where Marcel is going to sit down to write the novel, and when he sits down to write the novel, you have finished the novel, and time, literally, is defeated. At the end of *LETTERS,* you are holding in your hand not the novel that Jerome Bray aspires to compose, not the mad limiting case or the pure form, but something that has fallen from Plato, although it participates in Bray's idea.

HZ I think there is a kind of opposite motion between the documentary novel which, even while drawing its substance from history, nevertheless makes history fictitious in the process; and the epistolary novel which, even while being written, in your case, by 'fictitious drolls and dreamers', still does, through their interrelationship with the real author, become actual. Do you agree that this adverse motion really does exist and, if so, is it possible that it constitutes a dialectic and that the Platonic form might now be said to consist in this dialectic as opposed to a static idea expressed?

JB That's a wonderful thing to say: I hadn't thought of it, but I love it. There *is* a kind of opposite motion between the documentary novel and the epistolary novel. There is another element to that motion, too, which may or may not have anything to do with the Platonic line that we have been touching on. Back to Borges again and to the recognition in stories like 'Tlön, Uqbar, Orbis Tertius' that things can imagine themselves into objective reality. The best example of that is fiction itself. The story 'Tlön, Uqbar, Orbis Tertius' is a piece of imagined reality which, nevertheless, has an objective existence and does work in the world. Fiction is made up; and yet, having been dreamed into existence by the writer, it does actual work in the world — witness the novel of Harriet Beecher Stowe to whom, as you know, Abraham Lincoln himself, in the midst of our Civil War, said, 'You are the lady who caused all this.' Fiction does work in the world. The characters in a novel don't ever take on the kind of reality that real people have; but people can be moved and changed and touched by them, as by one's friends and intimates. Regarding the documents of history: surely these documents *are* history. And I suppose the documents which interpret those documents also constitute history, in that they do work in the world. They cause events and, in a sense, *are* events. I don't know where that leaves us with Plato.

HZ   Perhaps the Platonic idea, because it presupposes substance, can't really serve as an analogue for postmodern literature.
Your concept of history in the novel seems to be more useful, as it
suggests that documents constitute history while being, at the same
time, interpretations of it. Substance doesn't really exist then.
Nevertheless, doesn't this suggest the possibility of a sort of
dialectic at work in your writing which, although it does away with
the notion of substance, can nevertheless, through sheer continu-
ance — the sheer length of the novel, for instance — create
something like a substitute for the Platonic idea, a substitute for
substance?

JB   I hope so. I like the idea. Our friend John Hawkes, in the
conversation which we had in Cincinnati that was later published
in the *New York Times*, made a remark which touched me much at
the time and seemed, to me, to look deep into my preoccupations
as a writer. Jack said that he had the feeling about my novels,
especially the long ones, that they were spun out against a kind of
nothingness, almost as a shield against a kind of nothingness. I
guess, leaving Plato aside for the moment, that there is an impulse,
if not in all long novels, certainly in my long novels, that somehow
they will assume a kind of substance, or pseudosubstance, or
similitude of substance by their mere persistence. I think that's an
exorcism of nothingness, of the vacuum that one fears might exist
if one stops to look at the void. It's a long exorcism of silence, too.
As for the quality of this persistence: I believe it takes seven years
for every cell in the human body to replace itself. One should write
a novel that would take just that long to read — maybe this one
will — so that the reader, at the end, is literally not the reader who
began the novel. Not just in a mild Heraclitean sense, but literally.
No material cell that was in the reader's body on page 1 is still
there on page 772. I would love that.

HZ   So *LETTERS* reconstitutes itself just as does the reader's
body?

JB   Also the writer's.

HZ   I think that what you just said can be related to one of the
characters in your novel. In *The Floating Opera* Todd Andrews
held that *nothing* had intrinsic value; in *LETTERS* he has changed
his concept and has come to believe that nothing *has* intrinsic
value, which I understand to mean that nothing *contains* intrinsic
value or may lay sole *claim* to intrinsic value. Therefore, 'everything has intrinsic value'. Does this imply that, in a sense,
everything can be juxtaposed, opposed, or interrelated? By

accumulating, in your novel, so very many facts which really are connected only by coincidence (I am thinking, for example, of the long catalogues of dates and lists of persons born on one or the other particular date or of things that happened on that date) do you intend to give intrinsic value to every word?

JB Mind you, Heide, I regard both of Todd Andrews's propositions as strictly unintelligible. The two fates that await all of the principal characters in the novel are either (a) that they will literally re-enact crises from earlier on in their lives or their careers, or (b) that they will realize an opposite notion or be driven by a notion that is exactly the reverse of the notion that drove them previously.

Todd Andrews's notions are his and not mine, and they were in the original case, too: chess pieces on the board. I have never been a nihilist in the complete and naïve way that Todd Andrews was in *The Floating Opera*. But Andrews's notion, which he fears himself and admits to himself that he doesn't quite understand, is that perhaps his earlier nihilism is the reverse of the truth. If that is extended to other aspects of the novel, it would lead, of course, to the absolute chaos and anarchy of indiscrimination that threatens the novel, that threatens all lists, catalogs, anatomies and the rest. But against which, in fact, I hope novels like *LETTERS* are shores or buttresses. I might add, too, that, by the rules of dramaturgy, it's fatal to come to the kind of conclusion that Todd Andrews comes to. He is risking death in the same way that you risk moral chaos and paralysis by flirting with the notion that everything has intrinsic value. When Todd Andrews says that nothing *has* intrinsic value, that's as much as saying that everything has intrinsic value — just by the old rule of logic that whatever is true of everything in general is true of nothing in particular. That's fatal intellectually and morally. And because we are writing novels and not talking philosophy, it's also fatal in the other sense: a character must die if he comes to the realization that Todd Andrews did. Or at least he risks death.

HZ That's what I thought his notion of taking the tragic view of the tragic view of life implies. It's true that Todd Andrews is only one character in the novel. On the other hand, he is very self-conscious, very self-reflexive, and he knows, himself, that whatever opinion he holds he risks being wrong.

JB That's right. This does not paralyze him for action, though it always threatens to, and I will say, unabashedly, that I am more sympathetic to Andrews's character and ideas than to those of any other character in the novel. It's not a case of Todd Andrews *c'est moi* at all, but it is a case of there, but for the grace of God, go I. Andrews is a sensible man, a rational man, yet one whose view of rationality is, if not tragic, at least skeptical. I go along with that. When Todd Andrews is talking about the tragic view, he is certainly echoing ideas close to my own thought — especially when he wonders if he must take the tragic view even as the tragic view, because it doesn't always work. I feel that way, too.

HZ   Would it, then, make sense to say that you take the tragic view of character in *LETTERS*? Drawing a line from, let's say, Ambrose Mensch's realistic description of his East Dorset family to the letters which Todd Andrews is writing to his dead father, or which A.B. Cook IV is writing to his unborn son or daughter, to eventually the author's own fictitious and elusive personality within the novel, one could say that the concept of character gradually seems to disintegrate. On the other hand, if one understands Ambrose Mensch as the *alter ego* of the author, then this would become a reaffirmation of character or — because the author is involved — characterization.

JB   I would subscribe to that — with an amendment which acknowledges that the characterization which they and I realize is completed by the end of the novel, but what they have become are completed fictional characters. The tragic — or skeptical — view of characterization, I suppose, would be the recognition that, even in the hands of a great psychological realist (which I am not), even in the hands of a Tolstoy, let's say, the characters that are achieved are finally fictitious characters. The tragic view of characterization is that we cannot, no matter how hard we try, make real people by language. We can only make verisimilitudinous people. That view itself is on the minds of the characters themselves in a novel like *LETTERS*, and it's very much on the author's mind in a novel like *LETTERS*.

But as to the countermotions that you mentioned: those characters who don't actually dissolve by the end of the novel do indeed come through as characters should in a plot — if not to an affirmation of themselves, then to a kind of integration of themselves. But what is integrated is not a person, but a fictitious character. I want the reader to be left with the feeling — it has just the right flavor — that these are remarkably lifelike puppets going back into the box. I want them to act like real people in the reader's imagination for a time, but I want them to begin by seeming made up and to end by seeming made up. I take the tragic view of the tragic view of character.

Donald Barthelme

Donald Barthelme was born in Philadelphia on 7 April 1931. At an early age he moved to Houston, where his father became a well-known architect working in the style of Mies van der Rohe and Le Corbusier. Barthelme's experiences in Houston, as a reporter, a university publications writer, a founding editor of the University of Houston *Forum*, and an art museum director, were to influence the form of his later fiction. In 1962 he moved to New York City to edit the only two issues of Harold Rosenberg's and Thomas Hess's art and literature journal *Location*. When this journal folded in 1964, Barthelme remained in New York, devoting himself full time to fiction, occasionally teaching as Distinguished Professor of English Prose at the City University of New York. He has received both a Guggenheim Fellowship and the National Book Award, plus numerous other literary prizes. Since 1963 Barthelme's fiction has been appearing regularly in the *New Yorker* and sometimes in other magazines as well.

His Texas experiences play an important, if indirect, role in Barthelme's fictions. On the one hand they serve as a foil to, and seem to heighten his awareness of, New York language and New York life; on the other hand they appear to have been crucial in tying in his fiction with art and music. Among the forms of art, Barthelme prefers the collage, the apparently random accumulation of disparate items frozen, nevertheless, into meaning by their simultaneous presence, thus conveying a stifled, yet rebellious sense of plot. In music, Barthelme juxtaposes New York's contemporary music, which he describes as noise, with classical harmony. By making conscious the dissonance between the two, he reveals a longing for order which becomes tantalizing precisely because of the impossibility of fulfillment. Thus, when Barthelme compares his short fictions to pieces of music or to things in a still life, he points to what is, for him, their necessary ontological function: illustrating the irresolvable, just fleetingly bearable, yet overwhelmingly important conflict between sign and meaning. His stories always reflect upon their own limitations; they remain, to use the word of one of his characters in 'See the Moon?', fragments.

Thus, although many of Barthelme's fictions seem to be written with critical intent, they should not be viewed as satires. Barthelme himself has called a number of stories in *Guilty Pleasures* (1974) 'political satire directed against a particular Administration'. Other stories, most notably the well-known 'Report', could be added to this number. But all these stories lack an underlying ideal, the essential prerequisite for genuine satire, and there is not the hint of conscious moralizing. Pervading all of Barthelme's writings seems to be an ironic fatalism that would verge on nihilism, if life and language, for all their repetitiveness and superficiality, were not so ineradicably present. The story 'Nothing: A Preliminary Account' explains the privileged position of Barthelme's favorite form: the list. 'Only the list can present us with nothing itself, pinned, finally, at last, let us press on.' By extolling the principle of substitution instead of contextuality, the list keeps reminding us of possible exhaustion, of the emergence of nothingness at the end of the series, yet nothingness is never allowed to appear, to 'nothing' our world, because even a list that would 'get it all *inscribed*, name everything nothing is not' would then leave us with the list itself: trying to name nothingness makes nothingness — and nihilism — impossible.

'But if we cannot finish, we can at least begin.' Barthelme's fictions are a series of constant beginnings, abortive attempts to use lists as thrusts into an ever-receding nothingness, for lists require a context of meaning in order not to lose their dynamics. Barthelme's first collection of short stories, *Come Back, Dr. Caligari* (1964), makes extensive use of the ironic juxtaposition of sign and meaning, as in 'The Viennese Opera Ball', where a beautiful girl, eventually to be spotted by a *Glamour* editor, pretends to be thoroughly thrilled by the continuous 'discussions' which, consisting more or less of enumerations, include, for instance, a guest's list of sixty-seven nouns beginning with the letter *s*.

The epistemologically revealing, but semiotically meaningless use of much of contemporary language becomes one of the central concerns in Barthelme's first novel *Snow White* (1967), an episodic retelling, for the America of the mid-1960s, of the Grimms' and Walt Disney fairy tale. Initially the increasing meaninglessness of the new language of advertising, psychology,

education, and political manipulation actually ensures the dwarfs'
equanimity. In fact, they want to be 'on the leading edge of this
trash phenomenon, the everted sphere of the future', because at
the rate that the trash production is going up the point may soon
be reached where language becomes one hundred per cent trash,
at which point 'the question turns from a question of disposing of
this "trash" to a question of appreciating its qualities'. Only their
fondness for Snow White disturbs the dwarfs, because Snow
White, in waiting for a prince who will 'complete' her, is yearning
for someone who will use a new language, but a language that will
be meaningful to her, that will redefine the circumference of her
identity. *Snow White* thus illustrates the tension between progress
and love.

This tension continues to dominate Barthelme's fiction, especially the following three collections of short stories, *Unspeakable
Practices, Unnatural Acts* (1968), *City Life* (1970), and *Sadness*
(1972), although the tone in these volumes seems to change from
affirmative defiance in the first to resigned acceptance in the last.
In 'The Indian Uprising', the first of the stories in *Unspeakable
Practices, Unnatural Acts*, the pitch is set high. One of the
characters declares that she plays Gabriel Fauré's 'Dolly', a piece
set for four hands, whenever she is either sad or happy. '"I
accelerate," she said, "ignoring the time signature."' Her remark
implies that progress, the accomplishment of the hitherto impossible, demands not only ingeniousness, but the willing departure
from meaning, which becomes the loss of clearly marked emotion.
In *City Life* Barthelme appears to have attained an ironic stance,
an ambivalent balance between the conflicting notions of progress
and love, which seems most notable in the two related centre
pieces, 'The Explanation' and 'Kierkegaard Unfair to Schlegel'.
The two stories, written in a formal question-and-answer style and
interjected with black spaces, are studies in the disruption of the
identity of essence and phenomenon, an identity Kierkegaard
regards as the basic requirement for truth. Thus, these stories are
meant to be studies in irony, since with irony 'the phenomenon is
not the essence but the opposite of the essence'. Furthermore, for
Kierkegaard, the actuality of irony is poetry. But precisely at this
point Barthelme's confidence breaks down and gives way to the
reverse question whether any display of irony can be poetry,
because for Barthelme poetry should do what Kierkegaard would
claim only faith can achieve: reconcile progress and love. *Sadness*
states that this reconciliation is impossible through art. When the

narrator of 'The Sandman', in answer to his girl friend's frustration over not having succeeded as a concert pianist in her youth, nevertheless opts for buying a piano instead of continuing psychoanalytic treatment, he willingly takes a stand for love at the expense of ultimate artistic failure, for 'what an artist does, is fail'. Barthelme seems to agree.

Barthelme's second attempt at a novel, *The Dead Father* (1975), consequently reverses the idea of progress by turning it into a quest for love, yet making clear from the very beginning that this quest can only end in death. The Dead Father, at first still unwilling to give up love, is being led to his grave by his — unbelieving — son Thomas. Only when the Dead Father finally acquiesces in his burial and gives up his sense of self, can he become the Dead God, a monument revered by his people, '*working night and day for the good of all*'. His huge left leg, which is entirely mechanical, contains facilities for confessions which are '*taped, scrambled, recomposed, dramatized, and then appear in the city's theaters*'. By illustrating, in terms of technology, the archetypal struggle between father and son, in which eventually the father must always lose the right to love to his son whom he has taught how to hate him, *The Dead Father* comments not only on the loss of love entailed by progress, but also upon the necessity of that loss.

This final acceptance of the 'mechanical age' leads to a less ironic, almost nostalgic, stance in Barthelme's latest two collections of short stories, *Amateurs* (1976) and *Great Days* (1979). (The recent *Sixty Stories* collects stories published since 1961.) In 'At the End of the Mechanical Age', the last of the stories in *Amateurs*, one of the characters almost comes to deplore the passing of an age which did, after all, provide 'personal well-being and comfort'. And in the story 'On the Steps of the Conservatory', included in the collection *Great Days*, the moral of Never Enough is probably meant as a piece of self-criticism on the part of the author: if the artist must always fail, he should be generous enough to view his own art as only a small contribution to his age and times.

Interviews with Donald Barthelme

New York, 25 April 1978

HZ   Given the proposed title of our book. I suppose I ought to ask you about liberalism, but when I think of your fiction, I find it difficult to formulate a question that is directly related to any concept of liberalism. On the one hand, you seem to subscribe to a humanist position of leaving people and things alone so as not to interfere with their development (you state this explicitly in 'Brain Damage'); on the other hand, in your fiction, you are equally critical of the value of liberalism, conservatism, radicalism or any other position; they are all satirized or — more or less resignedly — accepted. It seems to me that, for example, there are several stories in which you allow different kinds of values to exist alongside each other — 'The Viennese Opera Ball' for instance, or 'Florence Green Is 81'.

DB   I don't have a clear idea yet what you mean by 'liberalism'. I think we have to get that defined before I can say whether I feel it's relevant or that it is not. I might point out that both stories, 'Florence Green Is 81' and 'The Viennese Opera Ball', are, from the aesthetic point of view, about noise (there is a lot of noise in both stories), noise in the sense of that which is not signal. Electronics technicians, for example, distinguish between signal, that is, intelligible message, and noise, which is static or garbled transmission. What I tried to do in both of those fictions in different ways was to make music out of noise.

Now we must talk about what kind of noise this noise is. It has to do with sensory assault; it has to do with bombardment. Both of these stories were written while I was still living in Texas. The noise level in Texas is, in every sense, considerably lower than in New York City. Still, I must have felt, when I wrote those stories in the early 1960s, a high noise level. And that's a structural concept because that's the way the pieces were put together — in a mosaic fashion, by adding one little piece of noise to another little piece of noise. I don't have the texts in front of me, so I don't recall what they are; but I do remember that they were rather carefully built up of interesting bits. A 'bit' again is a computer term. I think a 'byte' is eight 'bits'. A 'bit' is the irreducible computer input. But, as in a collage, you select. A lot is left out of both pieces. I think 'The Viennese Opera Ball' begins with some kind of quote from a surgical manual. The guy is discussing the use of the forceps. He says, in essence, although his language is more elegant, 'Be careful!' There is a kind of model character or beautiful young model whose name, as I recall, is Carola Mitt, who moves through this rather noisy Viennese opera ball which has inputs from many times — historical times. Similarly in 'Florence Green', who is an old, old lady. It's not her fault that she is rich or that her husband was an oil man who drilled into the ground and had a lucky strike and found already distilled gasoline in a great gigantic pool — Texaco was the brand name. He found it as crude oil but in the story it is Texaco, which is like saying that he found Dannon yoghurt under the ground. So this is not from a political idea, but from an aesthetic idea. The aesthetic idea being what it would be like if we had all of this noise pulled together and then turned up very high — increase the volume. What is the aesthetic effect? That's what I'm interested in. There may be political coloration to the individual 'bits' — of course there is. That is where my morality comes in.

HZ   Can your morality be connected with the fact that these stories are structured like pieces of *dissonant* music? You obviously did not try to achieve the effect of harmony ...

DB   No! It's late twentieth-century music, which is, clearly, noise. That's what we are subjected to all day long if we live in cities. Our lives are *enhanced* by Beethoven; we're *subjected* to a day of noise.

HZ   But can't the rendering of noise become a metaphor for the need to accept all kinds of other dissonances also?

DB   I don't *accept* the dissonance. I *notice* it and write about it. The greatest dissonance of my adult lifetime was the Vietnam War, which many people did not accept. But the weight of the anti-war movement was eventually felt. Grace Paley across the street was a heroine of the anti-war movement. She devoted almost full time to ending the war. I published a story called 'Report', about 1968, which I hoped would magically end the war overnight. It didn't, although it is a rather strong story in propagandistic terms. A guy in the middle of the story pulls out a big sign and says 'The government is misbehaving! Stop it! Stop it!' It didn't do any good. Well, maybe it did some good, a thousandth of an inch worth of good.

HZ   Could it be that the problem of ineffectiveness is at the heart of any social satire? Because when you are trying to create aggressive social satire you need the foil of an ideal concept, and this ideal concept tends to deconstruct the satire from the very beginning.

DB Social satire is of minor importance not only in the world, but also in what I do — I am of an ironic turn of mind. What I'm most interested in is language and making a kind of music. If I told you, as a straightforward proposition, that eating people is wrong, could you agree with me? 'Yes', you might say, 'on balance, eating people is wrong'. So, as I told you, I have made a proposition in the English language that is sensible, that is moral, and to which you can only give assent. But I haven't told you anything that you don't already know. What I'm trying to reach is a realm of knowing that cannot be put precisely into words, but must be gotten as music is gotten. Take a piece of music which is not program music, not describing, let's say, 'The Fountains of Rome'. You cannot say precisely what this piece of music means; on the other hand, you cannot say that this piece of music is meaningless. It has a meaning and a very strong meaning, but you cannot say precisely what that meaning is and perhaps should not. It's this kind of thing I would like my writing to do.

HZ Is it important to you that there's a difference between music and language, that language refers to objects more directly than music does?

DB What I am trying to do is to make a language that does not do that. The question is, is it possible? I don't know yet. I find myself moving toward an increasingly abstract language which has the bad effect of leaving more and more readers confused and unhappy. I greatly regret that, but I can't help it. Possibly this degree of abstraction can't be done. A second possibility is that it can be done but shouldn't be done.

HZ You say that you are of an 'ironic turn of mind'. Now, in 'Kierkegaard Unfair to Schlegel' you explicitly deal with the concept of irony, trying, it seems to me, to question subjective irony as defined by Kierkegaard. Irony, in your fiction, seems to be a defensive strategy against objects rather than a means for the subject to become negatively free. Let me put it differently: You say that you want to create a language that is, in a certain sense, independent of subjective consciousness, that becomes something like an object in its own right. You want language not only to be an objective correlative of your thoughts but to become autonomous expression — like noise. Is that why you object to Kierkegaard, with his stress on the subject becoming free through irony?

DB My account of Kierkegaard's theory of irony is accurate insofar as I am quoting, with attribution, his *The Concept of Irony*. I consider that all through my work there are thousands of tiny pinpricks of statements which, if one analyzed them or added them up ... I don't want to make any big moral statements. I think Rilke can say: 'You must change your life', and that's probably true; I wouldn't disagree. But I can't make a statement that big; or I have not achieved a statement that big, one could argue. But what I do manage, or what I try to manage, is to make a thousand little statements — half-turns of the screw in the direction of what I consider to be the Good. The accumulation may not be noticeable; but that's my contribution. In that story, 'Kierkegaard Unfair to Schlegel', irony is equated with masturbation, explicitly in the beginning when the guy says: 'I use the girl on the train a lot.' That's a masturbation fantasy; and again at other points in the story. This has never been noticed by any critic. So irony is considered to be masturbatory. The Danes, for example, have a saying that masturbation is to intercourse, to making love, as eating at a hot dog stand is to having dinner in a restaurant. My conception of what that story says is that irony is, finally, of not much use. Nevertheless, there is an ironic cast of mind that you have acquired or whatever. And everything you write is stamped with it; you can't get away from it. It's a struggle sometimes against irony. These are the types of issues that the story tries to engage.

HZ   You mean that the subject cannot become free—even negatively free—by being ironic?

DB   Irony *is* always a kind of push in the direction of freedom. You are trying to disassociate yourself from something that is going on around you, usually something in which you are in some way involved. So that, if you are at a social function and suddenly find yourself dressed in a very stylized (what we call 'black tie') formal dress, you feel like a fool by being in this thing, which we also call a 'monkey suit'. So you make a joke about it in order to disassociate yourself from the whole affair. You look at what is going on and you say: 'This is not me. I am not wearing this funny-looking suit. My ordinary self spends ninety-nine percent of the time in blue jeans and an ordinary shirt. I am being false to myself by wearing this absurd costume.' You are trying to liberate yourself from this ridiculous formal constraint by making jokes.

HZ   So then your irony does relate to your environment, right? It is a strategy to deal with objects or situations in order to avoid escapism or daydreaming. And Kierkegaard was probably wrong when he thought that, through irony, you can disengage completely from reality; because reality is inescapable and you are always part of your environment and the world.

DB So then I come back and am absolutely serious by saying that what I am really trying to do is cope with Kierkegaard's disapproval of me; because, as a moralist, he is obviously my superior and I concluded that, viewing my life's work, Søren would disapprove. Not only disagree, which I could stand, but disapprove, which I couldn't. I don't disagree with him. But, you know, Schlegel, to me, represented the aesthetic side of the problem and I don't think that Kierkegaard gives adequate consideration to that. Nevertheless, Kierkegaard's is the most sophisticated analysis I have read of the operation of irony, and it is a pleasure to disagree with him.

HZ In *Snow White* Dan evolves the theory that the 'filling' or 'stuffing' part of language has '(1) an "endless" quality and (2) a "sludge" quality'. And 'the "sludge" quality is the *heaviness* that this "stuff" has'; that is, if I understand you correctly: the 'sludge' quality of language — by becoming infinite in quantity — assumes value, meaning. Thus, language itself seems to have become inherently ironic. But would you consider this to be an aesthetic or an ethical phenomenon?

DB Well, I don't know if I would be speaking to your question if I said something which I feel is pretty obvious: that is that irony is originally, at base, a defense. Then what one has to ask is: a defense against what? I think it is a defense against nonsensical impositions by other people who force themselves into your life. For example, we have here in this country a thing called the Internal Revenue Service, the authority charged with the collection of taxes. Fine folks, lovely men, they are the Robin Hood's band of the government. Very meticulous, all well-schooled, and they know the numbers very well. There is no defense against the Internal Revenue Service except irony, and that is not much of a defense. It's like trying to use irony against the telephone company. It doesn't register with them. Of course, wit can hurt as hard as a killing. But the first problem of wit is that it requires a witty audience. If you have an audience of sheep, wit is an ineffective weapon. Gregory Bateson (an American psychologist) said that the great alternative to psychosis is humor. Or, to quote the great Irish writer Flann O'Brien, 'Maggots chuckle dementedly in the grass at this remark.' That satisfies you, but doesn't really deal with the situation. It's an escape valve. It doesn't do anybody any good but, on the other hand, it is a kind of necessary defense mechanism.

HZ Do you really see humor, wit, and irony so pessimistically? Perhaps irony can be seen as the source of meaning in a fiction. In trying to understand your language theory in *Snow White*, I linked it up with Clem's theory, in that novel, about life in America, and with his statement 'that Americans will not or cannot see themselves as princely'. Could we say that an increase in ironic language is meaningful because it mirrors increasing trashiness, because it mirrors an increase in democracy?

DB I certainly do not equate democracy with trash. Trash is waste. Democracy is the best idea we have come up with that I know of politically — a Greek-Christian kind of social organization. So I would not say that democracy equates with trash at all. Trash is not produced by democracy but by economic organizations, which are different from political organizations. In political organizations you get any individual guy and voter (poorly educated or well-educated, it doesn't matter) — he pretty well knows what he is about, what he hopes for, what he thinks. It is going to be pretty well clear to that guy. He is going to know what scares him, what worries him, what he hopes for. In a democratic organization — according to whether he's more worried or more hopeful, and so on — he is going to vote for X who answers his own needs, or he's going to vote for Y because this man seems to be more in tune with him spiritually. That's one thing. This guy is also, as a person, oppressed by and seduced by and, in some cases, vividly interested in the proliferation of trash being purveyed — as on television or in the local supermarket where he is being offered an unspeakable thing called Pringles, which are phony potato chips, (I don't know how you can make phony potato chips; it escapes me, but there is a thing called Pringles and it is a phony potato chip). Finally he will sort all of this out; he will stop buying Pringles and he will possibly stop buying other such rubbish. This guy is really pretty smart because he knows what his problems are. He is not smart in the sense that Lionel Trilling is smart, but smart in other ways. And remember, these people are being subjected to enormous pressures of seduction — media bombardments as they are called. But people finally get it sorted out.

HZ *City Life* begins with a story ('Views of My Father Weeping') based on the discrepancy between a rigorous aristocratic order and everyman's human emotions. It ends with a story ('City Life') where hierarchical order has been supplanted by complete democracy as a world system where everything seems to take place on the same level. Is it, then, that with this book you want to stress a gradual or rapid process towards a better social order? Is there no disenchantment? No point where aspiration and hope become satiety and disillusionment?

DB I think that the 'City Life' thing was originally two stories which I collapsed or folded into each other. They had to do with confusion and with the new young women coming to the great city — just as if they were coming to Rome or Mandalay, from China. They find and orient or just arrange themselves. And I think those ladies in the story, as I recall, are having trouble with this man, who is successful, who is a moralist except for his relationship with a revolutionary who is thick, thick, thick. This is pure disappointment in one of the girls's opinion; she has no luck at all. This describes many people I know — bad luck, bad luck. So I suppose that the contrast between the two is a contrast of expectations partially fulfilled and expectations totally unfulfilled. It is really a kind of stab at a description of the city, of people coming to Rome or Paris expecting great things — a kind of sociological essay clothed in fictional terms.

HZ Let me pursue this issue of disorientation, of disappointed expectations. On the one hand, 'City Life' can be read as a critique of the old aristocratic order, as a reluctant celebration of the virtues of democracy. On the other hand, 'Views of My Father Weeping' indulges, as it were, in a nostalgia for the old days, when everyone at least had his proper place and knew where it was. There seems to be an ambivalence here: genuine commitment to the radical criticism of elitism, but also genuine dubiousness about the alleged 'blessings' of democracy. The resultant mood appears to be one of resignation, of reluctant acceptance of disorientation.

DB I think you are asking for a *pure* critique of this, that, or the other. I think the question as posed asks for a pure critique, whereas I think that these critiques are always mixtures, admixtures of old values floating in the good soup of new values. They might pollute the good soup of the new values a little bit, but they are irrevocably there. So there is no purity.

HZ It seems to me that this struggle between old and new values is at the centre of *The Dead Father*. Do you think one could say that *The Dead Father* is based on the proposition that you can overcome the idea of fatherhood or godfatherhood, if you replace the idea of omnipotence with the idea of vastness? For vastness is synchronic in that its appropriate dimension is space; whereas the concept of omnipotence is diachronic: it implies the notions of inheritance, authority, tradition, and so on. The result might be that, if vastness undercuts the time-bound historical value of omnipotence, it can thereby overcome the hate relationship between father and son — but only at the price of a gradual wearing down of moral difference.

DB   I think that, in that book, the son figure would insist quite as strongly as the papa on the moral imperatives. It is not a situation in which moral distinctions are blurred or obviated. I'm afraid that the young man, whose name is Thomas, would insist as vehemently as the papa on the old rules learned from the papa. It is a situation in which one person is replacing another. The young prince is taking over; the old king is being conveyed to his grave. There is a slight shift maybe in values — now your word 'liberal' comes in handy. The younger one might be expected to be a little more liberal — and God only knows what that means to his people — than the old king. And he does take the old god-king to the bulldozers with a certain amount of respect. I mean he is not disrespectful, he is doing it rather ceremoniously. Yet there is some hint that, under the new regime, things will be done differently — maybe not much differently. He will turn it down a little bit, things will be a bit quieter.

HZ   Would it be possible to say that you prefer experience over meaning? For example, in your story 'The Balloon', the balloon, on the one hand, is said to be 'a spontaneous autobiographical disclosure' of the protagonist-narrator who inflates and anchors it in the middle of Manhattan as a subjective compensation for his temporary loneliness; on the other hand, it is an objective reality, so much so that 'at that moment there was only *this balloon*, concrete particular, hanging there'. Covering subjective and objective, that is, distinct realities, the balloon resists definite *meaning*. However, it can be *experienced*. Could this idea — that the world can be grasped and coped with only through an immediate and spontaneous response on the part of the individual — be said to recur in your fiction? And could it, moreover, be said to be mirrored in the fact that you prefer writing short pieces of fiction to writing long ones?

DB   I don't quite know how to answer that ... Turn your head in this direction and you will see a still-life by an American artist named William Bailey, which has something to do with the Italian Morandi and his still life paintings. Bailey is a young man; Morandi the Italian is quite an old man and he spent most of his life painting bottles. Morandi is wonderful, Bailey is quite accomplished. There is something about that painting which compelled me to hang it on my wall. You may observe that it is very strict in palette, not much fireworks in the colors. The palette is so strict, it's rather somber. But I like it very much. I can look at it for many days running. What does this do for your question? I think that maybe it is the idea of limits, of doing small things. Short stories are small things, very limited. A short story is, to me, like a small painting, or whatever, as against the Sistine Chapel which would be the pictorial equivalent of the novel. I like studies, studies for paintings, as the artists say. Jack Barth has been writing books that run to a thousand pages and which I greatly admire. But I can't do that; I have never written anything that ran two hundred pages. Maybe this is condensation, maybe it is a good preparation — who knows? But I don't trust big canvasses or can't do big canvasses.

HZ Yes, I understand why you like the sketch. Does this predilection relate to the idea that a long novel must not only develop a plot and characters, but also an underlying idea, a prolonged immanent argument? What I am trying to understand, or trying to ask, is whether, perhaps, you distrust idea or argument, whether you trust only the immediate response?

DB May I talk about what I'm doing now? I am writing a novel and the main subject of this novel is fear. Trying to understand fear. Fear has, as you know, far too great a part to play in our lives. I'm trying to figure out how fear arises, I'm trying to think about fear. For fear is a very interesting although despicable subject. People don't like to think about fear or read about it. There is not much written about it. If you go through the literature you won't find it — psychological or otherwise. You find very damn little about fear. There is a little in Kierkegaard.

HZ I felt that fear is also the most pervasive idea in *Sadness*, fear of the necessity and, at the same time, impossibility of finding and defining one's self. For example, in 'The Rise of Capitalism' you say that 'self-actualization is not to be achieved in terms of another person', whereas the protagonist in 'Daumier' tries in vain to institutionalize the idea of an ego-surrogate as a barrier to the ego's insatiability. But the most precarious position seems to be that of the artist, whose self-actualization, as you state in 'The Sandman', seems to consist in the very failure to bring 'here' what he feels is 'out there'.

DB To begin with, the phrase 'self-actualization' is a joke about sociological jargon and what it finally means is that you can't say to yourself that, by investing a lot in another person, the other person can save you. The other person can't even save herself or himself;

and no one can save anybody else. What was the second part of that question?

HZ There are really two more parts. In the short story, 'Daumier', do you try to set forth the idea that by consciously thinking of yourself as another person you can limit the desires of your own ego?

DB The fundamental idea is that the self is insatiable, and I think it is a mouth, a maw. It can never be passive. It cannot be told often enough: 'You are a good kid, you are a good person, you are a nice, beautiful woman, a handsome man, etc.' It can't ever get enough praise. The American writer James Purdy says: 'There are two things I like — praise and encouragement.' And I certainly agree. The hungry and fearful self can never be encouraged and praised enough.

HZ And what position does the artist hold in this struggle for self-realization — being, as I understand him, responsible not only for himself but for his creations as well?

DB In the story I called 'The Sandman' there is the line that says that what the artist does is fail. And the artist fails again, again, and again, repeatedly. He fails to do what he knows can be done. Even great achievements are failures. Even Shakespeare was a failure as an artist, because, by definition, there is always a level of achievement that could be greater.

HZ Measuring what the artist achieves against an ideal, this seems to be very true. But it could be argued that artists only need to set standards — standards of *possible* achievement — and that, if there had been no Shakespeare, the standard of dramatic art would not be as high as it is.

DB I'm sure Shakespeare felt that he had done a pretty good workmanlike job — not bad, but not what might have been done. But here we look at Shakespeare and say: 'My God, I could never do what Shakespeare did.' And it's true: we cannot do what Shakespeare did. If I were to do what I consider to be the highest thing, I would write poetry. But I'm not able to write poetry. I can go back and read Blake, for example, and I say: 'Well, my God, I wish I could do that.' And so, instead of trying to do Blake, I might steal a little from Blake. As Michelangelo said so beautifully: 'Where I steal, I leave a knife.' He knew how to steal. My father, who was an architect, said: 'Get out there and steal, but improve what you steal.' He told his students what stealing is, from an architect's point of view: 'Take the details and reduce them — Corbu or Mies or

Neutra — and improve on these guys.' Or else your stealing has no meaning.

HZ Doesn't that mean that some artists are at least lesser failures than others? Or to put it differently: that subjective failure doesn't imply that the artist fails objectively? Objectively, he may reach great heights and be a very good artist and still feel himself to be a much greater failure than lesser artists do.

DB It's a sadness that is part of life. Harold Rosenberg argues, for example, that what is interesting about Cezanne is Cezanne's anxiety. He finds anxiety everywhere in Cezanne. I can imagine works better than I can do. It is like that famous philosophical proposition: 'I am thinking of a happy island more beautiful than I can imagine.' It really does describe the situation.

New York, 23 August 1979

HZ Out of the sixteen stories that comprise *Great Days*, most reviewers concentrate on the seven dialogues which do not introduce specific characters, because for you this is a new form. Now, I remember you don't approve of the term satire as applied to your work. But I find that the stark juxtaposition of voices in these dialogues tends to beg the question of social satire. 'The Crisis', for instance, seems to deplore the success-and-failure ethic of American life, 'The Apology' the dominance-and-submission theme in sexual relationships, etc.

DB The intent is far from satirical. There may be satirical elements. What *is* the intent? I think, as always, to make a picture. When you use the word satire, I have to think back and try to remember what satire is used for. It's a destructive attack on its object — usually rather murderous and with the intent of doing away with something or changing something. These pieces aren't satirical in that way, although they could be *construed* as satirical. I think they are an accurate picture of how things are; but with little satirical intent, little satirical effect. They do try to capture extreme states, but my feeling is that these extreme states are now more or less normal. What would formerly have been considered an aberration has now become extremely common.

Someone commented the other day about the relationship between parents and children and the burden of the comment was that sarcasm was not much used any more by parents. Manuals of child-raising will tell you that sarcasm is the poorest of the parental instruments; irony is the next poorest. But whoever made that comment seemed to feel that sarcasm and, by extension, irony is just not much used any more. I think the reason for that is that parents are so buffeted, so knocked around by twentieth-century life that they don't have the confidence to employ sarcasm. The brute confidence has been taken away from parents by the conditions of contemporary life. In the same way I think you have to be a bit of a fop to be a satirist. I hope these pieces are really accurate psychographs.

HZ   Does this rejection of satire qualify your notion of the ideal also? In the story 'The Leap' you quote Kierkegaard as saying that 'Purity of heart is to will one thing'; whereas one of your interlocutors says: 'Purity of heart is, rather, to will several things, and not know which is the better, truer thing, and to worry about this, forever.' Do you believe that today idealism is bound to consist in willing several things and in worrying about the necessary choice? In other words: that, as compared to Kierkegaard, the very concept of the ideal is subject to historical change?

DB   Wouldn't it also be fair to say that there is no such thing as a single ideal? For example, Communism or Christianity or whatever. Since we have lived through and experienced the partial failure of many things proposed to us as ideals, there are always mixed feelings — mixed feelings is our condition, our mental set. Not one ideal — mixtures! All of these ideals are useful, but none are absolutes.

HZ   Is this intellectual and emotional condition of our times mirrored in the form of the dialogue in *Great Days*? Because I don't think that this form demonstrates what the first reviews of the book said it was to demonstrate, namely the artificiality of talk, or the impossibility of communication. I think these dialogues show a very real effort at communication, although not always an effort at good will on the part of the characters. They concentrate, I think, on special preoccupations or prejudices, on the only way a character can express himself or herself. Are these pieces, then, pictures of characters in some sense, or are they again meant to be only like pieces of music, self-sufficient because of the lack of authorial intrusion or comment?

DB   I would opt for music. I think we spoke before about music as a goal, about a kind of relevant meaning not immediately accessible to reason. Yet you hear the music and it means something. Again, that's what is being attempted here. The dialogues are no great formal invention. You find similar dialogues in Joyce and you find parallels in Beckett's novels and a lot of two-character dialogues in the plays. So formally it's nothing inventive, just a choice among available modes.

The form is attractive not because it presents any particular concept of character, but because it permits the use of a certain kind of language. This language can be very personal, very allusive, very quick. You are allowed to get to the center of a situation very quickly. There is, as you say, a stripping away of a lot of authorial intervention. It is a stripped form, a very meagre form, a Giacometti-like form in the best case. All my references would be to painting. Come back to Morandi whom we discussed before: it's a *poor* form.

HZ   But doesn't it allow for a clearer stating of contrasts? In all of your fiction, but especially in this book it seems to me, you have a tendency to juxtapose various types, if not of character, then, as you say, of language: technical language and some particular idiom, or highly cultured language and slang, etc. May not these dialogues heighten any such contrast, make a story more comic, for instance?

DB   Yes, it's a liberating form for me. How long it will remain so, I don't know.

HZ   I think that one of the most interesting stories in the collection is 'Cortés and Montezuma', because it combines the historical perspective with the notions of religious belief and romantic love. Montezuma loves Cortés as if he were a god and he wants to sacrifice himself to this god. Cortés, not being a god, cannot accept the sacrifice. That is, he cannot redeem Montezuma, which is what Montezuma desires. Do you want to demonstrate, in this story, the failure of ideal or romantic love, which here takes the form of religious belief?

DB   I think, historically, Montezuma had been taught that the god Quetzalcoatl would come back to Mexico. He had left Mexico on a raft of snakes, as various accounts have it. Montezuma presumably felt himself a kind of caretaker god, a caretaker for a greater god. Cortés, at least initially, was what had been prophesied. That is, the coincidences between the description of what Montezuma was waiting for and what Cortés appeared to be are striking, almost incredible. Cortés took advantage of this fact. But all of the accounts show that Cortés also admired Montezuma inordinately. There was great mutual respect.

An interesting question, which perhaps I didn't sufficiently explore in the piece, is what Cortés thought he himself was doing in this situation. There was a revulsion against the Aztecs' form of sacrifice. There was an intent to substitute the Christian gods for the traditional ones. Cortés was going by the book in this instance. The question of Montezuma's end is disputed. Some scholars argue that the Spaniards murdered him. Others argue that, as in the story, Montezuma was fatally injured during an uprising by his own people. I chose the second idea, which may have been softheaded of me but felt more nearly correct. From a practical standpoint Montezuma was much more useful to the Spaniards alive than dead. There is no doubt that Cortés was despondent. You can't characterize either Cortés or Montezuma as anti-romantic. They are both as romantic as men can be under the circumstances.

There was also an immediate military situation. Cortés's men were under attack by another Indian faction. The Indian leadership decided that Montezuma was fatally compromised and so they launched a very heavy military attack. Cortés had to withdraw from Mexico City under very superior attack. It amounted to a rout. He went across that causeway, then went across the lake and got shot up pretty badly. It's one of the saddest stories I know. Not mine, I mean historically.

HZ Would it be possible to say that, like 'Cortés and Montezuma', 'The Death of Edward Lear', is, among other things, a story about the interrelationship between fact and fiction? Edward Lear knows when his own death is going to take place just as a reader would know how many pages of a novel remain to be read; and once he is dead and his dying is re-enacted on the stage, he seems to become the ghost of the actors who incorporate him. Thus, the distinction between fact and fiction seems to dissolve. Does Mr Lear try to demonstrate that for him as an artist his own death is nothing out of the ordinary: no philosophical or existential issue, but just another piece of art?

DB I tried to suggest at the end of that piece that Edward Lear also partakes of Shakespeare's Lear. Tolstoy's story 'The Death of Ivan Ilyich' is usually thought of as the, or at least a, classic rendering of the fact of death overtaking an ordinary citizen. Ivan Ilyich notes something is wrong, and for a long while he doesn't understand what is happening to him. Then, at the very end, something does happen to him and he dies. But he only has about fifty percent consciousness of what's going on, what's happening to him. Edward Lear was not an anonymous citizen, he was a very celebrated citizen of England. He was an artist, he made things happen. In the story it's suggested that he made art of his death, that he made a highly dramatic event out of his death, but at the same time insisting on its ordinariness. So there is a kind of quadruple flip there. One is that he is not an ordinary man, he's an artist. He presents his death as a managed event or almost as a painting of his own. Two is that he insists on its ordinariness and at the same time, at the very end, he protests against it, and he is making a Lear-like or Dylan Thomas-like 'Do not go gentle into that good night' version. What's the point of such a maneuver? The point is that it suggests various conventions to try and render the thickness of the event — multiple aspects of it.

HZ   You say that 'The Death of Edward Lear' refers to literary or historical models, for example to Shakespeare's *King Lear*. From many of your fictions I get the impression that you are interested in the change brought about by a shift in historical perspective, if this shift is mirrored in a change of language. 'The Question Party' seems to be a striking example, because the ridiculousness and hypocrisy of the characters in the original story are revealed, not through parody, but through the fact that you leave the story as it is and just add a few lines to it. But these few lines put the story in another perspective.

DB   You are right. There is no parody involved. Most of the story I did not write, most of it is a 'found object', an *objet trouvé*. But I did cut it a bit and edited it and added a few lines. I don't think I could have taken that 1850 story and just presented it purely as a museum exhibit. Yet it's just another picture.

HZ   Although I like the idea of the picture, I am afraid I question it at the same time, because it seems to me that the meaning of some of your stories derives from the juxtaposition of different historical contexts; and the picture, of course, would not necessarily have such a context. May I give another example? In 'The New Music' you contrast the old belief, the ancient belief of the Greeks, with the new music, the new belief, which at present seems to be something like 'Christianity'; but of course 'the new music will be there tomorrow and tomorrow and tomorrow'. There will always be the *new* music. I thought there was a movement within the story away from a belief in nature, the representative of which is the Demeter figure Momma, and toward a belief in history and change. Again, this would be more than a picture; the story would then deal with a development, I think.

DB   It's a lament. I worry about these two men. They seem quite decent fellows, but something is missing. The story doesn't really suggest that there are any great prospects. There is a line: 'I called the number for help and they said there was no more help.' What has happened to these people? The story does not, perhaps, provide an adequate answer to that question. Its meaning is mostly in the overtones, it's a question to me of how the overtones register, since I proceed by a kind of system of allusions and you can only guess at how many of the allusions strike home with any particular reader. It's based, in part, on an old jazz tune called 'Momma Don't Allow' which catalogs what Momma doesn't allow. In the jazz performance there is a kind of chorus chanted which says, for instance, 'Momma don't allow no trombones played in here'; then the trombone player comes in and plays. This is left out of my version: you don't get that catalog, that violation of what Momma don't allow. Momma is given a very important role here, whereas in the normal rendering of the traditional jazz song Momma is controversial, because the trombone player comes in and plays. Momma don't allow no banjo played, but the banjo player comes in and plays the banjo. These guys are wry bachelors, although they apparently have lady friends. They are a bad case. They go to bed and put on their fancy nightshirts, but get up without much expectation for tomorrow. It's a very depressing piece.

Let's psychologize for a moment and ask the question: What can these men in this story hope for? Other men are going ahead, rising in the ranks of organizations, saying momentarily important things on the floor of the United States Senate, running for office, making money, having love affairs. You will notice that these men are doing none of that. They are separated from all notions of, or all belief in, progress in the world.

HZ So between memory and hope, the two poles of the 'emotional terrain' of your stories, as stated by the jacket flap, they will only have memory. But doesn't that imply that your 'psychographs' deal mostly with those who are underprivileged —either through circumstance or through ill-fortune? I am thinking further of stories like 'Belief', 'Concerning the Body-guard', 'The Zombies', or 'On the Steps of the Conservatory'.

DB That's true, but these stories came from such different impulses that I find it difficult to parallel them. Take a story like 'On the Steps of the Conservatory'. The Conservatory is kind of a holy city. One woman is in it and one woman is not. I subsequently wrote a sequel to that story in which the two women are again called Hilda and Maggie, and Maggie is the one who is in the Conservatory and is theoretically trying to help Hilda to get in. In the sequel a glorious messenger comes riding up and tells Hilda that she has been appointed to the Conservatory by presidential order. She goes to tell Maggie that she too is in the Conservatory now and Maggie says, 'That's wonderful, but I have to tell you that a lot of the Conservatory people are leaving the Conservatory and going to this new place which is called the Institution.' And then Maggie tells Hilda about the Institution, which is much, much better than the Conservatory — and, of course, it's very tough to get into. And of course Hilda wants to get into the new place, the Institution. So it's exacerbating. Poor Hilda! I think it's the absolute condition that Hilda will never get into the Conservatory or the Institution or whatever — even if the Conservatory were a different place. There is no straight explanation for that. It's a picture of Never Enough.

Malcolm Bradbury

Malcolm Bradbury was born in Sheffield in 1932. As a consequence he was one of the first beneficiaries of the 1944 Education Act, which made free secondary education available to everyone. He suffered from a heart defect which was not rectified until he was in his late twenties, when he was among the first adults in Britain to be offered a newly-developed form of heart surgery. It saved his life. Indeed it was while he was in hospital awaiting this operation that he completed his first novel, later ascribing some of the pessimism of the concluding chapter to the fact that at the time he felt he might not survive. The book was begun in the early 1950s but did not appear until 1959, after Kingsley Amis's *Lucky Jim* had demonstrated the market potential of the university novel. Malcolm Bradbury took a BA at Leicester in 1953, and a PhD at Manchester in 1964. After teaching at Hull and Birmingham he has, since 1970, been Professor of American Studies at the University of East Anglia, Norwich.

Both of his first novels feature liberal protagonists, trying to deal with the fact of personal and public disintegration. Despite an underlying pessimism, which made the characters evidence, and to a certain extent agents, of the forces which they opposed, the comic method in some degree recuperated a threatened humanism. Indeed it was as a comic novelist that he principally attracted attention, Bradbury being seen as a Waugh-like satirist, more especially since his second novel, *Stepping Westward*, published in 1965, offered a mordant view of America, rather as Waugh had done in *The Loved One*. But in fact it was a book which, beyond its satirical edge and parodic tone, developed a theme which became increasingly central to his work — the confused passivity of liberalism and the amoral manipulations of those prepared to enforce their definitions of the real. Usually the latter are presented, or see themselves, as being radicals, but his concern is less with radicalism as such than with those who make a coercive use of history, who manage to function in a world which seems to have unnerved the liberal, and to be slowly draining of its human content.

As a student he went to America as a Fulbright scholar, and as an academic he became first a lecturer and then a professor of American literature. In fact he moves easily between the two cultures. As a literary critic he is in a tradition typified in England by Richard Hoggart and Raymond Williams, and in America by Lionel Trilling, which is to say that he is a cultural critic, concerned with locating writers in terms of their social and cultural context. But he has been by no means hostile to the developments in linguistic, structuralist and poststructuralist criticism. Indeed his internationalism is evident in his criticism, in his concern, in particular, with the achievements of modernism and postmodernism. Monographs on Evelyn Waugh and E.M. Forster underlined primary influences on his work, while studies of the contemporary novel emphasize his concern with new directions in writing on both sides of the Atlantic. He is joint editor of the Methuen *Contemporary Writers* series.

His third novel, *The History Man*, appeared in 1975. It bore the marks of his sense of a shift in the social and literary sensibility. Like his first two books, it was a comic novel, but the comedy was no longer recuperative. In an introductory essay to a reissue of *Eating People is Wrong* he observed a move away from a 'generous comedy' in his work and that of others, towards a humour which emphasized irony and contingency. And in *The History Man* comedy no longer intervenes between the individual and the consequences of his actions, no longer offers to heal social or psychological wounds, no longer conceals the force of contingency or the vulnerability of those who hesitate to intervene in a world which appals their moral and aesthetic sense and who thereby compound its estrangements.

Like his two previous novels, *The History Man* is set in a university presumed by Bradbury to be a setting in which one can legitimately expect to find humane values surviving. But this time the university offers only an environment drained of human content. It is a world of concrete buildings and squalid underpasses, of alienating surroundings and alienated individuals. Liberalism survives only as a vestigial presence in some way implicated in the creation of the situation which oppresses it. Power seems to have passed into the hands of those who spin their fictions and manipulate those around them in the name of history, the liberal lacking the will to engage a twentieth century so at odds with values forged in another age when history apparently bowed to the power of individual will and imagination. And now the narrative voice makes no concessions. The characters are isolated from their roots in a private and public past by a narrative which operates in the present tense. Alienation has evidently infiltrated the style and structure of the novel itself, posing questions about the nature and function of art and the status of the writer. The narrator is no better placed and shows no greater inclination to enter the consciousness of the characters.

The only character who invites the reader's empathy betrays that trust. It is a novel which bears the marks of a profound unease, not merely about the direction being taken by contemporary society — though the book's action is carefully located in time — but about the role of the writer. Adapted by the dramatist Christopher Hampton, it became a highly successful television serial in 1980.

Bradbury's new novel, *Rates of Exchange*, as he explains in the accompanying interview, is to be concerned with the fictional content of all exchanges, the numerous and arbitrary values ascribed to currency in Eastern Europe providing a paradigm of this. He is also the author of many short stories, the most recent collection, *Who Do You Think You Are?*, appearing in 1976. He has written a number of television and radio plays, and is a fellow of the Royal Society of Authors.

Interview with Malcolm Bradbury

Norwich, 3 July 1981

CB You were brought up in what I suppose you would call a lower-middle-class family and you were educated in a provincial university in the early 1950s, presumably one of the first beneficiaries of the 1944 Education Act. In other words your background was rather different from that of those who had previously dominated the English novel. Did you have a sense of that difference?

MB Yes, I did. I suppose I am in that sense a prototypical figure from 1950s fiction, because my kind of person became a characteristic hero of novels during the 1950s. And so, to some extent anyway, did that kind of author, producing that kind of novel. But indeed I was a beneficiary of the Education Act of

1944. I think I was in the first year that went free to the grammar schools, and then I went on to a university as a first generation university student — that is to say, my parents hadn't gone to university. I suppose I then entered academic life with a certain kind of chip on my shoulder, feeling to some extent that I was an outsider in the university system. I think it is that kind of perspective that has encouraged me to write about universities, and also made the university into an appropriate subject matter for postwar British fiction, because a number of university novels were written by people who found universities as strange as going to Russia or as strange as a world of fantasy. It became an appropriate imaginative world to write about because it was new, because it wasn't part of the cultural heritage in which you had grown up.

CB You started writing your first novel while you were still a student at Leicester so that the incestuous relationship between critic and writer started very early. When you began to write, did you have a strong sense of writing in a particular literary tradition? Who at that time would you have claimed as your ancestors?

MB Well the two writers who interested me most were E.M. Forster, whose fiction I have written about since, and who, although he published his last novel in 1924, was of course still alive and very much an intellectual and moral influence in British culture in the early 1950s, and Evelyn Waugh, on whom I also wrote. Waugh was in some sense the opposite to Forster, you might say, because of his Catholic background, his ironic detachment from British cultural life. But he is one of the great comic writers for me and will always remain that.

It was a mixture of liberalism and comedy, really, that seemed to me to be the starting place for the kind of writing I wanted to do. As far as the liberalism that Forster represents is concerned, I think it is worth recalling that in the postwar period there was an enormous retreat from the kind of revolutionary politics that had been around in the 1930s. This was the time when people were writing books with titles like *The God That Failed*, books where they were asserting that the commitment to Communism, which they had taken up in the 1930s, was a mistake, that now the dominant political threat was of a new totalitarianism which was represented by Communism and no longer by Nazism. So that the conversion process from a kind of anti-Fascist position, which led naturally to a Communist position, into an anti-totalitarian position, which led to a liberal position, seemed to me the dominant mood. In this sense it seemed to me also the primary subject matter of somebody who was starting writing fiction at that time.

So when I started writing novels I wanted to write about this latter-day liberal atmosphere — what in America is often called the 'new liberalism' — with engagement but also with a certain kind of detachment because I also found it to some degree a comic performance. This was partly because it did involve an ideological change, you can say almost an hypocrisy, in the people themselves, and I felt myself to be part of a generation which was a successor to that particular switch, extremely interested in liberalism, extremely committed to it, in one way, but at the same time observing it as something that belonged to my seniors.

CB   Yes, that is the characteristic note of your work, isn't it? In a way you are celebrating liberal values but also exposing weaknesses in the liberal position. And along with the comic method and a basically liberal stance there has always been an underlying pessimism, even in the first novel. What is the source of that pessimism, and isn't it essentially antithetical to a classic liberal stance?

MB   Well, I think it is and that is really why I suggest that the detachment is partly present as a result of my sense of recent intellectual history. That is to say, in some sense I felt I came after liberalism, after the heyday of liberalism, after the liberal generation, without, I think, having anything except a kind of satirical irony to substitute for it. And so my posture might be said to be destructive, in that I have never quite been able to make sense of my own ideological position. I don't have a clear politics. But in another sense it is indeed a kind of pessimism that derives from my feeling that I would like the world of liberalism, a world dominated by liberal values, to prevail, but I don't see the historical conditions that can make it prevail.

CB   I wonder, though, in a way, if what you call liberalism is always clearly distinguishable from conservatism? In *Stepping Westward* the protagonist reacts against what he calls myths of dispossession, taking something away from someone and giving it to someone else, and he says, you remember, 'I'm for people, people keeping what they have struggled to have. I don't think we can yield up what exists for the possibility of what might; that is my idea of liberalism, kindness to what is, to those who now exist.' Do you think that what you have been calling liberalism all these years has been infiltrated by conservatism?

MB Well, I think it has, but not by what I see politically as conservatism, that is to say not by the conservatism of, say, Mrs Thatcher's monetarism. In that sense I think conservatism, too, is a peculiar quantity; as far as I am concerned, in Britain it is largely a mercantile and business philosophy, a philosophy in which I have no real interest in that form. But you might say that this is the Evelyn Waugh side of my work. I do see, I suppose, some sort of idyllic nineteenth-century past where the equation of individual and society is balanced in forms that I value; that is to say intellectual forms and social forms as well. The intellectual form, I suppose, is that which sees individualism as coequal with an account of society: that is, the individual may be counted as quite as important as any account of the social and political world. So determinism doesn't prevail; the individual is not a product, an outright product, of society, determined, ideologically, or in terms of entitlement to action, by exterior forces, but has a moral function within himself or herself, a power to act autonomously. So, at that level, I think I see my liberalism as nineteenth-century liberalism and because it is nineteenth-century liberalism it must take a conservative cast, I suppose.

In terms of a social order, well, again, I am disposed to identify with the world in which that version of man has power, in other words a world in which certain kinds of structures of individualism seem capable of being balanced against the social order. In that sense I am against state intervention or collectivism as I am against determinist theory, and I think my political priorities start from there, my political thinking such as it is. But at the same time I see this as an ideology that precisely does belong to the past, an ideology that is not consistent with the direction of history. It certainly is not consistent with the direction in which statism is developing, is not consistent even with my own sense of the importance of postindividualist theory, in psychology, let us say Freud and what that implies, or in sociological theory.

CB But if you don't believe in determinism what does a phrase like 'the direction of history' mean?

MB I think it just means having some feeling for the evolutionary process of history as it has developed over the last two hundred years; that is to say it is possible to perceive a direction, to perceive a set of forces at work without necessarily believing that those forces are an outright system of inevitability. They are nonetheless a direction, and I would say that my liberalism is very much infiltrated by determinism precisely as it is infiltrated by pessimism; that is to say, the two things may be connected.

CB   Your liberals, presumably as a consequence of all this, are nearly always presented as ineffectual. There is no toughness to liberalism as you present it, from Professor Treece, in *Eating People Is Wrong*, who is basically seen as a symptom of the things that he dislikes, to Annie Callender, in *The History Man*, who doesn't so much succumb in spite of her liberal values as because of her liberal values. Is that now definitional of liberalism as far as you are concerned?

MB   In terms of what I have just said, I think it is. That is, I can't see liberalism as anything more than a set of virtuous principles which are secreted in our culture without necessarily being functional in our culture. We are having this conversation on a day in which monetarism has intervened radically in the university system. All the laws of practicality and the laws of a declining economy and recession have attacked things that I actually regard as profoundly valuable, and to this extent of course one of the reasons I write so much about universities is that I do see them as bastions of liberalism in a society which on the whole is far less liberal than they are. And in this fashion I see a world of liberalism encroached on constantly from outside by the rules of economics, the structures of Freudianism and the psychoanalytical account of the self.

One of the ways in which this is important to me is that I suspect that most contemporary fiction is faced with the same sort of struggle. One way I would express it is to say that one of the fascinating things to me in fiction is the idea of character, which basically is a nineteenth-century idea and a liberal idea. In nineteenth-century fiction it is very easy for a writer to write the character, and the way in which this is done is part of a total equation of relationships between a person, the object world, the world of goods and chattels — the world of specifically real things outside the self, like society and history and nature. In the great nineteenth-century novels all of those things equate, as a set, and this allows the idea of character to be functional. In twentieth-century writing we have seen the disappearance of many of those ideas of character; in modernism it dissolves towards consciousness, and in an awful lot of postmodernist literature it dissolves towards text, dissolves away from a clearly figured subject.

There is a theory behind this, there is a necessity at any rate behind it, which is in part that it is extremely hard to substantiate the human figure in relation to the things that I have just mentioned, that is to say the object world, the world of nature, the world of society, the world of history. That securely centred figure has gone, and because this is so it seems to me that the writer of novels is persistently being driven to what I think of as a strangulated humanism. An awful lot of twentieth-century fiction, particularly late twentieth-century fiction, seems to me to be constructed exactly on this area of anxiety. The human figure is displaced in some fashion; the idea of character is dispossessed and then resought. Perhaps that is why people write novels, actually to rethink this question, to reach back to it. An awful lot of the fiction we talk about as postmodern, American fiction, French fiction, seems to be deeply structured on this idea of a lost human subject and a lost human voice, a voice which cannot personalize, which cannot signify.

CB But how, then, do you deal with those absences? *The History Man*, for example, doesn't really contain the values which it implicitly urges. Those values are expressed through their absence. But that creates a difficult problem I would have thought for the writer — how to sculpt the absence — and a difficult problem for the critic — how can he legitimately deal with what is not in the text but which nonetheless may be the crucial element?

MB Yes, yes, exactly. Well what I was trying to do in *The History Man* was to write a book in which there is no character who is securely there in a traditional sense, that is to say a character with whom you can identify. There is one character whom you can identify with, but she betrays you. So what this does is to force the reader into trying, as readers do, a set of equations where you do try to identify with one character then another, with each character performing a kind of act of fictional treachery or textual treachery against the reader. So in the end the safe houses that the reader can associate with disappear one by one. In this sense you are forced back again into the story. It was very hard to make this work when it was adapted for television, precisely because you can't go back over a television play; you see it once and that's it. In a novel you can go back, and I think to some extent the reader is forced to go back and to ask about the missing story — say the story of the wife, Barbara, which is absented from the book to a very large degree, but which becomes important at the end of it when Barbara becomes not only the one unexpected victim of the story but also the one person who has not yet betrayed you. In that fashion, I think, you start to create a new story to the book through her. But this does textualize the book, and the textualization perhaps locks in with other kinds of unease that I am trying to build all the way through — unease about this particular landscape, the landscape of a new university.

As I said, I do tend to associate universities with castles of liberalism, and yet at the same time this university itself is physically dehumanized and abstractified by its own architecture, and by the dominance in it of a kind of deterministic thinking, a particular kind of deterministic sociology. The result of this is that you end up by reading the book with a sense that there are successive displacements, maladjustments, which you as a reader then must comprehend. It's even more apparent in a more blatantly postmodern text like a Donald Barthelme short story, the classic one being the story, 'Robert Kennedy Saved from Drowning', where what Barthelme seems to be doing is to offer to portray a human figure, in this case a known historical human figure, and then develop the text by a set of half-factual, half-imaginative displacements around that figure. So you get a portrait, but not a logical coherent portrait, not a portrait you can hold, and what you remember is the way it is written, not the subject about which it is written.

CB   But in your description of how *The History Man* works, aren't you relying on the survival of the values outside the book which inside the book you suggest to have disappeared?

MB   I think that is probably true, but this is the problem with much of this sort of writing, which I do see as a culturally dominant sort of writing. Let us take another writer, Peter Handke, whom I admire very much and whose work can be read in two quite different ways. Handke's *A Moment of True Feeling* is basically a story about a man who lives in a totally disconnected world in which he experiences events as they happen to him, but he has no feeling about them, he can't actually create a feeling towards them or a connection with them. The book, then, expresses in one sense I suppose a classic schizophrenia. Does he ever achieve that moment of true feeling? Should he achieve it? That is the sort of question the reader might ask. At the same time the text is so powerful in its manifest expression of absence, what is not there, that you accept it as a total condition. You then read the words very very carefully as a kind of vision. It becomes almost a fantasy, and so many of the classic things which happen in fantasy, that is to say a sense of displacement, a sense of moving into another world, a sense of being estranged, being taken into a strange place, are also very important to the book. Estrangement I think is a very important part of contemporary writing.

CB I still don't feel I have got to the bottom of this. If in *The History Man* you create absences and you rely on the reader standing outside the text filling those spaces with values which inside the text are evacuated and do not exist, is there not on the simplest level, a contradiction at work? In other words the book relies on the fact that those values have not actually been wholly evacuated from our culture. And secondly, how can you as a writer control those responses to something which is not there? Or would you even wish to control those responses?

MB I think this raises the problem that so far in this conversation we have started with ideology or belief and then moved to fiction, whereas I suspect that the important issue is the reverse. I use fiction as a way of finding things, of discovering what I think or what I feel, and what I wish to say, and to that extent I wouldn't wish to put the liberalism that we were talking about prior to the way in which I write. I do see writing as a continual discovery.

CB Does that mean that from your point of view this uneasy debate that has been going on over the last few years about the nature and function of the novel is not a real debate at all. After all, the debate suggests that, on the one hand, there is John Hawkes, who says that plot, setting, character, and theme are the enemies of the novel, and on the other hand you have John Gardner, calling for moral fictions. Fictiveness appears to be located on one side and a kind of renovated, reinvigorated realism on the other. I take it from what you are saying that you actually don't accept the terms in which the debate is conducted.

MB No, not really. I think in this I would climb both the sides of the fence at once, which is a liberal thing to do. The problem I have with this kind of argument is that I think it is extremely hard theoretically, as a critic, to stabilize what we mean by realism or the moral effect of a novel. So that to assume that, let's say, John Hawkes's novels are not moral is to assume too much, because in fact Hawkes's way of allowing his imagination to flower and function — which I think he does better and better; I regard Hawkes more and more as a very important writer — is a 'moral' enterprise, to pick up Gardner's language. Gardner, I think, is making a bid to possess the moral voice of fiction in a way to which he is not entirely entitled. I have sympathy with him; I want writing not to withdraw from moral perception. But beyond that, there is the question about realism and what we mean by it. The idea that we now live in a world in which reality is in some fashion less available than it was has become obviously a very important one, affecting the debate we just talked about and helping to explain why writers like Hawkes write the way they do. It seems to me that perhaps the biggest question that displaces me from being the kind of nineteenth-century liberal realist novelist I was talking about is a very strong commitment to fictionality — or to what I would call nominalism. I think to be a good liberal you need to believe there is a real world out there, and that the real world is penetratively real, that it affects everything you do. In other words, liberalism and empiricism have some intimate connection.

CB   How then do you explain the author's note to *The History Man* which suggests that the characters, the place and the year in which the novel are set are fictions, as was the 'real 1972'.

MB   Classic nominalism. Let us come back to monetarism again — it fascinates me at the moment. The novel that I am writing now is called *Rates of Exchange*, and it is about money as fiction. I think money is a classic fiction: money is the way we talk pieces of paper into currency, into value. And now of course we have a confident theory of realism in money, though the more you penetrate it the more it turns out to be very questionable. That is to say, any economist that I have talked to in the course of writing this book says, well, the first problem is that we don't know what money is, we can't define it, or only by naming it after motorways, M1, M2, and so on; and the result of this is that they are using a set of fictions or hypotheses quite as mysterious as those we employ in literary criticism. They have come up with a critical definition of reality which is, for the moment, an economic law. Well, we all know what 'law' is in literature and science; it is a hypothesis working at the moment, though in the case of monetarism it seems to be working less and less well. Our sense of our definitions of reality or of history being true seems to me to be questionable according to perfectly recognizable and familiar criteria. We create reality by hypothesis. And the more we examine any accepted version of reality, whether it be a daily newspaper, or a computer language, or an account of 1972, the more we find it is constructed fiction.

CB   So they are plausible fictions.

MB   Plausible fictions.

CB   But just now you were invoking it a little less cautiously when you were looking back to the nineteenth century and saying that you need a sense of the real. Was your sense of the real already shot through with fictionality?

MB No, I'm talking about something that has come to preoccupy me and quite a lot of other novelists more and more. As a novelist, I started much more realist than I am now. My first two novels seem to be quite a long way from me now, precisely because, although they are sceptical about liberal realism, they employ the methods of liberal realism for their stylistic method or their code. To this extent I am describing a stylistic change which I do actually think is a change in perception which has run through the culture at various levels, and is apparent in our writing at various levels. That is, if you take the history of British fiction over the period from the late 1940s to now, I think you can see a curve running through it, so that what happened is that after the war a new generation of writers began to emerge — Angus Wilson, Kingsley Amis, Iris Murdoch, and so on — all of whom see themselves as postmodern in the obvious sense; that is to say, they are located after modernism, but the way in which they reconstitute the novel in this period tends to be with a very strong drift towards realism, a realism invested by new liberal values.

As I have said already there are historical reasons why that reinvestment could occur at that time — to do with the political state of the world, the need for the recovery of democratic institutions, and so on. This liberalism then gives a very strong sense of realism in British fiction, a rather protected realism in the sense that it has to be provincialized.

There is a very strong local, empirical, provincial streak to it: here we have good old commonplace British reality — Kingsley Amis's world of the pub round the corner, the bottle of beer and the blonde. In more sophisticated writers, like Iris Murdoch, it is a much more complicated equation, of course, but realism is back. In America, with Bellow, Malamud and Mailer and others, there's a related but different affair. It seems to me that what happens in American fiction after the war is an enormous renewal of history, or rather of historical concern. On the whole, American fiction prior to that date might be said to have been mythically, even idyllically inclined; but after this date there is a lapse into history, which has a great deal to do with the fact that many of the writers who were writing at this time are Jewish and are conscious of Europe, modern history, the holocaust, and their own status as survivors. So they are profound examiners of a new political world in which not just the American continent or the American dream are at stake, but the larger historical world of which America is now part. So there is pressure towards a kind of realism, and a sense of writing as dealing with profound moral issues. What is a human being, what is a person after the holocaust? So you get enormous pressure, again, I think, toward moral realism: in England, in the States, indeed in France, with existentialism, where these questions are also dominant. That's the climate in which I started writing.

By somewhere around 1960 these issues had been subverted or overturned, I think, by a quite different way of looking at things. And this different way of looking at things is signalled, I suppose, in France by the *nouveau roman*, and in America by what we call postmodernism. Now one of the interesting things to me about postmodernism is the incredible number of books that actually do start over again with the metaphor of World War II. If you think of Hawkes's *The Cannibal* and so on, if you think of Pynchon, who uses the war as a great barrier both in *V* and *Gravity's Rainbow*, if you think of Heller, with *Catch 22*, that metaphor of a world changed by the Second World War, so that it has somehow fallen into new systems, is dominant. But in these writers it is the systems that are terribly important, and war implies psychic dislocation rather than moral recreation. A classic book is *Slaughterhouse Five* — which on the one hand has the realism of the Dresden section and on the other hand has the fantasy of the Tralfamadore section. In the tension between those two lies a kind of equation of postmodernism, realism enforcing displacement, enforcing estrangement, so that Vonnegut is displaced into Billy Pilgrim to start with and then Billy Pilgrim is displaced on to Tralfamadore, where he learns new message systems. The new message systems have to be played back on to Dresden, and so it goes, as they say.

CB   So that again you wouldn't go along with Gerald Graff's attack on postmodernism for what he calls its inability or refusal to retain its moorings in social reality?

MB   No, I wouldn't go along with it entirely. I share the anxiety, but then you see my point really is that so does postmodernism, or the best postmodernism. I think there is a soft postmodernism, an easy option; it becomes an easily-played experiment. But in the best writers I see a very strong anchorage in social reality, but also a pressing question about what social reality is.

CB   I suppose another thing about postmodernism is that it is drawn so strongly to a comic mode, which is interesting also in terms of your own work because certainly on the basis of your first two novels you were presented as a comic novelist. Obviously your comedy remains in *The History Man* but it has undergone an enormous transformation. How do you see the transformation of your comic approach?

MB Well I think again it ties in with the things we have been talking about. In one sense it might be explained as a switch from one kind of comedy to another. I think there is a central tradition of the English moral and social comedy and I have drawn on it for the first two books. Forster would be an example, but you can also trace it elsewhere to writers like Jane Austen, or Meredith, or in the eighteenth century to Fielding. But there is another more disordered kind of comedy which I would associate with writers like Sterne rather than Fielding, Peacock rather than Jane Austen, with Dickens rather than George Eliot, and Waugh rather than Forster, which seems to me to portray the social world not as something which is set up for moral inspection and virtuous improvement, but as painful, chaotic. So the comedy is vastly more devastating, ironic, apocalyptic. In America this is what ends up in black humour. I feel that *The History Man* is veering more to that kind of comedy, though not all the way, because it is not a totally anarchic book.

The way I felt I was commanding the book when I wrote it was through irony, and the ironic voice that I managed to derive for the book was the most difficult thing to get. The way in which this is done is a retreat from that sympathetic posture of value which the other kind of comedy goes for. When I said earlier that you can persuade people to sympathize with a set of characters, one of the easiest ways to do that is to make them funny; an awful lot of unpleasant, unsympathetic characters have been made very manageable by making them funny. I tried not to do that in this book. I didn't want to make Howard Kirk funny. I don't think Howard Kirk is funny. I think it is the other characters around him who are funny.

CB I want to ask you something about narrative technique because the technique of *The History Man* seems to share something of the perspective of the principal character himself; that is to say neither Howard Kirk nor the narrator make any attempt to go inside the consciousness or the sensibility of the characters. Is there a degree to which you are offering a critique of a literary mode?

MB There is a critique of a literary mode and in a sense it is my own literary mode, it is the way I have written books before. As I have already said, there are very strong influences on that book which come from the British tradition of fiction. I was trying very hard as a writer not to do what I had done before; that is actually one of the things that make writers write. An awful lot of fictional activity is an attempt to break through to a new point, which is why postmodernism is interesting, because it does seem to me to be persistently curious about creative action as such. It opens the doors of creativity to many writers. But as far as the blindness of the narrator of *The History Man* is concerned, it is indeed a chosen blindness. Obviously I could if I had wished have gone into the minds of the central character, or of all of the others. The choices I made not to do this are very deliberate and they are choices having to do with my own questions about the relationship of motive and psychic action to the way the world works, to what people actually perform, what they actually do. Life in the book is indeed very much seen from the outside so that I am partly posing figures against landscapes or cityscapes and so on. The analogy that I had in my mind was that of camera and there is a certain sort of staging going on in the book all the time.

CB   But in the case of a writer like Jerzy Kosinsky, who uses a similar alienated prose, what you don't have is this kind of moral pressure, invisible in the text, against which you are invited to judge the text, whereas in your book I do feel that that is implied and that that judgement, that space, is important and that those judgements are important.

MB   Yes, and I think you are right. I wouldn't want to over-insist on that world outside the text. I think it would be impossible not to if you happen to read my previous two books but as far as that book stands on its own I think its presence is there in the implications of the withdrawal, the blankness that you were talking about, that is to say that I do persistently pose my characters against settings which I clearly don't like very much, the world of concrete and multi-storey car parks, shit in underground subways, and so on. I am on the one hand trying to suggest an element of aversion, of satiric aversion. On the other hand the aversion is perhaps not so much from Howard as such as from the world in which he has to live. And perhaps the largest element of implicit distrust is with the late twentieth-century technological and urban world. Again I think this is true of a lot of postmodernist writing. I keep using the word postmodernist not to try to say that I am one, but because I think that there is a relationship between various kinds of writing that are going on now and which are deeply flavoured with a kind of anxious fear about the relationship between human selves and systems, and the nature of the landscapes and cityscapes that we are building up for ourselves. I want that to be a presiding anxiety in that book.

CB   There is another level on which the book offers some degree of self-criticism, isn't there? You have always been interested in the process whereby people manipulate other people, create plots and then invite other people to inhabit them. Obviously Howard Kirk's seduction of Annie Callender, which is at the heart of *The History Man*, may be a cautionary tale about the liberal's desire to be screwed by history but on the other hand you are the novelist who is permitting it to happen and I take it that in a sense, not literal I hope, you are Annie Callender; you are being screwed by history. But you are also the person who collaborates with the forces which allow this to happen to Annie Callender. Now I take it that this is a conscious element in the book.

MB   Yes. The way I would explain it is that the reason I wanted that scene to be there, or the reason I meant the book to go in that direction, is that Annie Callender, as you suggested before, represents values with which I am sympathetic, but which I also think are inert or inactive. So I put at the centre somebody who takes a quite different line, offers to speak for history, offers to speak for change. Howard is the only person who acts in the book, the only real actor; all the other characters are in a sense self-satisfied. Howard acts out of principles which I don't share, but one of the reasons for making him a sociologist is that I did indeed want to associate him with Freudianism and the determinism that I see as necessarily penetrating liberalism, and changing it.

I think the great question I see behind both my work and a lot of other work is whether there is an individualism that can be reconstituted, how the idea of a person can be reconstituted from the present intellectual compound. Intellectual ideas are very important, they become social ideas, they become ideology and the problem is whether there is any idea of individualism that can be reconstituted that is not of itself deeply disappointing and vulgar, that is more than Marin County California individualism, more than the hustling individualism that is what the United States seems to be able to offer as the alternative to a collectivist future.

CB   I suppose one of the things I am trying to get at is whether your anxiety about manipulation, about people who want to inhabit other people's worlds, extends to your own role as a writer, as a manipulator of fictions?

MB   Yes, in the end an awful lot of novels are about themselves, that is to say that what one is conscious of doing in the book is indeed trying to relate passive agents to active plots. The derivation of a plot in a novel is a crucial affair, if you believe in plot, which I actually do. The organizational structure interests me, the making of a developing set of events which perhaps has some power or fabulous quality rather than just being a loose spinning of text, an open text. So the question of plot becomes part of the enquiry; why does one *have* a plot? Well I suppose I decided myself that one has plots because history does, too, and one has plotters because history does too; so making Howard into an historical plotter was quite an important part of the making of the book, in its simple sense as a construct.

CB   When you implied a little while ago that the English novel was parochial I presume that you were locating that in a particular time. I take it that you don't believe that the contemporary English novel is parochial.

MB   No, I don't. I never really completed what I meant to say about that. I did suggest that there has been a change in American fiction, a striking change in American fiction; I think the same thing applies in British fiction as well. One of the marvellous things about a number of writers I very much admire in the 1960s is the extraordinary opening out that they gave to what I thought was a narrowing novel. I think of people like John Fowles, in particular, who in *The French Lieutenant's Woman* manages to pose many of the equations of the decade, by using the liberal nineteenth-century novel form and setting, but at the same time asks all sorts of fundamental questions about the logics in that procedure, and interrupts it constantly at various points in order to vary it. So in a sense he gives an account of why the novel today is written in the way it is; his book is the result. The other book I think of is *The Magus*, which is an extraordinarily European book and in that there is a great opening out. There are lots of other examples, but I think that the Europeanization or internationalization that was going on in the sixties is really coming to enormous flower now; many of the most interesting British writers now seem to be interested in enlarged twentieth-century panoramas — like D.M. Thomas in *The White Hotel* — or in very elaborate equations of historical and fictional referentiality — like J.G. Farrell, who seems to me a very fine writer. Indeed many of the best writers of the fifties have gone through the same sort of change, like Angus Wilson.

CB   As will have been apparent from the way you have been talking you are of course both a critic and a novelist, a university professor, indeed, and as you know Gore Vidal has had some fairly caustic things to say about people who combine the role of novelist and academic critic; in fact he implied that postmodernism is virtually a product of that system and of the professionalization of literary study. Is there any substance to the notion that that symbiosis creates a particular kind of novel? Do you feel that pressure on your work?

MB   Yes, I think there is some truth in this, in the same sense that it is true that *A la recherche du temps perdu* or *Ulysses* wouldn't have been written if there hadn't been Paris. That is, all writing is conditioned by the environment in which its creator lives, and in which it is received. Vidal seems to be objecting to the fact that books seem to be written in one seminar room and studied in the next one, and clearly there is some danger in this. But the important thing that has always invigorated the novel, in my opinion, is the relationship between those who produce it and some serious aesthetic debates and intellectual debates, and you may find this in Bohemia, you may find it on campus, you may in Gore Vidal's case, find it on the one hand in American political life and on the other hand in his Italian city home. The point is that I think all writing needs a seeding-ground for its activity, and this involves some sort of audience that is prepared to recognize the terms in which the art is being done. What has been striking about the academic environment is in the end that it has produced some very good writers indeed, particularly in the States of course, and many of the writers that we have mentioned today are academics, or at least working on campuses.

CB   So that the loss of innocence has its advantages as well as disadvantages.

MB   Yes. It seems particularly important in this country, in Britain, because in fact there is almost no alternative intellectual scene, there is no literary meeting place, there is no café system for writers to sit down and meet, there is no Paris, Paris being of course a very small city indeed in an intellectual and artistic sense. So the university to some extent does provide parallel functions. What is curious about it is that in Britain — despite the fact that there are a certain number of writers like myself working in universities — contemporary literature is still very little studied. Maybe from Vidal's point of view that is a good thing. I actually approve of the study of contemporary literature.

CB   I'm sure it isn't by design but you have actually produced a novel for each decade and you are moving towards completing a 1980s novel, *Rates of Exchange*, which you mentioned earlier, and there is a sense in which each one of those books has captured things that are happening in the culture, cultural change, political change, changes in style, modes. What direction is *Rates of Exchange* taking us? Already a long way removed I imagine from *The History Man*.

MB   Yes, it is. I think it is true that I do tend to think of books as objects for particular cultural periods, partly because I think all writers do anyway, but also because I write very slowly and therefore it takes me almost a decade to write one. As far as this book is concerned, what I am trying to do in it is to preoccupy myself — amongst other things — with money, which I think is the important focal symbol of post-oil crisis, recession-obsessed Europe, and America too, and in the course of that book I am also trying, to some extent, to globalize the subject by making it a story of Eastern Europe and Western Europe. So it is set in an imaginary Eastern European country. One of the problems of my work is that I am called a university novelist and this is my first non-university novel. The only problem is that this imaginary Eastern European country seems awfully like a university. At times I feel in danger of short-changing what is a fascinating political theme. I have set the book in 1977 which was the year of the Royal Jubilee in Britain and also Charter 77 in Czechoslovakia following the Helsinki SALT talks, and so the issue of human rights or, again, what is a human being, seems to me to be set-up very usefully in the image of an exchange. But the question of how you try to exchange the Western value system or, you might say, Western currency in an Eastern European society is one important theme in the book. The other is language; the imaginary country has an imaginary language which changes in the course of the novel, rather like the French parking system. You know how in France you have to move to the other side of the street half way through the month, well how about if they had countries like that with languages that changed — Serbo in the first half of the month, Croat in the second? So that was the idea.

CB   May I take it that the comic mode is preserved?

MB   You may.

Robert Coover

Robert Coover was born in Charles City, Iowa, in 1932 and was educated at the universities of Southern Illinois, Indiana, and Chicago. He saw active duty in the US Navy from 1953-57.

He has taught at a number of universities and is a recipient of the Faulkner Award, the Brandeis University Creative Arts Award, a Rockefeller Fellowship and a Guggenheim Fellowship. He is married and has three children. For a number of years he lived in London but recently moved to Providence, Rhode Island.

Robert Coover's first novel, *The Origin of the Brunists* (1966), was received as an attempt to revive naturalism, while grafting onto it fantastic and even surreal elements. And he himself admits, in the accompanying interview, that it could be seen as his attempt to prove his skills in handling a conventional form in all its depth and complexity before occupying new territory. But in his picture of the efforts of a rational individual to penetrate mystery, in his flattening of the moral perspective, in the pressure which slowly breaks down moral assurance and a controlled social and aesthetic texture, there are signs of the work which was to follow. The form barely withstands the pressures which it is required to contain. There is a constant seepage which surfaces in the form of hysteria, madness, religious passion and sexual assertiveness. The final scene, indeed, in which the Brunists, an unlikely but all too familiar group of mystical zealots, experience a confused epiphany, collapses not merely into literal riot and spiritual excess but into stylistic and emotional anarchy. The perspective shifts rapidly. Reality dissolves and the re-establishment of consonance in the final pages is charged with unreality.

Robert Coover is concerned not merely with displaying the creative imagination but with moving it to the centre of attention, making that the source of the moral world rather than a reflection of it. The stories in *Pricksongs and Descants* (1969), for example, are in a sense concerned with deconstruction in so far as they disrupt conventional patterns, refuse to operate in a recognizable temporal and spatial world. Character is flattened, plot turned against its own implied rational structure. But the process is not presented as the simple disassembly of meaning. There are other orders than those proposed by time, other forms than those inherited from familiar literary modes. Art becomes less an analogy for life than an expression of it. The stories examine the process whereby control is exercised; they are equally an expression of the resistant imagination which operates in more dimensions than those suggested by the simple triangulations of the natural world. William Gass, indeed, has called *Pricksongs and Descants* 'examplary adventures of the Poetic Imagination'. But the mind which proposes cannot always dispose. The manipulator is not a wholly confident being. And if clarification rather than mystification is his primary objective it is achieved principally through exposing the processes of that mystification which, once clear, is no less mysterious, merely clearer in outline.

Similarly, in *The Universal Baseball Association* (1968) Coover creates not simply an analogue for the natural world, a metaphor which offers itself as an explanation and demonstration of intermingled free will and determinism. It is equally a novel about the special delights and pains of fiction-making, the sense of creating the world within whose boundaries we operate. J. Henry Waugh invents a complete baseball league and, with the use of dice and a complex system of mathematical tables, plays out the required fixtures, by degree and over time establishing a history and a tradition which provide another level of constraint and another source of satisfaction. Yet while being deeply moved by the events which he creates and observes he remains aware of another level of reality. But, in his god-like state, he is tempted to intervene, to break his own rules, to exercise the privilege of the creator. The effect is disastrous. The allegorical dimension plainly exists. But it is not primarily this which concerns Coover. His interest lies more directly in the processes of invention, in the moments when these inventions detach themselves from their origin, in the interplay between the given and the possible which is the essence of writing no less than of life.

Coover's concern with language, with the manipulative imagination, with the degree to which we inhabit imagined worlds, made *The Public Burning* (1977) more a natural extension of his earlier work than it might otherwise appear. Ostensibly concerned with the execution of the Rosenbergs for treason, it turns in fact into a bitter but funny account of private and public paranoia. His characters act out their lives in an increasingly bizarre world, adjusting themselves rapidly to the madness which they inhabit and in part create. Sexuality is presented as a distorted image of those assaults on the psyche which seem a natural product of personal relationships and public intrusions alike. Richard Nixon is a central character, as he was in fact in the hounding of the Rosenbergs, but here he becomes a parody of that collapse of self and of the moral world which he in part initiated and of which he was the paradigm. But behind the games, behind the metaphysical speculation and the layers of self-doubt, there is a genuine anger born out of a world in which values can be assumed to exist if only because their threatened collapse can generate a reactive art, because the writer feels obliged to challenge public fictions on their own ground.

Interview with Robert Coover*

London, September 1979

CB You have said that when you were at Chicago you felt dissatisfied with the traditional novel and also you sensed there were fundamental shifts going on in the way people perceived reality. Can you elaborate on that? What were the sources of your dissatisfaction with the novel as it was, and in what sense were we beginning to perceive things differently?

RC At Chicago I was taught that all rational discourse was like a kind of game, with its own inherent possibilities and limitations, and that the history of that discourse was like a kind of history of changing fashions, a swing from possibility to possibility, often accompanied at first by eurekas of discovery and ringing manifestos, but then a moving on when each possibility in turn revealed its own inevitable limitations. Some of these shifts or swings took place from generation to generation, petty squabbles often, but some were more fundamental, and it seemed to me that we were on the threshold of a more fundamental change, moving into a new metaphysical age like that of the seventeenth century. Probably I only wanted to dramatize my own emergence or something. But what I read in physics, psychology, sociology, what I saw happening in the arts, all seemed to suggest a basic shift

---

*This interview was transcribed and largely edited by Robert Coover.

in underlying assumptions, underlying principles. The comforting structures we'd been living with for three centuries or so were giving way suddenly to a less conveniently ordered view of the world in which everything seemed random and relative, and in which all the old isolated disciplines found themselves flowing into each other, their old ways of organizing the world being recognized as essentially convenient fictions. Though any new ways they might think up would have to be fictions too, of course. So fiction itself became something central to the human experience, or so I flattered myself — all conceptualizing seen as a kind of fiction-making, that is, such that fiction embraced the world. *All* the disciplines, as we call them, seemed to be reaching out like that and absorbing the others: the particle physicists, for example, with their quarks and charm and color — almost as though to emphasize the universality of this underlying particle activity, its escape from the confines of mere physics. All the new cross-disciplinary studies, the so-called multi-media experiments, the collapse of old dogmas about matter and energy, sanity and madness, mind and body, the stave losing its power over music, and so on: all signs, I thought. And in the midst of all that, the governing principles of traditional fiction seemed like dead restrictive dogma too. Beautiful art objects, some of them, but not much truth left in them. I felt we had to loosen fiction up and reinvest it with some of its old authority as a self-aware artifact, a kind of self-revealing model, as it were, for the universal fiction-making process. At the time I felt I was all alone in this, but as it turns out, a lot of writers, unknown to each other, were all approaching fiction in this new way at the same time, and so we had a brief season then of self-conscious and formally innovative fiction. Something in the air after all ...

CB   You've spoken in the past of the impact that the work of Samuel Beckett had on you at this time.

RC   Yes, he helped to sweep the board clean. He was intransigent, yet full of humor — like a great Zen master.

CB   You also said of him that he offered you a way of making art without affirmation. Is that your objective, something you are after in writing?

RC   You hear it said by a lot of people — critics, religious types, and some writers, too — that the act of writing is an act of affirmation, a way of affirming the essential goodness of the world. Faulkner said something like that when he accepted the Nobel Prize, as I recall. Beckett writes without loading these kinds of sentimental values on his art. He's a wonderful exemplar of the act of creating art without any justification whatsoever for what he's doing, yet not without integrity ... He'd probably laugh at the idea of trying to construct an order among men that would make any sense, given their appalling limitations. He just listens to the voices, as he says, reports on them as he hears them, without any kind of romantic expectations. He's the least arrogant writer I know, and as a young writer I found him a healthy antidote to the high-minded aspirations of the romantics, though these were also attractive to me.

CB On the other hand, your narrator in *The Universal Baseball Association*, J. Henry Waugh, does say that invention implies a need and need implies a purpose ... Is he saying that the act of invention cannot help but suggest form, causality?

RC I seem to recall a certain irony ... I mean, he's working in a self-justifying system that he has invented for himself, and even so ...

CB Ah yes, but his desire to invent that system implies a need of some sort on his part. Does that need imply purpose ...

RC Maybe. I mean, maybe need implies purpose. But I doubt it. Possibly what's involved here, besides the spinning out of an interesting and appealing metaphor, is a certain nostalgia for that kind of idea ...

CB You speak of our having moved from an open-ended, anthropocentric, humanistic, optimistic starting point to one that is closed, cosmic, eternal, supernatural, and pessimistic. On the other hand, are you offering literature, fiction, as a liberating device, as a way of escaping that sense of exhaustion, or closure? Literature as an escape?

RC No. Nor has it ever been. Serious writers always tell the truth, and that truth has to do with the metaphors or clusters of metaphors they've chosen to work with. Inside his metaphors, the fiction writer is a truth teller, or is at least open to the truth. The metaphor chosen may allow for humor or for horror, for intellectual amusement or existential *Angst*, but the writer is still trying to penetrate reality, not escape from it. He approaches it with what Borges calls 'that lucid innocence': eyes open for the worst. I think of myself in that sense as a realist, and I imagine so do the others, though of course: new realities, new forms.

CB But in view of your dissatisfaction with fiction as it was, why did you write *The Origin of the Brunists*, which is arguably not a new kind of fiction?

RC   For some time I'd been writing the kinds of stories which are now in *Pricksongs and Descants*, especially in the 'Exemplary Fictions' section, and it was what I meant to keep on doing, but at the same time I felt the need to show — myself as well as others —that I could write a traditional mimetic novel. Partly this need was imposed on me by others, since I was getting nowhere with the more innovative fictions, but mostly it was to prove something to myself. I wanted to go down into that mine myself and emerge from it, hopefully, with new perceptions, a new confidence about what I was doing, and maybe hone a few skills while I was at it. I had a lot of guiding lights in this. Cervantes's own first pastoral novel, for example, Joyce in his poems and stories, or the realistic early work of the likes of Picasso and Matisse. It was a four-year struggle, and I learned a lot, especially about scale.

CB   But the realism isn't quite sustained right to the end of the book, is it?

RC   I think, inside the terms of the book, it all happens as it would happen. I don't believe there's anything unreal in it, not as far as event is concerned. Of course the genre itself, as I learned, is oddly paradoxical ...

CB   On the question of 'the real' both of your first novels have religious sects in them, people who try to explain things by reference to myths or fictions, but which we *know* to be myths and fictions because of our privileged position as readers. Isn't that privileged position something of a problem? Doesn't it imply a clear distinction between the real and the fictive which you eleswhere wish to deny? The characters within *The Universal Baseball Association*, within that fiction, don't know that they are within a fiction, they suspect it every now and then, but they don't know it. But the reader knows, doesn't he?

RC   Does he? I think that would reflect a false sense of confidence. It's not absolutely clear which is the fiction and which the real world in that book, for example — nor indeed in the reader's own world. It is true though about the religious sects cropping up in both books — in others, too, the plays, the new book — it's something I seem always to be coming back to, the way our fictions get pushed into dogmas, invested with a force of reality, a sense of literal truth, that they were never meant to have. These fictions, these imaginative ways of grasping the universe, can't be imposed on people, they can only be shared, and I suppose in everything I write there'll be this need to stick holes in overinflated world views and let the hot air out.

CB Can I move on to *Pricksongs and Descants*? You've said that you regard the story 'The Elevator' as an anchor story —which is a curious word of course to apply to an elevator which may or may not go plummeting to the ground — but in what sense is it an anchor story in the collection?

RC It *is* curious. Yet another misquote no doubt. 'The Elevator' was in fact a generative story for that collection, not an anchor story. It gave me an idea for constructing a new kind of book of short fictions and I used it for awhile like a structural analogy for the book as a whole, in terms of what the stories would be like and how to organize them, pattern them out, and so on. Eventually I moved away from such a rigid plan, but it was what got me going. If there's an 'anchor' story in the set, it's 'The Magic Poker'. Having got the basic idea, concept, of the book from 'The Elevator', and some of the story ideas as well, I kept moving toward the completion of the book, watching for the story that would say, now it's done, this completes it. And that story was 'The Magic Poker'.

CB But why that story and not, for example, 'The Babysitter'? There's a similarity between them, isn't there — a series of alternative fictions, possibilities, styles ...?

RC Yes, well, that's true of 'The Elevator', too, 'Quenby and Ola' ...

CB Exactly. So what was different about 'The Magic Poker'?

RC Well, all the stories in the set touch on or reflect or embrace the others. But in 'The Magic Poker' this embrace is more complete. Or so it seemed to me. It's a kind of fictional presentation of some of the assertions in the dedication to Cervantes, for example, and its form, more elaborate and subtle than the others, reflects the form of the book itself. Even its setting up in Rainy Lake, where I did my earliest serious writing, is a secret metaphoric embrace. It's still the one that gives me the most pleasure when I go back to it ...

CB You said, talking about story, that you wanted to restore the love of story; in other words, narrative mattered. And yet at the same time, of course, another of your techniques in that book is to disrupt narrative, constantly disrupt narrative ...

RC Yes, but this is to give a new life to narrative. What's so dull about most conventional fiction is that the narrative is essentially dead matter, and what you get interested in is the style, the craft, the development of character, some of the delicate or sensationalist imagery, a brilliant smile or two ... What I wanted to do was call attention again to narrative itself, the movement of story.

CB Isn't it misleading to talk about stor-*y*? I mean, aren't you talking about stor-*ies*? In 'The Babysitter', for example ...

RC No, there's only one story there. Every line is part of it — it came to me all in once piece.

CB So you don't see yourself as presenting a series of alternative fictions? I mean, a given situation can be projected in a number of different directions — which is what I took you to mean — each one of those projections being equally 'real' in its own terms, deriving from its original situation: that's not what you're doing in the story?

RC Yes, well, maybe that *is* the story. Still singular. One part of it ...

CB In talking about the Cervantes stories, you said that they 'struggled against the unconscious mythic residue in human life', but you've also said that literature is a link with the past, it's 'a mythic reinforcement of our tenuous grip on reality' — now, are those two ...?

RC No, they're not contradictory ...

CB You're producing new myths ...

RC Yes, but fiction, myth, these are necessary things. I'm not against them. I doubt we could function at all without fictionalizing in some way, without making up something about the world, falsifying it with a name, or names, that allow us to operate in it. But the world changes, or our perceptions of it or our needs in it change, and new fictions come from it. Fiction then, self-conscious fiction, has, as I see it, a double purpose. On the one hand it draws into itself what seem to be the truths of the world at any given moment, and on the other it struggles against the falsehoods, dogmas, confusions, all the old debris of the dead fictions — and this struggle itself is self-revealing in ways that remain important across the ages.

CB Is that what *The Universal Baseball Association* is doing? Setting up an old myth and destroying it?

RC Perhaps. But I confess it's hard to talk about it like this. These thoughts are far from my mind when I'm actually writing. It's more innocent than that. I find something that interests me and I set off to explore it. I expect to make some discoveries and get some pleasure out of that.

CB But isn't there a problem in applying a metaphor or an allegory to a perception of a disordered reality — in that the form that you're using implies order; the thing that you're trying to describe involves contingency?

RC Well, the writer's experience is paradoxical. Like life itself. The imposing of order on a disordered reality — that's how cities work, how sciences develop, how diseases are treated. Fiction only reflects all that. Only with more irony, since it's also more self-aware about what it's doing, exposing its own activity as it goes along. This is partly what accounts for the peculiar structure of contemporary fictions: they're revealing this paradox, and in a sense imitating it, so the forms themselves are seemingly not as coherent as old-fashioned narratives, the mock histories and case records.

CB But isn't that sleight-of-hand? Isn't that like the conjurer revealing the process — and then going ahead and tricking you anyway? I mean, you disrupt a narrative and draw attention to the fact that it is a narrative, and then you continue with the narrative and the disruption is forgotten ...

RC ... or healed. I like the allusion to the magician, though, except for the notion of sleight-of-hand as mere trickery — what you call trickery is the magician's art, after all. We can appreciate his act, even knowing how he does it. I like the allusion because of the skill involved — no tricks to fiction really, it's an open gesture: more like a high wire act ...

CB I was hinting at hubris, actually ...

RC Yes, well, trying to grasp the ungraspable — any attempt at that takes a little hubris, I guess, a bit of cockiness ...

CB But there's a central point here that worries me. How is a view of history, for example, as a series of fictions, or a series of myths, or metaphors, or explanations — how is that consistent with a *moral* sense which requires an agreed, perhaps more static version of behaviour?

RC Ah, is that so? Is morality tied to some kind of stasis? I don't know, it seems to me that out there in the flux our moral values are being generated and regenerated all the time. Our politicians and sociologists, historians and literary critics are constantly up to that, creating value-generating metaphors or fictions by way of which we understand things, derive our sense of morality, as you call it — and looking at fiction in a broad way, this is what always happens and must happen, it seems to me. I see self-conscious fiction as a willed passage beyond the functional definitions of the world, out where it can wrestle with the shapeshifting universe. That, for me, is a moral act.

CB Is there any way, though, of avoiding replacing one form of coercion with another? You talked about various mythologies, implying that they have a kind of coercive power, and what you're doing is substituting what seem to you to be truer, more appropriate versions, fictions. May they themselves not attain a coercive power?

RC I'm afraid the kinds of fictions that professional story-tellers have been engaged in since the decay of the prehistoric priesthoods have had very little impact on the world. To my knowledge, no poet has yet changed the world. There are ways of looking at, say, John the Seer's Patmos revelations as a fabulously coercive short story, but this is not quite fair because he was clearly not perceiving himself as a fiction writer. On the whole, most coercive fictions come from outside the self-conscious artistic fictionalizing processes.

CB No, but say you are contributing to a version of reality which is relativistic, in which there are no centrally agreed moral values. How would you, in such a world, indict the concentration camp guard? By reference to what set of agreed values? Couldn't he simply say that my fictions are different from your fictions?

RC In a purely relativistic world, he could, but there's no such thing, there isn't apt to be, and I'm not consciously contributing toward it. Communally held moral values come and go — indeed, communities themselves come and go — but the basic thrust toward community, toward larger and more integrated social organisms, is a constant. It probably has to do with the way the brain works. The fiction-making process is itself in part a groping for some communicable truth, a group truth, as it were. The tools are poor and the truth itself may be metamorphosing on us all the time, such that the process is endless and riven with inevitable dispute, but it's not simply relativistic. We're all, as the saying goes, a product of our time and place. We might want to escape this, and indeed a lot of what art does is to show this dark desire to break away from the oppression of community, to rebel against it, but even rebellion is a kind of adherence.

CB Do you see this as actually evidenced in your work?

RC Yes, I'm sure. I have respect for it and I assume it shows itself. Certainly in the novels — even while I'm struggling against what I see as perverse mythological forms, ones that are distorting the people caught up in them and affecting adversely the people outside them. But I wouldn't hold to any universal or timeless 'morality'. I think this is purely a human invention; I don't believe it exists in the world as such, there's no 'good' behaviour and 'bad' behaviour in universal terms, just actions and our communal judgements about them. In the end, if you don't like the concentration camp guard, you just have to *do* something about it.

CB Is this actually a direction you're moving? I read in an interview that you'd become more interested in delving into the American communal experience, more interested in sociopolitical than formal and literary questions. Is this in part what led you to write *The Public Burning*? Was it a sort of artistic problem, or was there a sense of anger, of affront ...?

RC All I've written so far — the novels, stories, plays — have all emerged from a small kernel of an idea, something that in each case could be put in just a few words. But once examined more closely, they all hinted at a lot more packed away inside, and my task then was to unpack them, unwrap them, make them reveal themselves. This is an artistic problem and it's what I'm always most interested in: this intransigent penetration of a metaphor. It's a little like chasing a vision. Most of the time, I might say, you end up in the dark. The germ idea behind the Rosenbergs project was a simple one, and partly set off by anger, I suppose, and an affinity with the times — this was the mid-sixties, Vietnam War days, a time of gathering protest in the United States, countered by a mounting right-wing reaction. I chanced to come across a book on the Rosenbergs and wondered with some embarrassment why we'd forgotten them. I was working with some theater ideas at the time and it occurred to me that we ought to restage the execution, some theater in Times Square maybe. I elaborated the idea a little — and then came that pregnant kernel: what if I wrote a *story* about doing this? That is, what if I wrote a kind of documentary history of the event, only instead of holding the executions at Sing Sing prison, transpose them to Times Square as a kind of circus event and bring the nation there to see it? That was all there was to it at the time and I thought of it as a short piece, thirty or forty pages long. Only when I started working seriously with it — *morally*, you might say — did it start to fatten out into this large complex communal metaphor we have now.

CB Were you at that time involved in any of the anti-Vietnam War activities?

RC Yes, the marches and so on ...

CB Why did you choose to stress the involvement of a number of the characters in amateur dramatics — Ethel Rosenberg, Nixon, Eisenhower?

RC   It was a metaphoric way of showing how mythic reinforcement works, how certain ideas and attitudes get implanted in us as we
grow up, and then become unconscious determinants of our behavior. This is what 'morality' usually is in the common sense. And a
good thing too. But as hand-me-down attitudes they must constantly
be re-examined. Also these plays Nixon and the others had been in
were ripe with images that resonated with the rest of the book.

CB   This concern with role-playing: is this why you have the
dramatic intermezzos?

RC   Yes — but also there was something inherently theatrical
about a lot of the documents I was reading and I wanted to express
that in some way, make it available, as it were. I was already doing
something like that with *Time* magazine ...

CB   Putting it into verse ...

RC   Yes. A lot of theatrical possibilities occurred to me, but the
one that really caught my attention was what is now the last Inter-
mezzo, the one based on the Rosenbergs' separate accounts in their
Death House Letters of the visit of the Bureau of Prisons director. I
hardly had to touch them, the whole thing was set out like a stage play
in their letters. Then, the next thought along these lines came when I
was reading Eisenhower's speeches during the six months between
his inauguration and the Rosenberg executions. I was astonished by
the strangeness of the vision that lay concealed in them, a weird
Manichean view you ordinarily don't associate with the man. Maybe,
a bit awed by his new office, he'd merely made the mistake of trying to
think, something he was not famous for, and had got lost for the
moment in all this spookiness. Certainly there's a lot less of it before
and after this six-month period. But during this run-up to the executions, his speeches are full of it, and all I had to do was extract the
scattered lines and put them together in a coherent verse form.
There's nothing of mine in any of those three Intermezzos. Every
word spoken comes from some document or other. Finally, once I
had these two, it was easy to see what the other one should be —
together, the three pieces virtually tell the whole story ...

CB   Do you feel any responsibility toward real people and real
events? You transmogrify them, you change people and you change
events, and you restructure them. Is there any responsibility you
should owe to events, to history in that hard sense, and to the people?

RC   Well, everything in the book, except the more speculative
material in the Nixon sections, comes from public data — from
newspapers, magazines, memoirs, interviews, and the like. I took
history as a fiction itself and created my own fiction out of these

fictional but referential materials, attaching them to my own metaphors while trying to keep intact their essential integrity as reported data, to distort them as little as possible. Moreover, this is not itself a record, a document, it's a work of the imagination —my original subtitle for it was 'An Historical Romance'. I didn't think anyone in his right mind could possibly confuse my version with the so-called real one. In my version, there is a clear set of transpositions meant to enliven our perception of some of the things that happened by throwing a new — radically new — light on them.

I've never yet had anyone come up and ask: 'Were they really executed in Times Square?' This idea of the large circus event emceed by Uncle Sam is so obviously metaphoric — it's like Gulliver in the land of the Lilliputians: no one takes this literally, yet no one misses the literal aspects either. The main thing, I think, is that anyone reading the book is aware from the first line that he's reading a book of fiction, something he may not be aware of when he's reading say, a history book, or a newspaper. My metaphors are different, but on the whole I don't tamper with the data any more than do the histories of the time. I explain some of this in the *New York Times* and *Time* magazine chapters. So, although admittedly it's a kind of confrontation with History, the liberal dogma of History, its sacrosanct nature borrowed from the old authority of the Bible, it's also a kind of enhancement of it, a celebration, a deep respect for the moment itself, which I'm trying to make more vivid, more memorable — more 'real', as it were ...

CB   This might be true of the circus sections, but what about Nixon?

RC   Well, though his sections are also based on biographies, speeches, public data, there's admittedly a bit more distortion. Through an excess of intimacy, you might say. But the book demanded it. And he, you might say, volunteered. He's a great one for getting down in the arena, how could I keep him out of mine? And I was not cruel to him. Few killers in world history have been treated with such kindness.

CB   Can I end by asking you why your interest in fictionality and theatricality hasn't drawn you to write for the theatre more often?

RC   For one thing, theater is struggling so to continue to exist. Outside of this city there isn't much of it around — and even here in London it's got a fragile life: take away the tourist traffic for one year and it's dead. So it's hard to get a play, especially a provocative or difficult play, on. Without funds, it's almost impossible to get it on right or get an audience to it. And from the experience I've had so far, I know how much creative time and energy get consumed by the production effort. That's true of films and television, too, though there's more money available and a larger audience. In spite of the difficulties, though, I've a great affection for all these forms and a lot of ideas I'm likely to pursue, if invited. Especially theater. I like the ephemerality of it — a breath of the *real* world — and a good antidote to the illusory stone-tablet experience of hammering out a novel.

Stanley Elkin

Stanley Elkin was born in New York City on 11 May 1930 and spent his youth in Chicago. His father was a travelling salesman with a gift for story-telling whose professional jargon and imaginative powers were later to dominate much of his son's fiction. From 1955-57, Elkin served in the United States Army, where he developed his fascination with radio, a preoccupation that would later give rise to a novel. During his student years at the University of Illinois, where he received his PhD in 1961 with a dissertation on William Faulkner, he worked on *Accent* magazine, which published one of his earliest stories, 'Among the Witnesses', in 1959. For this story and 'In the Alley', published in the same year by the *Chicago Review*, Elkin received the Longview Foundation Award in 1962. In 1963 he won the *Paris Review* Humor Prize. He is the recipient of Guggenheim and Rockefeller Fellowships, as well as a grant from the National Endowment for the Arts and Humanities. Having lived and written abroad, primarily in Rome and London, he now teaches as a professor of English at Washington University in St Louis.

The conflict between idealism and sensuality dominates much of Elkin's fiction. Apparently ennobling — but secretly disabling —ideals are confronted with life-affirming — yet trite — sensuality. His style portrays this conflict by welding precious, highly stylized metaphor to persistent cliché. Elkin's descriptions of his characters' fall from the heights of idealism produces the humorous effect he is noted for precisely because this idealism is tainted from the outset by supercilious and self-serving innocence. The experience of sensuality teaches the protagonist to accept his own humanity: his capacity for greed and hate as well as for love and suffering. Thus, the grotesque or farcical in Elkin's fiction ultimately always partakes of the reconciliatory mood of true comedy.

Elkin's attitude towards his art parallels his protagonists' attitude towards their own lives; the hierarchical relation between author and character is consciously deconstructed: the author's art becomes life, the character's life becomes art. Thus, Elkin's protagonists usually have professions that demand highly developed rhetorical skills, like salesmanship or broadcasting. Moreover, they tend to view their lives as a loose series of performances — as if in response to the episodic structure of their author's fictions — the contours of which are threatened, or perhaps brought into focus, by sudden existential crises. The protagonist of 'The Making of Ashenden', for instance, one of the three novellas in *Searches and Seizures* (1973), experiences the transition from the high level of aristocratic taste to the sheer affirmation of life, from an elitist death wish to the unexpected delights of sodomy. Moreover, by becoming the main figure within the setting of an already existing painting the protagonist creates, through his erotic act, a new piece of art; like the artist, he reinvigorates a tradition. At the same time, the portrayal of the protagonist's experience of immediacy betrays the artist's yearning for the company of his characters, which would relieve him of his solitude. In Elkin's latest novel, *The Living End* (1979), God, the ultimate artist, annihilates the world out of the same frustrated desire: 'Because I never found My audience.' God created human beings so that they would not only inform His story — history —with life, but read it at the same time and thus satisfy His longing for peers. Creator and created, author and character were made to relate to each other.

But this narrative mood makes secondary the characters' relationships among themselves. The mode of interaction between the protagonist and his surroundings is decided, for better or worse, by his all-out activity. Thus, as early a character as James Boswell in Elkin's first novel, *Boswell: A Modern Comedy* (1964), tries to inflate his ego by a madly comic quest for celebrities that parodies the pursuit of the famous Dr Samuel Johnson by the eighteenth-century biographer. In a dream, through a crying out of his unconscious, Boswell finally comes to understand that if his design of participating in every great discovery were to succeed, he would drain the very source of his energy supply.

In his collection of short stories, *Criers and Kibitzers, Kibitzers and Criers* (1966), Elkin dramatizes the conflict between idealism and sensuality through the opposite emotions of despair and hope, presented, and — as the form of the title indicates — held in tenuous balance, by the criers and kibitzers respectively. If, as Elkin says, the despair of the criers is founded on a system of thought (which, it could be added, has been falsely absolutized), while the hope of the kibitzers is based on nothing more than a (spurious) belief in anecdote, then it follows that the complete man will be he who can bear the pain of irreparable fracture inherent in any existential crisis — like the protagonist of the title story, who, after the death of his only son, learns to face the fact that his idealized progeny and heir was a cheat.

But learning to bear the pain of that fracture entails the blurring of the dividing line between good and evil; for not only does the distinction between the ideal and the sensual no longer coincide with that of good and evil, but the distinction as such becomes questionable. Thus, the title of Elkin's second novel, *A Bad Man* (1967), is doubly ironic. Leo Feldman and Warden Fisher appear as the antagonists in the struggle between good and evil. Feldman's ego — like Boswell's — unfolds in acts of self-aggrandizement. Having learned to respect only mercantile values, Feldman's philosophy requires that he see all things as equal under the law of supply and demand: he is, by a Christian culture's standards, 'bad'. The Warden's concept of the 'good', however, implying that 'virtue is system, honor is order. God is design, grace is covenant, a contract and codicils, what's down there in writing', results in hypocrisy and violence: the uncompromising reign of the good means the loss of human dignity. The ensuing linkage of individual freedom and evil, good and mass terror, has its roots in the structure of power. The paradoxical sense of human dignity arises from the recognition that one's life counts only as a number, yet that as a number it counts. There is reason for laughter in the midst of despair.

The Dick Gibson Show (1971), Elkin's third novel, shows the protagonist dealing with the artist's problems as artist. Dick Gibson is involved in a wide range of radio activities from news broadcasting in the early days of the radio to the talk shows of the 1950s and the confidential phone-in shows of the 1960s. Using the radio as metaphor, the novel centres on the human voice as the agent of communication through projected meaning. Incessant talking trivializes meaning, yet it guarantees that the voice can never be completely divested of its humanness; at the price of an infinite process of devaluation, the medium in Elkin's novel can never become the message. Accordingly, for the protagonist, cliché can assume the role of myth. Living by cliché, he will rise to the promises of the American Dream. In other words, the increasing triteness of the American Dream becomes its saving feature by ensuring its expansion and thus its durability.

In *The Franchiser* (1976), Elkin's next novel, the artist seems to reach out and redefine his own role through an exploitation of the possibilities of character. Yet this novel cannot be read as an autobiographical disclosure; instead it attests to a perpetual unfolding of the artist's imagination as such. The freedom provided by this process — concomitant with the ego's expansiveness — is genuine precisely to the degree that it is independent of real-life experience. Ben Flesh, a travelling franchiser, who claims responsibility for the homogenization of America, becomes another example of a complete character: he consciously curbs his hopes through the acceptance of his disease while transcending his despair by endorsing the necessity to expand his franchise business even against the odds of an energy crisis. His career, started by his godfather's bequest of the privilege of borrowing for life at the then-current prime rate of interest, becomes a metaphor for the career of the artist himself who, within the given limits of his own tradition, is granted the privilege of borrowing from language for life and of employing the returns to his own advantage.

The Living End substantiates the artist's claim from a metaphysical, if precarious, angle. Through His lack of a sense of humanity God the Father, omnipotent artificer, is seen to fail the standards which the artist must set for himself. He cannot bear the pain of the fracture between life and death. Thus God becomes the ultimate kibitzer, whose creation is founded on absolute whim and who will not let His hopes be modified by even a tinge of despair. He would rather annihilate the world — earth, heaven, and hell — and see the living end than admit of a failure that He, after all, is completely responsible for. God, it turns out, is a bad artist. It remains for the human artist to carry on.

Interview with Stanley Elkin

St Louis, 16 September 1979

HZ   Do you think that it is possible to speak of your fiction as a fiction of compassionate satire? I am thinking of *The Franchiser*, for example. There the name of Ben Flesh itself seems to be, on the one hand, a satiric reference to the American franchising system: rawness as the core of the intricateness of the system, or the notion of selling your body to the Devil. On the other hand, the narrator seems to sympathize with Ben. For example, after the speech Ben gives in the dance studio, his own shortcomings can be understood and forgiven against the foil of his listeners' outrageous behaviour. That's why I thought that your fiction might be seen as satiric on the one hand, but that the satire is transcended through compassion on the other.

SE   Well, I think there is only the other hand. I don't really think there is much satire in my fiction. It would seem to me that satire is probably one of the most conscientious forms. The satirist always knows what he is doing. He always goes around with his targets three feet or thirty feet in front of him. But they are never very distant. They are near at hand, they are close to home, and they are in the forefront of his mind. For that reason I don't really think I'm a satirist at all. Occasionally I will satirize somebody's way of talking, or a kind of syntactical impediment, but I don't satirize institutions. You said something about the name Ben Flesh and the rawness of the name. I accept that, and indeed it is primarily as a body that I want the reader to look at Flesh. He is flesh up front, and then spirit, perhaps, stands behind that. But it's primarily body that Flesh is talking about and that I am talking about.

Of course my works *are* taken for satire all the time. It's a word I quarrel with. I don't like satire myself, I don't like to read it. Sometime during the Vietnam War there was a satiric play on Lyndon Johnson called *MacBird*! Philip Roth did a satire on the Nixon administration. The targets, as I say, are always specific and the intention (even of Philip Roth and Barbara Garson) is always compassion, because the intention is always to do something right by humanity. I don't really have that intention and I'm not particularly interested in pulling the rug out from under institutions.

HZ   Maybe I can approach what I see as a central issue in your fiction from another angle. In the short story collection called *Criers and Kibitzers, Kibitzers and Criers* ...

SE   — a collection I don't particularly like any more. I like a couple of stories in it, but I'm not particularly proud of that book.

HZ   ... there seems to be an underlying theme which I nevertheless find very interesting and which, I think, could be partly related to the idea of satire. That is, the protagonists in that book all seem to concentrate on some kind of ideal or an *idée fixe* which is then shattered. In the title story Greenspahn's grief for his dead son collects additional poignancy when he has to face the fact that his son stole money from him; in other words, when his ideal image of his son is destroyed. Again, in 'On a Field, Rampant' the false ideals of the assumed aristocrat are undermined. Could I therefore modify my earlier question and ask whether you criticize any adherence to an erroneous ideal? To an ideal that is too narrow and too single-minded and that doesn't have any potential for future development?

SE   Well, let me talk about that story. When I was studying for my prelims for my PhD I read maybe twenty Restoration comedies and I was struck by the fact that in all of these Restoration comedies someone ultimately turned out to belong to an order greater than that which he thought he was a member of. He turned out to be a prince or something even higher than a prince. 'On a Field, Rampant' was a transvaluation or inversion of that notion. Khardov, the boy's father (and he *is* his father) plays a kind of practical joke on his son by planting these phony notions in his skull. He acts as a sort of retainer, butler, footman, counsellor to the unnamed protagonist. So whatever ideal the character might have is something that has been pushed on him, and he is obsessed with the notion: 'Well, gee, I may be somebody important.' When he discovers that, in fact, he is not somebody important, that is essentially the punch line of his father's joke. It is not a question of stripping this ideal off of that ideal until we get down to the essential onion which is only more onion. It's a question of a ruined life. I regard that kid's life as absolutely wasted, because of the temperament inculcated in him by his father. I don't think the story has much point beyond that.

Incidentally, this story has a kind of companion piece which is 'A Poetics for Bullies', a story *I* like. In that story the son from 'On a Field, Rampant' returns as John Williams, the antagonist to Push the bully. He *is* a kind of royalty case. He is not really the same person, but I *was* thinking of 'On a Field Rampant' as I wrote 'A Poetics for Bullies', though the stories were several years apart.

HZ   But even if a protagonist's wrong-headed idealism turns out to be, after all, only his father's practical joke, is he not, as a doomed character, preferable to the people you call criers and kibitzers?

SE   The criers in the title story have despair, but that's all they have. The kibitzers only have hope and that's all *they* have. In that story, 'Criers and Kibitzers, Kibitzers and Criers', I am trying to say that there are two kinds of people in the world, those people who are always saying 'Woe is me', because behind the 'Woe is me' is a system of thought; and those other people who say 'Ho, ho, ho', and behind the 'Ho, ho, ho' is only anecdote, no system of thought at all. To say that one is preferable to the other would be false. It would seem to me that the complete man is that fellow who says 'Woe, ho, ho. Woe, ho, ho.'

HZ   What about Greenspahn? Isn't he that kind of person?

SE   That's right. Greenspahn identifies the different groups. Greenspahn is a whole man.

HZ   But isn't he a whole man only as long as he can cling to his ideal?

SE   Now we are talking about final things, not fiction. Sure, I suppose Greenspahn is Greenspahn so long as he stays serious. The criers are serious people. The kibitzers are not serious people. I think that Greenspahn is both serious and playful, but if I were asked which weighs more — the seriousness or the playfulness — I would have to say the seriousness.

HZ   Is that the reason why the comic in your fiction is less related to, say, the burlesque than to the grotesque? For instance, it seems to me that *The Dick Gibson Show* makes a particular claim to the grotesque by putting the comic under the pressure of a modern society. That is, if one were to argue that the harmlessness of comic laughter is generally dependent on values as they are being reassessed within a traditional social context, then *The Dick Gibson Show* ought not to appear as a comic novel at all.

SE   Because that's not what comic values depend on. That's not what comedy depends on. Comedy depends on character. It depends on character repeating itself and repeating itself like a stammer. Indeed, I'll make an aphorism or try to make an aphorism: Comedy is the stammer of personality. It seems to me that it is always linked to obsession — to an individually articulated obsession. It arises in, and of, and from personality. It is a defect of the soul and whatever is comic in my fiction is comic because of the defect in soul behind my character's mannerisms and bad manners.

HZ   But isn't the comic partly dependent on the reaction of the audience, that is, on social environment or, simply, on the situation?

SE   Yes, I wasn't thinking of the audience. Feldman in *A Bad Man* says, 'How can I be Feldman, if there is no one to be Feldman to?' In other words, how can he be a bad man, a super salesman or a pitchman if there is nobody there to hear him be one? So that, when he is in solitary confinement in that novel and has no relationship to the outside world and no audience except the guard

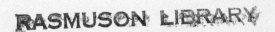

who doesn't answer his questions (the warden later on comes and creates a little drama), what must he do? What *can* he do? He falls back upon masturbation, he falls back upon individual pieces of his memory, he remembers when, in fact, he *was* Feldman. But nobody is comic in solitary confinement. There must be a public and the public is the other characters.

HZ   And the other characters reintegrate the comic character by reassessing the values from which he has defected? So that the effect on the reader is one of relief?

SE   It seems to me that you can say the same thing of tragedy. Tragedy is also a kind of social reassessment. At the end of *Oedipus*, Oedipus is a calm man for all of his grief. It's a calm grief. He isn't the flibbertigibbet that he was during the course of the play. All of the terrible things that have happened to Thebes are over, the ban is lifted. Since the essential nature of fiction, it seems to me, subsists in conversion, either a social conversion or an individual conversion, everything is a kind of reassessment, properly speaking, a reworking or retelling of whatever drama there is or of whatever principles have pre-existed.

HZ   But in tragedy, it seems to me, it's the values of the individual which are being reassessed, whereas in comedy it's those of society. You say that comedy, for you, is connected with character. The obsession of your comic character reminds me of Bergson and his theory that laughter is a social phenomenon due to mechanical repetition where you would expect variegated human behaviour. But the stress in your concept of comedy seems to be on the individual or on tragedy. Does this explain the tragicomic or the grotesque effect of, for instance, *The Dick Gibson Show*?

SE   Most of *The Dick Gibson Show* takes place on the radio. That suggests certain limitations. It seems to me that the great joke of contemporary life or, better, of history, is that of somebody without power facing power, someone between power and powerlessness. Kingsley Amis, who I do *not* think is the best writer in the world, nevertheless makes marvellous use of this particular joke in *Lucky Jim*, where Jim makes monkey faces behind power's back. Now, if Jim were simply some kind of lunatic who walked down the street making his Eskimo faces and his angered Indian faces and his outraged cockney faces, you would simply be afraid of him and cross the street. But he is a very civilized man and when we see that civilized man standing behind his boss's back making all those moves and crossing his eyes we laugh. We laugh for a complicated series of reasons: first we laugh because the boss doesn't *know* that this is being done to him, second we laugh because it *is* being done, and third we laugh — and this is most important — because this is all that Jim can do. There is a kind of failure of potency in these faces that he makes and so his revenge is essentially an almost effeminate blow that he is striking for himself.

Now, my character Dick Gibson, on the radio, cannot always make the kinds of remarks that he would like to make because the radio is itself an inhibition. In that all-night radio show where Pepper Steep tells her story and the druggist Bernie Perk tells his story these are absolutely astonishing to Gibson — the fact that such things should be going out over the radio. It outrages the decorousness of the form and he is helpless. The only time he can make any reaction that we can see is when he *thinks* the reaction. I think that most of the humor in this section — except for the specific jokes that Bernie Perk makes and the comedy of the little ten-year-old singer and various other characters — depends upon Dick's being sort of honor-bound to still perform decorously on the radio while his guests take each other's pants off.

The essential tone of voice of most of my protagonists is sarcasm — not satire, but sarcasm. Sarcasm is essentially their basic speech pattern. Sarcasm is itself always less than what the person would really like to do. Sarcasm is the voice of powerlessness. Sarcasm *is* powerlessness. Sarcasm is the same sort of almost epicene blow that Lucky Jim makes behind his boss's back.

HZ   Would it be possible to say that sarcasm is ultimately transcended in *The Living End*? Not because the novel relates to heaven and hell, but because it is ultimately concerned with art, with the art of story-telling as the final redemption?

SE   There is a great deal of sarcasm in *The Living End*. I think the funniest line in *The Living End* is when Ellerbee says to the angel of death, '"But if I'm dead — you mean there's really an afterlife?" "Oh boy," the angel of death said.' Every time I do a reading of that story I crack up when I come to '"Oh boy," the angel of death said.' Because the angel of death is not saying all he could say. He is being sarcastic. To be sarcastic is to be dead, is to be muffled.

HZ   But doesn't Ellerbee discover for himself that everything is true — 'the philosopher's best idea and the conventional wisdom, too?'

SE   It's astonishment! This is the essential emotion that Ellerbee is left with after they take everything away from him and he comes to the realization that, by God!, everything is true, everything. He is simply overwhelmed by that idea, as I am, because I believe that everything *is* true. Anything I can think up the world has already thought up. I find that astonishing.

HZ   But for this insight you need to be a member of mankind, right? Because heaven and hell, at least in your novel, seem to comprise the realm only of conventional ·wisdom. Throughout his life Ellerbee always tried to do the right thing; for example, he tried to abide by moral conventions and moral standards. Yet after his death he is rejected by God: not because he did not keep to these moral standards in life but on petty grounds — for having twice used God's name in vain or kept his store open on a Sunday, etc.

SE   What I am really saying is: I believe in whim. I believe in bad luck and in good luck, I believe that the world spins on an axis made out of whim, just pure whim. The ultimate whimmer is God. When God permits Ellerbee to view those pearly gates, it's only because He wants him to know how much he has lost by going to hell. God is the most whimsical thing in the universe.

HZ   And He is omnipotent.

SE   That's right, and He uses His omnipotence to execute His whim.

HZ   At the end of the book, when all the saints are assembled, God asks them why did He create the world? They offer the explanation that He created the world in order for them to exercise their goodness. But God insists that 'it was all Art'. Do you believe, then, that the artist is whimsical in the same way that God created the world on a whim, or exercises His power whimsically?

SE   That's right. That's exactly what it is, only it's controlled whim. Art is the decision of the artist and it can be anything he decides. I want to be permitted to do in my fiction anything I want to do, and what I want to do is what I *can* do. I don't see any reason why, if I do what I can do well enough, people, good readers, can't say, 'Well, this is art, too.' It doesn't perform according to this rule or that rule, it performs according to its own rules and givens. Hence I really don't have society in mind, I don't have America in mind when I write — though there is some of that in *The Franchiser*, of course, and in *The Dick Gibson Show*, too, but only minimally.

HZ   There is one question I would like to ask in that connection. In an interview published in the *Paris Review* you say that your fiction is not autobiographical and that, in fact, you dislike autobiographical fiction. On the other hand, you say that there is only one psychological assertion that you would insist upon, and that is that the self takes precedence. Now, if the artist may be as whimsical as he wants to be, is he not indulging his own self? And is his fiction then not autobiographical?

SE   Well, in that sense, of course, my fiction *is* autobiographical, because it is the didacticism of my own personality. It is concerned with the self, but not with the events that occur to the self. Joe McElroy and I were talking about this last night and Joe asked me if I would ever write an autobiography. I told him what I have heard John Irving say when asked about autobiographical fiction: that he writes fiction because nothing, in fact, has ever happened to him. Well, nothing has every happened to me either. I think if I were to write an autobiography it would have of necessity to deal with the last two weeks, because I can't remember anything psychological for more than two weeks. If I had to depend on the events in my life to make drama, it would be just dreadfully boring. It's boring enough as it is without my depending upon my own life.

Another word for whimsical is arbitrary and I do regard my 'art' as totally arbitrary. In other words, it's what I happen to be thinking at the moment when I am writing it.

HZ   Do you mean that, as a writer, you cannot make use of the situations and events that happen in real life because they lack arbitrariness?

SE   That's quite true. I'll tell you an anecdote. When I was in the army, back in 1955-57, my wife and I were invited to a party in Washington, D.C., which was given by a cousin of mine who had a lot of dough. He didn't live in Washington, he lived in New York. The party was for his daughter who was at that time living in Washington, and he invited the entire family. There must have been about one hundred and fifty people there. I was a soldier. I didn't have any money. I had one pair of clean pants, but they were torn. There was a little L-shaped tear in the left knee, and so these were the pants I was saving to wear to the party which took place, as I recall, on a Sunday afternoon. My cousin had rented a whole series of motel rooms for everybody. We each had our own motel room and he was paying for it. I showed up and I was talking to his daughter. My legs were crossed and she noticed the L-shaped tear in my pants and she said, 'Stanley, what's the matter with you, couldn't you find it in your heart to wear a whole, entire pair of pants to this affair?' I became furious, this was my best pair of pants. It was either punch her in the face or get up and get out. So I didn't punch her in the face — which I should have done — I got up and said, 'Come on, Joan, we're going back.' And we drove the hundred and some odd miles back to Fort Lee, Virginia, where I was stationed. This was just the culmination of a series of putdowns I had endured that weekend. All of my cousins, people my own age and maybe one or two years younger than myself, were doing very well in established Eastern firms, and here I was, an enlisted man in the army. I had nothing going for me and they were patronizing me. They were very nice in a way, but they were really very dismissive of me. And I was going to get them in a story called 'Next Year in Jerusalem', and I tried for two years to write the story of that weekend and I came a cropper every single time. It was just impossible for me to do. It was impossible for me to do because *my* rage would not have been the audience's rage.

One of the basic mistakes that young writers — people in my writing classes — make is to think that whatever particular contretemps they have just experienced, which is interesting to them, will also be interesting to a reader. One kid came to me just last week and said that he wanted to write a story based on a situation that happened to him that summer. He had been hitchhiking in Colorado and the cops picked him up for hitchhiking and put him in jail in Denver. They strip-searched him and did all sort of things to him, and he was very upset by this. He was still upset as he was telling me the story. I advised him not to write the story, because what was an outrage to him would have only been mildly convincing, perhaps, to a reader. You've got to make stuff up.

My fiction is completely arbitrary and whimsical. However, I *do* go to the well of self also. In *The Franchiser* I gave Ben Flesh multiple sclerosis which I have, and I suppose that was a way of dealing with my disease. But it ended up as a way of dealing with life itself rather than with the disease.

HZ   Isn't *The Living End* supposed to show another way of complementing the idea of the artist as being completely arbitrary and whimsical? Ellerbee, when he is cursed by God, because he prays to Him to end hell, 'to close the camp', is commented on by the narrator, who says that Ellerbee wouldn't have had it any other way ...

SE   Because now he could hate the son of a bitch forever, world without end, the real McCoy son of a bitch God that dealt with him.

HZ   But also, say, Ladlehaus in 'The Bottom Line', although he too hates God, because God mistakenly sent him off to his grave as the only person ever to be properly dead, nevertheless learns to think fondly of God's tendency to make mistakes.

SE   Because he can now *use* God, He makes mistakes. He thinks: I'm going to tell God that Quiz is a musician, that he is the composer that made up all this wonderful music. This stupid God makes mistakes. That's why he thinks of God fondly: He is going to kill Quiz for him.

HZ   But at the same time he admires God as a very superior kind of person.

SE   He admires His power! There is the classic confrontation that I have been talking about: powerlessness and power. God has all the guns. Ladlehaus, Ellerbee, and all the rest of that crew, including Jesus, Mary, and Joseph, don't have shit! They have nothing. So, I guess, in one way *The Living End* is the final working out of whatever is comic in my fiction by being the ultimate confrontation between all power and no power.

HZ   And yet I wonder: wouldn't the eventual effect that *The Living End* has on the reader be that a powerful, anecdotal, whimsical God on the one hand and powerless human beings on the other hand are, after all, preferable to nothingness? And that even a vast lie, a huge mistake which God might make, is better than annihilation?

SE   Yes, and a mistake is better, as far as the story is concerned, than a well-executed plan. That's true. The world as it is now arranged, according to the lights of *The Living End*, is a better world than a world where children don't suffer, where people don't get multiple sclerosis, and all the rest. But God is *still* a son of a bitch and *still* annihilates, at the end of that book, everything, absolutely everything. He annihilates the universe because there is no one in the universe who can appreciate what a good story He is telling.

HZ   I thought that God's act of absolute annihilation at the end of the book was, in a sense, a metaphor for the dangers of art. Because by creating the world the way He did, God has made Himself dependent on mankind; in creating a story He needed an audience. Thus He cannot fairly blame His audience for not understanding His story because He Himself created this audience. It's just as if the artist were expecting his own characters to understand him.

SE   I like that, and it's true. It is perfectly consonant with the spirit of my intentions.

HZ On the other hand I think that the conclusion of *The Living End* places the *reader* in an almost metaphysical dimension. For only the *reader* can pity and understand God.

SE But not just pitying God; he has also got to pity the victims of God's little jokes, and I'm as much on humanity's side as I am on God's.

HZ I felt that pity was due the human beings anyway. So I found it interesting that, in the end, the reader even comes to sympathize with God. For me this seemed to imply that you would prefer emotion to justice, and absolutely any emotion to nothingness.

SE One of the things that is most moving to me is the end of Faulkner's *The Wild Palms*. The doctor, Harry, in his jail cell has just been sentenced to life for performing the abortion on Charlotte. Charlotte's husband, who is still Charlotte's husband, comes into the jail cell and gives Harry a poison capsule. Harry doesn't really want to live, because he has nothing very much to look forward to. He takes the poison capsule in his hand, says goodbye to his visitor, and when the visitor goes you have the sense that Harry is going to take this and swallow it. But instead of swallowing it, he throws it down on the creosote-soaked floor and grinds the poison into all the grime and schmutz of the jail and thinks, 'Between grief and nothing I will take grief.' Just saying that sentence chokes me up: between grief and nothing *I* will take grief too.

HZ Another way of approaching *The Living End* and linking it with your other fiction would probably be through the notion of cliché.

SE That's why the stories have clichés as their titles. That was one of the troublesome things about publishing this book. I wanted to call the book *The Conventional Wisdom*. My editor, Henry Robbins, objected to the title. Actually he objected to the title because one of his other writers, John Irving, who was very fond of the book (John reviewed it in *The New York Times* and he has heard me read it at Bread Loaf), objected to the title. He's the one who whispered in Henry's ear: you can't publish the book with that title. So Henry tried and tried to get me to change the title and finally I gave up — because I'm powerless! I figured: if I don't do what he says he's not going to push the book; I mean, he'll publish it and call it *The Conventional Wisdom*, but he won't get behind it. So I was running scared and said, 'OK, we'll call it *The Bottom Line*', which I wasn't particularly fond of, but I thought it was a

little better than what it was ultimately called, *The Living End.*
Then Leanna Boysko, my typist, looked in *Books in Print* to see
if there was any book called *The Bottom Line,* and, indeed,
Fletcher Keeble, a popular novelist, has a novel called *The
Bottom Line.* So that was no good. I couldn't call it *The State of
the Art,* because that wouldn't have made any sense at all. So we
went on this vast cliché hunt and I was at a party asking people
for various clichés, and they were suggesting clichés without
any of them working. But one girl, my chairman's wife as a
matter of fact, said, 'Ah boy, that's the living end.' She didn't
mean to give me a title, but as soon as I heard 'the living end' I
thought, 'That's terrific!' Because of the ambiguity of the title:
the living end is God and the living, in fact, do end in the novel.
So I settled for that. But I had to have a cliché as title for the
book, because everything in the book is built on some stereo-
typed notion of theology.

In *The Dick Gibson Show* the whole notion of clichés being
the real truth is articulated towards the end of the book. There is
a page on the nature of clichés and the relationship of cliché to
truth. You don't recall the paragraph, but it's when Dick wants
to avenge himself. Dick thinks that Behr-Bleibtreau is his enemy
—which is itself a cliché, the notion that somebody can *have* an
enemy. I don't have any enemies that I know of, I wish I did.
Here is the passage from *The Dick Gibson Show*:

> His thought was that here at last was something he could do.
> There was too much suffering. Too much went wrong; victims
> were everywhere. *That* was your real population explosion.
> There was mindless obsession, concentration without point,
> offs and ups, long life's niggling fractions, its Dow-Jones
> concern with itself. What had his own life been, his intermin-
> able apprenticeship which he saw now he could never end?

OK, here it is:

> All one could hope for was to find his scapegoat, to wait for
> him, lurking in alleys, pressed flat against walls.

Now, if you think about it, think of these images visually, we
are talking about melodrama, we are talking about clichéd
gestures in the cheapest kinds of entertainments.

... to wait for him, lurking in alleys, pressed flat against walls, crouched behind doors while the key jiggles in the lock, taking all the melodramatic postures of revenge. To be there in closets when the enemy comes for his hat, or to surprise him with guns in swivel chairs, your legs dapperly crossed when you turn to face him, to pin him down on hillsides or pounce on him from trees as he rides by, to meet him on the roofs of trains roaring on trestles ...

These are all things from movies.

... or leap at him while he stops at red lights, to struggle with him on the smooth faces of cliffs, national monuments, chasing him round Liberty's torch ...

These are, in fact, from Alfred Hitchcock's movies.

... or up girders of bridges, or across the enormous features of stone presidents. To pitch him from ski lifts and roller coasters, to Normandy his ass and guerrilla his soul. To be always in ambush at the turnings in tunnels, or wrestle him under the tides of the seas. Gestures, gestures, saving gestures, life-giving and meaningless and sweet as appetite, delivered by gestures and redeemed by symbols, by necessities of your own making and a destiny dreamed in a dream.

That's what it's all about, to find the truth hiding in clichés.

HZ   But the truth only hides in an accumulation of clichés, right? Just one cliché would simply refer back to the context from which it was originally taken.

SE   That's right. Earlier in the book Gibson says, 'The great life is the trite life.' That's true, I think. I mean, it would be terrific to have lots of mistresses, to have lots of money, to sell your soul to the devil, and then to be able to renege. All of these things would be wonderful and glorious and trite. But it's only in triteness that there is any truth at all.

HZ   Still, in writing, isn't triteness transcended through form?

SE   Oh, sure! Absolutely. But the kernel of organization is still trite. It's still triteness itself. Of course one hopes to transcend this, and in bad fiction the transcendence never takes place. What I'm trying to do is write my own bad fiction where it *does* take place.

HZ   At that point I simply wouldn't call it trite anymore.

SE   OK, then you turn the trite into true and this becomes a sort of alchemic act, a kind of alchemy. But the gold is still base metal.

HZ   Wouldn't it be possible to apply the Aristotelian notion to cliché that, through an accumulation, through quantity, it can eventually make the leap to quality?

SE   I absolutely agree. That's precisely the reason musical comedy works. There is nothing cornier than any given moment in a musical comedy. But through the accumulation of moments they become convincing and there is something almost exalted about a good musical comedy.

HZ   At the beginning of this interview you said at one point that we were not talking about art or aesthetics, but about final things. Does this apply to the cliché as well?

SE   Auden was right when he said towards the end of his life that no line he had ever written saved a single Jew from the ovens. That is true. It seems to me that the best artists make the worst propagandists. Because the best artists need the best audiences, and if they are in fact the best audiences, they are not going to be turned on by propaganda.

HZ   I didn't want to make the point of fiction having to be openly ethical or moral. What I was thinking of is something else you once said, namely that all fiction has a sort of Christian device behind it: that, through shape and form, you rescue the good and punish the bad.

SE   That's right. I am not saying that that *should* be right, but that that essentially *is* right. That is what happens in most fictions. It's because what the author is establishing primarily — and then the rest all comes along with him as his baggage and luggage — is a good character. I don't mean a *good* character, I mean a character who *works*. Because the character works, he generates sympathy, he generates empathy, we cheer for him in his victories, we weep when he loses, we cheer again when he recovers from his loss. But all of that is a kind of lazy man's morality. It really is. It is a hell of a lot easier to empathize with a fictional character than with a real human being. You don't have to give him any money, it doesn't cost anything. It's just supine good will, the hammock condition, your expansive sympathies almost sexually erect. It doesn't cost you any effort and you can't get hurt.

HZ   Still, I would try to make the point that there is more to the positive response of a reader of good fiction than just this lazy good will. I think that one could actually argue the other way round and say that the fact that you don't have to commit yourself to a fictional character, that you don't have to take any responsibility for him, may in fact open up possibilities of understanding which you would otherwise exclude yourself from — out of fear and distrust. This is a quality that I would like to attribute to all good fiction: that it creates sensibilities that cannot be evoked by any other art form.

SE   I agree with you. Saul Bellow calls this lazy good will, so beautifully, 'potato love'. But you are right, there is more to it.

John Fowles

John Fowles was born in Leigh-on-Sea, Essex in 1926 and was educated at Bedford School and New College, Oxford, graduating in French in 1950. He has taught in France and Greece, the latter experience providing some of the material for *The Magus*. Fowles is a recipient of the PEN Silver Pen Award and the Smith Literary Award.

John Fowles's first novel, *The Collector* (1963), is a study in power. A man imprisons a woman. The novel is generated by the struggle of each to impose a personal model of reality on the other. The patent paranoia of the kidnapper is pitched against the social truculence of his victim, a woman whose class perspective deforms reality as powerfully as the deranged sensibility of her captor. The battle between them operates on various levels as the imprisonment exists in more than the immediate physical fact of the kidnapping. Both their worlds are placed under pressure. Her death is in some degree her own fault. She fails morally. Challenged to find a point of contact with a being beyond herself she cannot do so, though there are signs of a crucial recovery. The novel stands, among other things, as a study of the pathology of a culture.

The Magus (1966) consists of an elaborate series of games, mystifications, enacted on the Greek island of Phraxos. A model of the rational mind's attempt to penetrate mystery, it probes the central question of power in its various guises. And out of this examination there grows a strongly assertive model of moral responsibility, an insistence that the self owes its shape and, finally, the justification for its being, to the acknowledgement of the rights of others, to the acceptance of their autonomy which can be engaged but not violated. And at the heart of this, as of *The French Lieutenant's Woman* (1969), is the sexual relationship, loaded down, as ever, with cultural assumptions, biological determinisms and social definitions not only of propriety but of socially-derived notions of sexual role. And though the chief

111

manipulator, the conjurer, the magus, is a man, the agent of moral education is a woman. Masculine egotism, indeed, is presented as a principle barrier between the self and its acknowledgement of responsibilities beyond an arrogant assumption of intellectual, moral and social rights. The novel is an assault on a hubris which derives in part from rational assumptions about the precision of language and the world's propensity to void its meaning totally and carelessly. Mystery remains a fact of the private and public world, an essential part of its reality.

The mysteries may be explained on one level. They are tricks, just as a novelist's gestures are tricks. But on another level the mystery remains. Why, after all, bother? Why the impulse to deceive, to corrupt in the direction of goodness? Conchis, the master magician, is Prospero, spinning worlds of mystery to protect something of value; but that something is a mystery located in the individual who is both his victim and his pupil.

Fowles clearly mistrusts trickery while necessarily practising it. Equally clearly he is wary of simple rationalism. He wishes to endorse neither as an adequate account of the real. He distrusts both a world too completely contained by enigma and one in which meaning is too completely displayed through language or contained by social structures. There is a virtue in refusing to be contained by plots generated by others but there is equally a virtue in the moment of self-abnegation which is the essence of love.

The Magus plays with myth and is myth. On one occasion he was persuaded to say, 'I was trying to tell a fable about the relationship between man and his conception of God.' But in this world God, too, is suspect; the pleasure of manipulation is not without its moral implications. The conjurer relies on deceit and the process whereby the individual is moved in the direction of truth is not without its ironies and, more important, its hypocrisies.

These lessons are all hard-earned, particularly in *The French Lieutenant's Woman* in which the protagonist is pressed beyond the parameters of his experience on a social no less than a sexual level. As in *The Magus* it is the woman who instructs, who draws him towards a world in which time collapses no less insistently than outmoded social models. An imitation nineteenth-century novel, the book blossoms out of that moment in which the familiar structures and assumptions dissolve. The book presents the reader with a series of alternative endings, offering itself as primary evidence of the possibility of taking radically new directions, breaking free of contours assumed too easily to be defining boundaries.

Fowles is committed to story-telling. The process of invention is itself the source of values. But it is also the origin of coercion. And in this respect he identifies an ambivalence which equally affects the individual, part constrained, part free agent. His form reflects and contains this debate, as in some degree does Iris Murdoch's (more especially in *The Black Prince*). To some extent, of course, the freedom which he offers is factitious. The author unavoidably has his thumb on the scale, but his gestures of deconstruction, his offer to let the text go where it will, is not wholly unreal or deceptive. The reassuring patterns, once disrupted, can never entirely re-form. The spaces have been opened up and the mind cannot help but begin to fill them. The wound may not be primal, but the imagination's power to people it suggests a level on which we evade control, or at least determine the texture and tone of our existence if not its fundamentals.

Daniel Martin (1977) is a confessedly self-indulgent book. Passages and incidents are sustained too long, drained too completely of their meaning, too ruthlessly pursued for their metaphoric significance. Nonetheless, the scale of the book is important. It ranges from England to America, restlessly searching for the real source of moral collapse. There is a powerful sense that in some ways Fowles's characters here inhabit a social world not really hospitable to the moral being. And yet the central task remains to discover a mode of living which bypasses the distractions, the trivializing flood of experience, the ready-made worlds of Hollywood or fantasy, for a purer world of genuine emotion and personal commitment. The real objective remains the moral self, a point not of stasis but of balance, of sustained tension, which is equally the aesthetic of Fowles work. He is both a traditionalist and an experimentalist. His admiration for the natural world, exemplified in his book *The Tree*, is not a sentimentality or a simple piety. There is a value to be found in the very fact of a vital existence, in a Zen-like awareness of process which contains both growth and decay, the contradictory but complementary elements of a world which, like his own work, operates by contrarieties.

Interview with John Fowles*

March 1979

CB Does the novelist's desire to transform the real coexist with a political desire to alter society or is it a sublimation of it? Have you been tempted to political action?

JF No. I make what is perhaps a peculiar distinction between desires and dreams. I have a dream of an altered society, and cherish that; but don't lose much sleep over desires I know I can't fulfil in practical terms. The most useful working quality in any politician is a lack of imagination. Novelists are ruled out. In any case, the novel is not the literary medium in which to advocate political action of a direct kind, simply because it never works. It has of course in the past helped remedy various social outrages. But I think its main power, in this context, is in enlarging or focusing sensibility — changing climates a little, not inspiring action directly.

CB While hardly a recluse you don't throw yourself into the public arena or even play a public role in the literary world. Do you feel in some degree an exile from contemporary England or from an English tradition in writing. Are you buying your freedom with isolation?

JF I feel exiled from many present English conceptions of society, social behaviour and so on. I think the notion of an English 'literary world' exists only in the mind of people who run literary organizations. We have no 'community of letters' that I have ever discovered. I feel in no way whatever exiled from the English tradition in a broad sense, though by the hazard of existence I am probably a bit more at home in French literature than most native writers today. I do find a lot of contemporary English fiction abysmally parochial, and of no conceivable interest to anyone who is not English and middle-class. I buy freedom with isolation in this sense.

CB And you see the novel as itself an instrument of freedom.

JF It is certainly an instrument for freedom — if self-knowledge is freedom — for the writer. But even the form itself, mainly because it is not a community art and because it is in economic terms cheap to produce, is potentially a freedom.

---

*The form of this interview was determined in part by the fact that, at the request of John Fowles, it was conducted by post. The responses are thus to a series of written questions.

Communication through printed symbol requires almost as much effort and 'creativity' — and as much sensitivity — from the recipient as from the sender, though much of this takes place in the reader at an unconscious level. In a sense all art is inherently totalitarian. Someone is trying to stamp his or her own sensibility and philosophy on someone else. The fact that the novel is handsomely the most despised of the contemporary major art forms in this country is of course painful for all of us who write fiction; but I suspect it also proves that the novel allows a greater freedom of reaction, and far more than the other narrative forms like the play and the film. There the audience is awed by spectacle and cost, and has all the moment-to-moment imagining done for it by the visual image.

CB The central character of *The French Lieutenant's Woman* sees himself as a liberal. If I'm right in thinking that your own convictions are liberal/socialist what is the difference between your own liberalism and his?

JF A century of intellectual ferment. My sympathies lie in present terms with the left wing of the Labour Party, though I have some quarrels even there.

CB You have implied (in 'Notes on an Unfinished Novel' and in *The French Lieutenant's Woman*) that we live in an age which is out to exterminate both the individual and the enduring. Isn't it arguable that in former ages freedom was simply a class prerogative and hence was illusory for the mass of people, and that there is now a swing back to respect for the enduring — indeed to a form of conservatism which is political as well as cultural in form?

JF A key phrase for me here is Gramsci's 'cultural hegemony' — the very cunning and sophisticated systems of brainwashing that so-called democratic Western societies have evolved to keep the ordinary man and woman passive and sheeplike. Of course economic and cultural freedom was and is largely a class prerogative, but how you should think conservatism can remedy that is beyond me. In a historical sense I am not at all sure that for most people the political and economic non-freedom of this country before the Industrial Revolution was *culturally* worse than the alleged freedom since. People who are shocked by this should read Pastor Moritz's *Journeys in England* of 1782.

CB Of course I don't think that conservatism can remedy this. In many ways it's the root of the problem. What I meant was that far from living in an age which is out to exterminate the enduring we seem to be living in an age with an undue respect for the enduring — at least in political terms. Right-wing conservatives struggle to sustain an England which has long since disappeared; left-wing socialists still believe in nineteenth-century economic theories and seek to preserve a model of England based on the political realities of the thirties, and a model of union structure based on the craft guilds.

JF I didn't fully take your point. By 'enduring' I didn't of course mean what are merely by-products of class or personal selfishness. I was thinking more of things like built-in obsolescence, exploitation of natural resources, contempt for craftsmanship ... and of certain values on the more intellectual side, such as a historical sense, community feeling, self-reliance, all the qualities that the over-powerful state, whether left, right or centre, tends to sap and diminish. The trouble is that many of these 'qualities' are simply forces, like electricity or nuclear power, and capable of serving very different ends. A historical sense can become a blindness to the present; community feeling, community brainwashing; self-reliance, a justification for economic greed, and so on. No doubt the threat to these ancient and potentially good values is simply the cost of social, economic, and technological advance in other ways. I still think it is a cost that the political left in particular persistently underrates. My general sympathy for the left does here get trumped by my biological beliefs. But then socialism's weakest point has always been in its attitude to nature and the natural sciences, which is far more damaging to it than its other and notorious inability to come to terms with art. The recent rise of the 'Green' parties all over Europe is in my view a direct result of this.

CB It seems to me that there is a continuing debate in your work about the reality and extent of individual freedom. Your protagonist in *The French Lieutenant's Woman* is a Darwinian in a tussle with social determinisms — that is, he seeks a freedom of action which, in a fundamental sense, he doesn't wholly believe in. On the whole you seem to insist on the reality and even the moral necessity of that freedom. How do you relate that to your strong interest in a natural world which is contingent and determined?

JF For most of my life I've been more interested in the natural sciences and in history than in literature. Behaviourism and evolutionary adaptations, in both human and non-human nature, fascinate me. My only sustained interest in the study of fiction concerns my own natural history (and behaviourism) as a writer, oneself as guinea-pig. I simply don't know the answer to the old enigma of freewill. In many ways I get more and more dubious of its existence as I grow older, and (for instance) now regard many past and supposedly 'free' decisions of my own as clearly conditioned; and especially in terms of choices taken during writing as regards character destinies and courses of events. But I am convinced there are degrees of being conditioned and that there is an area where many people — if society allows — can achieve moments or periods of comparative freedom. I think it is very necessary to cling to that, until science can categorically prove that all is conditioned. I now think of existentialism as a kind of literary metaphor, a wish fulfilment. I long ago began to doubt whether it had any true philosophical value in many of its assertions about freedom.

CB   Again and again I'm struck by the lyricism which you find in the natural world and which often stands in contrast to the prosaic formulae of human relationships and customs. And yet isn't that lyricism a false standard? The natural world is beautiful, calm, and restorative precisely because it lacks the anguished self-doubt and personal and ideological conflicts of the human world, it lacks that drive for meaning and purpose which provides both the irony and the impetus for change in human affairs.

JF   Nature may lack some of the things you name (though surely not 'personal conflict'), but you seem to be putting an extreme case, where the nature-lover attempts to turn *enfant sauvage* — or retreats to the blue lagoon. I hold no brief for that. Of course the 'restorative' in any aspect of existence *may* finally be dangerous, but I can't see why one must distrust a central experience because of a potential danger in it. Even if nature itself is 'amoral', our actual human relationship with it creates all sorts of moral problems, such as this one you've just raised. Nor do I understand at all what you mean by nature lacking 'a drive for meaning and purpose', which seems to imply there is no connection between human and non-human (or self-conscious and instinctive) drives. I see no hard frontier there, especially in matters like territorial impulse. A great deal of human behaviour (in ordinary conversation, for example) is quite unconsciously territorial in its characteristic sequences of assertion, backing-down, 'distraction behaviour' and the rest. Human males don't actually perch on their rooftops endlessly rehearsing their favourite operatic arias. But certain tunes have them — and most women — by heart.

Nature is above all for me rich in similes and metaphors of man. It is the poetry to the 'prose' of human behaviour, but not just lyrical poetry. I would claim my own experience of nature informs my work in many different ways. I've never been too fond of the strictly lyrical approach, in fact, except in a few poets of genius, and one or two prose writers like Thoreau and Jefferies. Even those last two I much prefer for their philosophical or quasi-religious understanding of nature.

CB You clearly try to get your reader to enact his or her own freedom, particularly in *The French Lieutenant's Woman*, by making him collaborate in imaginatively developing possibilities. For although all readers are in some degree inventors and can ostensibly project the narrative lines along parabolas of their own choice, you have yourself created those possibilities. That is a problem also in *The Magus* and is recognized as such by the protagonist who is uncertain as to whether his options have not perhaps been created for him by hypnotic suggestion or sheer conspiracy. How real, then, is the freedom which you offer. And, by extension, how real is the freedom which you seem to believe the individual has in a world surely shaped by hereditary and environmental forces of an unpredictable and unquantifiable kind?

JF Good question, and one I was very aware of during the writing of *The French Lieutenant's Woman*, as a close reading of some passages will reveal. In an internal sense, textually, I do not think a novelist can offer freedom to his readers, however aleatory his technique, however many forks he offers, however many 'clues' he suppresses. This is especially true in narrative and character terms. On the other hand, I think there is some sort of metaphorical truth in the use of alternative situations — that is, it suggests to the reader a possible method of escape in terms of her or his own life and its fictions and realities. It can't of course offer the actual escape itself. This isn't quite pure theory on my part. I am fortunate in getting plenty of letters from readers, and some at least have understood this function (the exemplary intention of the device in the book) rather better than the many academic students of the text.

The feedback from readers is in my view most important for a novelist — even when it is hostile — and I suspect most British novelists suffer increasingly from not receiving it. One can discover a great deal about contemporary sensibilities, needs, lacks, yearnings, from such letters and all this fertilizes one's work. If one's only feedback is from reviewers — especially English reviewers — one is seeing only half the reality. I know Doris Lessing feels exactly the same about this. It also partly accounts for my being something of a hermit in everyday terms. But I am a hermit who receives several hundred letters a year, and often very human and revealing ones, from complete strangers.

CB   Why do you associate freedom with women in your work?

JF   Because there is abundant historical evidence of a connection between periods of political and cultural progress (such as the Renaissance) and wider recognition of the feminine principle. I don't think it is worth arguing whether enhanced status for women follows an increased general liberalism, or vice versa; what is clear is that, once in motion, the two things feed each other. I can't see history as being solely determined by public events; I should have thought most public events are determined by social climates.

CB   Couldn't it be argued that the woman born out of her time, like the heroine of *The French Lieutenant's Woman*, and hence able to operate as the agent of change, may simply seem free because the rules she obeys are not yet socially enforced?

JF   Very possibly, but I don't see why this diminishes such a woman's value as precursor.

CB   No, but it may limit her value as an image of freedom if she simply stands for a different set of constraints.

JF   This seems to me a very idealistic objection. I don't see how any human can do more than predicate, in theory or behaviour, a more humane future social system. Inevitably that system, if it comes into being, will one day reveal faults and constraints of a different kind. I cannot conceive how any 'agent of change' could ever achieve a total, once-and-for-all freedom. Human examples and images of personal freedom must surely always be very comparative — adulterated by what is being escaped from, and therefore adulterating what is being escaped to.

CB   Both Sarah, in *The French Lieutenant's Woman*, and Lily, in *The Magus*, use sexuality as part of the process of moral education. And yet aren't they both guilty of an immorality more fundamental than a matter of sexual ethics in that both, in manipulating the other, become violators of what Hawthorne would have called 'the human heart', that is, they break some kind of moral contract.

JF   It has to be an excessively fastidious morality that condemns an oppressed race, class or sex for using the same weapons as its enemy. It is certainly not an evolutionary morality. Nor do I see how a contract that allows me an unfair privilege and denies you a just right can be termed 'moral'. Whether or not there was a heuristic, liberating and 'good' motive behind my imaginary Sarah seems to me not very important beside the fact that many such women, with such motives, have really existed.

CB   That strikes me as a little disingenuous. After all, the conspiracy in *The Magus* is directed to bringing home to the protagonist his selfishness — the fact that he violates the emotional integrity of others for his own purposes. My worry about Sarah and Lily is not that they use sexuality (as you rightly say, in a sense they are simply turning a weapon back on the sex which has always tended to see this weapon as its own prerogative) but that in doing so they become guilty of that same moral failing which Lily at least had set out to purge from the protagonist.

JF   Perhaps what is really revealed here is my intense dislike of general moral principles, or arguing solely from them. I've always found what one might call the algebraic side of ethics — 'All actions of type *y* are bad' — distinctly scholastic. Particular cases are very different. I'm not denying that inductively achieved moral principles are usually unjustifiable, and so on. *The Magus* was of course a deliberately artificial, model-proposing novel, and a good deal more about fiction than any 'real' situation, and I shouldn't go to the stake for Lily's morality (or her master's). Sarah in *The French Lieutenant's Woman* was always intended to be a sort of borderline case. I've long reached the conclusion that one principal function of the novel, or at least of my own novels, is to present such borderline cases. *Daniel Martin* was very intentionally conceived as such a one. I had during the writing harboured the notion that he would end by some fairly serious political 'commitment' — perhaps to one of the Marxist parties —but realized when it came to it that bathos was needed. So put him in the Labour Party. On grounds of 'pure' principle, I think he has no case at all. But do any of us?

CB   You imply that Charles's defect in *The French Lieutenant's Woman* was that he failed to recognize the power of passion and the imagination. Is this a critique of liberalism, which finds passion as difficult a subject as mystery?

JF   Yes. Of humanism also.

CB   You have said that you see man as a kind of artifice and woman as a kind of reality; the former as cold idea, the latter as warm fact. Isn't that a form of sentimentality, almost setting one up as the ego and the other as id?

JF   I don't think so, but on the contrary something true of the two sexes, for both biological and cultural reasons. There are of course many gradations from female males (no male novelist needs to be told why Hemingway felt obliged to wear such a *macho* face in public) to male females; and in the worst times of exploitation, such as the Victorian period, women have largely worn male faces and gone in just as stupidly for social status, kowtowing to authority and all the rest. But I still think that most men, and still today, are over-obsessed by order, logic and theory — that is, by various abstract games systems that allow them to compete more or less ritually for artificial status — and women by the contrary qualities, which also have their faults. I am not talking of values, or saying that in some way female qualities are *ipso facto* 'better' than male ones, or denying that logic and order have important virtues; but in terms of essential and mutually indispensable natures.

CB You react in your novels against social coercions and yet fiction is also a coercer, perhaps never more so that when it falsely pretends to surrender that power — a lesson clear enough from *The Magus*. Have you ever been tempted by more radical disjunctions of your narrative — the box novel, the novel organized by chance principle? Is it a resolvable paradox?

JF No. The purest aleatory technique and end product must always be caused by an original conscious and non-aleatory decision to write so. I regard all this as twentieth century rococo; I'd be happy to regard it as amusing nonsense...if only its creators would. The shock disjunction is the oldest trick in the world in one profession: that of the clown. The Monty Python group owe their success very much to their brilliant use of it.

CB Some of your more sympathetic characters are deceivers. Their deceptions are justified by the fact that they deceive in the name of moral truth. Isn't that a very dangerous principle to endorse?

JF If you take the novel as a straight reflection of reality, or desirable reality. I think of it much more in metaphorical or parable terms. And even if it is a dangerous principle, I must point out that it is deeply imbedded in the evolutionary system, which might be described as the triumph of intelligence over deception.

CB Do you believe in evil? I'm thinking in particular of the German torturers in *The Magus*.

JF Only as a very loose and vague (but useful) word applied to certain kinds of moral reaction to certain kinds of human behaviour. In a supernatural or religious sense, not at all. The exploitation of the Devil-myth by some contemporary writers and movie-makers does not appeal to me one bit. That is evil.

CB   There is a strong narrative drive in your work, a commitment to narrative, and yet there is an almost equally powerful urge to disrupt that narrative. Is that the outward expression of a debate in your mind between a liberal belief in causality, character, life as a process of discovery, and a sense of the contingent.

JF   I'm afraid I give good story-tellers far more credit than they deserve by other literary standards: and devalue writers who depend more on stylistic gifts than narrative ones. I don't defend this, it's simply the way I am. I do like the part hazard plays in evolution — and ordinary life — but nine times out of ten I break up or jump-cut straight narrative purely for fun...and also because readers seem to enjoy it, even if reviewers don't.

CB   The narrator in *Daniel Martin* says that the desire to create imaginary worlds is strongly linked with the notion of retreat. Do you see writing as in some ways expressing a failure of moral will?

JF   Not at all. A lack of politically activist will, perhaps. Novelists are all egoists, narcissists, parties of one, from the greatest to the least. But that is our principal social function — not to join, not to be what the contemporary state considers safe citizens. That can take rather more moral will, patience and courage than most non-writers ever care to realize.

CB   Yours was a generation which was confronted with matters of public policy which seemed to demand a personal moral response in a way which, perhaps, had not been quite so true for previous generations. *Daniel Martin* seems to suggest that a generation had failed in its responsibilites. What was the essence of that failure? A failure of action or imagination?

JF   Both, but I suspect they are only symptoms of the underlying cause, which was, and remains, a retreat into the self —a deep conviction that personal destiny matters more than public destiny. My generation developed (or had developed in us by world events 1939-49) a deep cynicism about anything that smacked of ideals and absolutes, indeed about all existing social and political theory. Our tacit motto became the old Navy catchphrase, 'Jack's inboard'. If I'm all right, to hell with you. Our self-fascination was certainly also aggravated by the fall in international status. This new treachery of the clerks has bred the dominant public spirit among the British intelligentsia during these last two decades: that of satire and sour grapes, of carping, complaining, cutting down to size, while I suspect the inward spirit — the underlying ethic, or lack of it — shows some curious parallels with seventeenth-century quietism. I am not suggesting that our self-defensive scepticism in public matters has not brought about some healthy demolition. One could argue that the main failure of my generation is not that we did not resist all this, but that we did not push it farther and destroy more. Instead, most of us in the professional middle classes have settled for Toryism, defence of a doomed system and comfortable fifth-rate lives. I think the bill is beginning to come in now.

Of course generations of moral failure — I'd rather say who fail to adapt to their historical situation — are commonplace in history, and perhaps because of our puritan conscience, especially familiar in British history. I don't think we're any worse than, say, the generations in power 1660-89 or 1890-1914.

CB   Although you seem to imply that the present younger generation displays a kind of honesty, at least in its idea of human relationships. Couldn't this be a form of sentimentality?

JF   A lot of it may seem sentimental to the jaundiced eyes of my class and generation. But I see sentimentality as an excess of a good thing, not of an already bad one. For me the Romantic Movement and the French Revolution are the same phenomenon. The best thing that could happen to the 1980s is the 1740s — a dawn of a swing on that old mind-heart pendulum.

CB   I know that you have said you were influenced by Zen in the sixties. Is that principally in the need for a sensitivity to the nature of your surroundings or in its concern with pursuing a transcendent self?

JF   I was at that time becoming far too science-besotted in my relationship with nature. Zen rescued me from that. I have no interest in its theology. I dislike all transcendental religion, and especially the oriental kind. However, I greatly admire some Zen 'aids' to experiencing and seeing. I try now to experience nature in both ways.

CB   You are constantly debating the significance of first and third person narration in your novels, as much as in your critical essays. What is the significance of that problem to you?

JF   Whichever person I start a novel in, I very soon begin feeling its restrictions, and remembering the liberties of the other. I think I'm settling towards the third now. The omnipotent power of gravity in the novel form is realism. I resist it less and less.

CB   What do you mean by realism?

JF   What is generally meant by the word. The attempt to reflect life, both in style and content, as it is *seen* by the majority; though not necessarily, of course, as it is *valued* by the majority. I suppose I mean something like 'traditional technique but original vision', which on the first ground would exclude Kafka and the later Joyce. For me Flaubert would serve as a paragon of realism; or Lukacs's hero, Thomas Mann. I don't in the least mean by this that I am in some way opposed to innovative technique. I am very certain that Joyce is the greatest novelist of this century. The liberty to express oneself as one pleases is the fundamental right of every artist, and I have no time for any literary theory or 'party' that challenges the general principle.

I suspect the crucial thing, in the novel, is how novelist conceives of audience. My own preferred contract is in the middle ground, and I am not ashamed of being widely read, since in my view that must always be an implicit hope in this particular choice (just as there are equally legitimate choices of audience that must exclude it). To the extent that liberalism is a teaching or converting belief, then I think realism must always hold a powerful attraction to 'liberal' writers; conversely, the always lurking suspicion of elitism in experimental or highly intellectual writing (in the novel) will repel them. So will strict 'socialist realism', in another direction.

I don't think one has to argue with the neo-Marxist view that the novel is an adamantly bourgeois form. This is just a way of saying that all art is elitist of its nature — beyond the majority in creation and very often beyond the majority in comprehension. All would-be egalitarian theories of art have their bottoms ripped out on the same reef: art may preach equality, but there will never be equality in the preaching, or among the preachers.

CB   *Daniel Martin* clearly relies on certain cinematic techniques and yet you are suspicious of the deadening power of the cinema itself. Can the novel usefully derive anything from the cinema?

JF   Quite a lot in technical terms, especially since all our conscious, and unconscious, imaging powers as we read — or dream — are now geared to 'seeing' narration in cinematic terms. I am sure it is also very useful for a novelist to be clear on what the novel can do that the cinema can't. I read too many writers who seem hell-bent on writing what the cinema can usually do much better ... and quite as much out of lack of thought as love of money. Deliberately writing a pseudo-scenario to ensure movie rights is bad enough; but writing one out of sheer ignorance of the special capacities of the novel form is absurd.

CB   In *The Collector* you draw a picture of an individual manipulated for selfish ends, in *The Magus* for selfless ends. Is the manipulation of others, then, to be seen as morally neutral, a condition of existence? If so, doesn't that open the door to the self-righteous despot, not to mention the didactic novelist?

JF The manipulation of others is certainly an almost universal condition of existence, in nature as well as man. I do not see why a necessary condition predicates moral neutrality; of course we must judge each human case for itself. I regard 'didactic' as a descriptive term; not necessarily an accusatory one. Speaking for myself, I soon lose interest in novelists who do not show their prejudices and their opinions; who do not try to sell me something beyond entertainment, wit, clever technique, exquisite prose...not that those aren't added pleasures.

CB Like your narrator in *Daniel Martin* you have written stories which avoid happy endings. Is that a fear of endings as such?

JF The passage where Daniel Martin worries about his fear of the happy ending is strictly autobiographical. Ending fictions has always given me terrible problems, as my editors know. I think this is mainly because I find the actual writing of a novel a deeply rewarding and pleasurable experience — both emotionally and intellectually — and for me the publication is like being locked out of my own self-created paradise. My printed texts are for me dead, cold, detached objects, almost like books by someone else. I analyzed this recently in connection with Thomas Hardy,* who I have a strong suspicion was in the same case. Of course one has to kill off the past text, count it as a failure, in order to gain energy and a motive for the next attempt. It is simply that for me the moment of assassination takes place while the victim is still alive, when that last chapter can be put off no longer. Whatever else I might have been, it is not a successful hit man.

---

*Hardy and the Hag', in *Thomas Hardy After Fifty Years* (Macmillan, 1977).

John Gardner

John Champlin Gardner, Jr, was born in Batavia, New York, on 21 July 1933. His mother was an English teacher and his father, a lay preacher, taught him to respect the language of the Bible and of Shakespeare. He also cultivated in his son a taste for serious music, and among Gardner's many literary productions are libretti for two operas by Joe Baber. As a boy Gardner lived in Batavia —which would later provide the setting for one of his novels — attended the local schools, and worked on his father's farm. He spent his student years at DePauw University, at Washington University in St Louis where he took a BA in 1955, and at the State University of Iowa where he took an MA in 1956 and a PhD in 1958. For his doctoral dissertation he wrote a — as yet unpublished — novel, *The Old Men*. Gardner has published widely in the field of medieval literature and has taught medieval literature and creative writing at numerous schools including Oberlin, Bennington, Skidmore, Southern Illinois, Northwestern, Chico State College, the University of Detroit, San Francisco State, the University of Rochester, George Mason College, and the State University of New York at Binghamton.

For Gardner, the poet and the priest are clearly related: both are concerned with the search for as well as the promulgation of Truth. But while their fundamental beliefs and aims are identical, their means differ radically: the priest strives to enforce Truth by threatening punishment in case of disloyalty; the poet attempts to persuade through metaphor. In other words, the artist provides the reader or listener or viewer with a dramatic equivalent of the prolonged intellectual process he himself went through in his search for Truth.

The True, the Good, and the Beautiful, each follows from the others. Thus Gardner states in *On Moral Fiction* (1978) that 'the Good is form: morality is function'. For he believes that the Good rests with the old traditional values which constitute the norm from which all subsequent moral actions derive. The artist's duty

126

consists in recognizing and reinstalling these archetypal values by divesting them of the diverse individual or ethnic rituals which attach to and obscure them. As early as his first published novel, *The Resurrection* (1966), Gardner seems convinced that the artist ought to create a new morality, since life, according to Gardner, always imitates art — not vice versa. Beauty, on the other hand, 'is the truth of feeling'. The Beautiful is not a given, but the result of the artist's acceptance of responsibility for the inviolability of the things of nature as well as those of civilization.

By these standards the importance of the artist's role in society leaves little room for play or irony. Even parody becomes the expression of a serious conflict between different *Weltanschauungen* as they are represented by various artists or philosophies. Thus *The King's Indian* (1974), a collection of short stories, sketches, and the title novella, parodies and opposes central beliefs in Coleridge, Melville, Poe, and Conrad through the appropriation of their respective styles. And in the epic poem *Jason and Medeia* (1973), which parodies the ancient myth, the intellectual aloofness of the West is pitted, through Jason, against the emotional spontaneity of the East, embodied by Medeia.

Gardner's literary effort is ambitiously comprehensive, ranging from the realistic to the fantastic but always centring on values which are typically American: the American dream and the pursuit of happiness. By an interfusion of matter and mind, nature and civilization, these values are then made to appear universal. Thus in *Nickel Mountain* (1973), the unpresuming protagonist ends up with an almost mystical insight into the 'holiness of things'. And the governing tyrant of — historically and geographically removed — ancient Sparta in *The Wreckage of Agathon* (1970), who becomes emblematic of the repetitiveness of evil inhering in any human attempt at political power-mongering, is rhetorically overcome by Agathon and Demodokos, the advocates of individual freedom.

Good and evil in Gardner's fiction appear either in a realistic context as social forces, definable as the pleasurable or painful impact which the actions of human beings have upon one another, or in a fantastic setting as innate attitudes which can be changed only through the magic of art. The novels *The Sunlight Dialogues* (1972) and *October Light* (1976), for instance, belong to the first category, the famous *Grendel* (1971) and *In the Suicide Mountains* (1977), the latest of his books for children and also a tale for adults, to the second. In *The Sunlight Dialogues* memory and compassion are evoked as positive values against the threat of entropy. In *October Light* each individual set of values is shown to become evil when its respective representative believes in his or her own self-sufficiency, and nothing short of the painful clash of these individual values will release the higher value of mutual responsibility. Ultimately, in both novels, it is the protagonists' ineluctable 'mortality that makes morality'. Whereas in *Grendel*, which retells the Beowulf legend from the monster's point of view, as well as in the tale *In the Suicide Mountains*, the figure of the dragon represents that indifference towards values which grows out of immortality. The good in both cases evolves as a struggle against this indifference, a struggle that John Gardner himself strives to share in each of his fictions.

Interview with John Gardner

Baltimore, 12 February 1978

HZ It's true, isn't it, that you *are* very much interested in the values that liberalism, as a political and philosophical attitude, has always focused upon, namely responsibility and freedom?

JG Yes, that's true.

HZ May I pursue the implications of this question regarding two of your novels, an early and a recent novel, *Nickel Mountain* and *October Light*? *Nickel Mountain* is subtitled: *A Pastoral Novel*, and the succession of chapters corresponds to the 'natural' stages of life: courtship, marriage, childbirth, temptation, guilt, forgiveness, death. The pastoral dimension seems to be further enhanced by a certain mysticism pervading life and nature, culminating in Henry Soames's understanding of the 'holiness of things' at the end of his life. Yet there is a tension between this pastoral background and Henry's struggle to assert himself as an individual character which might even link up with Bellow's thesis in *The Adventures of Augie March* that a man's character is his fate. Do you think that these opposing laws, the law of character and the law of nature, can ultimately be reconciled?

JG I think my position is almost identical to Bellow's. People do have free will, yet it's always true too, that a given human being has certain predispositions and inclinations — he has one foot planted in the determined physical universe — so that a man who is genetically a sensualist, say, can kill himself eating, can be greedily selfish, and so on; but he has choices all along the way, his second foot swings free, and by the usual luck of the universe — both bad luck and good — his freedom to choose is likely to be forced to his attention. Let me put it in a different way. Some people are born with an inclination to anger — you know, the adrenalin goes quicker — and some people are born with an inclination toward sloth. Obviously, each person is going to work out his individual fate at least partly in terms of those givens, the angry man slugging, the lethargic man wincing; nevertheless, each man does work it out if he's lucky. In a world of physical mutability luck's important. So Henry Soames can never be anything but a sensualist, but if life pushes him, life and the natural impetus toward love — and if he's lucky in love — he can be a responsible sensualist. He can finally love the mutable world, including physically and morally mutable people, in a way that's merciful, unjudgmental — which is what I think it all comes to in the end. He can learn even to be unjudgmental toward himself — his past, his faults, his slips. His body's a machine, 'mere nature'; but consciousness doesn't work with the simplicity of a ball on an inclined plane. It attaches to values, it generalizes, it dreams of a spiritual-physical totality whereby each of our important acts takes on meaning beyond itself, becomes not an isolated act but a ritual gesture, an affirmation of universal relatedness. Hence the focus you've pointed out in the novel — courtship, marriage, the ceremonialization of childbirth, and so on. We do the things physical objects and animate but mindless objects do — fall down, grow old, struggle to maintain our physical identity (as Whitehead might put it, even chairs 'concentrate', remaining what they are, insofar as possible, by 'negative prehension'); but in our consciousness that what we suffer is also suffered, in various degrees, by chairs and elephants. We rise above self: our necessary animal acts become ritual; we become knowing and (at our best) willing participants in the universal dance of creation and destruction.

Everybody in *Nickel Mountain* is set up as a kind of type, a variation on the universal archetype. Superficially, George Loomis is very different from Henry Soames, partly because he's been unlucky in love; but he's similar to Henry too. Mainly, both of them have curious relations to physical things, including their own bodies. In these two characters especially, the novel emphasizes the opposition between inanimate objects — all the sorts of things we associate with 'body' — and human spirit, 'consciousness', if you like. One thing I was thinking about as I was writing the novel was, you know ... a chair can't move an inch without our help. The whole physical universe is the helpless, idiot child of mind, yet without it we're nothing — probably not even conscious. Henry's relation to physical objects is, initially, a sentimental one; he loves them, even caresses them; he especially loves them if they're old and familiar, unthreatening; but he consumes them — drives his old car like a maniac, eats his way to a heart attack. That's not really having a responsible relation to things; and the same is true of his relationship to people. George Loomis is no better. He collects old guns and magazines and so on but doesn't really love them except as curios, valuable antiques — a different, more aristocratic kind of sentimentality. He finally loves as well as he can love an inanimate object, given his predispositions and his luck, but ultimately he kills a half-inanimate sort of person, the Goat Lady, because he doesn't take care of his truck right — fails to fix the lights. He doesn't take care of even the parts of his own body — he loses an arm, a foot, you know — sort of misplaces things. Both George and Henry could be doomed by their relationship to things. Henry comes out of it partly because he has the courage to love, which leads to his sense of community and responsibility; he learns the social importance of objects, including his own body. George doesn't. He's still a member of the community, because everybody else, represented by Henry and Mr Judkins, accepts George Loomis for all his faults, accepts the mutability that leads to George's guilt; but George himself doesn't accept. He's an idealist, a child of Plotinus.

HZ If, therefore, *Nickel Mountain* is concerned with responsibility, would it be correct to say that *October Light* is a novel about the longing for freedom? For James L. Page, freedom seems to come with life's 'struggle upward...against the pull of the earth', against gravity; whereas for his sister Sally it is a kind of escapism, a conjuring up and enacting, in her imagination, of the possibilities life has denied her. Her freedom is brought about, and at the same time symbolically represented, by the trashy novel-within-the-novel which she reads. A third approach to freedom appears to be a kind of nihilism, hinted at in Lewis Hicks's fleeting wish that his life would change entirely, a wish that at the same time is felt as a desire for death. How can these different concepts of freedom be related to each other? Are they irreconcilable, or do they complement each other?

JG They're irreconcilable when they come into conflict, but the conflict can lead to a higher idea of freedom, a reconciliation — or anyway that's my theory. I think what happens is that the three pursuits of freedom work fine until accident forces them to lock horns on one basic issue, the extent to which one does or does not tyrannize other people or allow oneself to be tyrannized. Any one of the three characters' ways of acting makes a perfectly acceptable 'reality', that is to say, you can live and not die by it. All three characters, James, Sally, and Lewis, both evade total reality and struggle to take care of things, certain of reality's components. Lewis is always patching things and fixing things — in fact he's a handyman by trade — but he avoids confrontation with his wife though he knows she's killing herself with cigarettes. He refuses to bully, and he refuses to *be* bullied. He's a dodger, an evader. It's admirable that he's neither a tyrant nor a slave, but the fact is that his solution excludes him from civilization in all its troubled complexity. He's half-Indian, symbolically, a half civilized, half natural man. His nearest approach to civilization, until the moment he faces up, is to civilization's physical objects —the chairs and doors he fixes for the people around him. You'll notice he never fixes anything for himself. His car — like George Loomis's truck — is a four-wheeled disaster. James Page, on the other hand, is a tyrant. His way of working is to force everybody and everything — beginning with his animals — to do what he thinks is good for them, because he has a notion of how life ought to be and, mainly from love and concern, he tries to force everybody into it; but he evades his own emotion — in fact he's forgotten the wife he loved. Sally is known for her 'goodness', but she's been terribly bullied all her life. She's a strong person, full of loves and hates, but she's been bullied by her husband, although he is a gentle-seeming man who likes Mozart and that sort of thing. In a mysterious way (I hope this is true) this ultra-civilized Horace of a man has suppressed her real character, as James, her brother, has in a different way suppressed her, until finally she says *No!* The three ways of living could run along parallel if the novel allowed everybody good luck. As long as she accepts being bullied and simply lives a fantasy life, secretly loving and hating but doing what other people want her to do, Sally will be OK; she could go on forever with her fantasy life. Lewis Hicks, as long as he escapes intense involvement by patching broken objects, could be fine forever; and James Page, as long as he's a successful bully, with no memory of what he's done, could also get along fine. But a moment comes when suddenly every one of them stops being lucky: their three roads converge. James destroys Sally's television — her escape — and the substitute escape she turns to, the trashy novel, ironically becomes, by the accident of its use at just this moment, not just a device of escape but also a weapon. And so the war is on. When Sally reads the trashy novel, she's not only given a means of passing the time of her rebellion — her 'strike', in effect — she's also spurred, by the accident of the book's subject matter, to more intense rebellion. She isn't willing to be bullied any more. She has laid back and let Horace set the standards during their marriage, and she's accepted James's standards (up to a point); but when she reads the novel, her potential for rebellion rises: the very escape — the trashy novel — becomes the trigger which fires her desire for something that's her own.

The point is that no matter what mode of action you choose, aggression, submission or evasion, eventually life demands fulfillment — or at least demands that you try for it. In the struggle of human evolution — that is, the soul's struggle for survival — fitness demands that we be supple enough to switch from aggression to submission, evasion and submission to aggression. It's an inevitable implication of our double identity as both individuals and members of a group — ultimately members of the whole cosmic business, the club of Living Things. And it's at this point, when our clashing identities strike together, that Sally fights James, and Lewis begins to assert himself in his role as husband, that is, 'house-bond'. It's at this moment, if ever, that 'alternative life styles' give way to something broader, universal. Everybody has to find common ground, the same principle of behavior: everybody has to be responsible to and for everybody else. Sally can't back off anymore; finally she has to take care of her own psyche and take responsibility for her secret aggressiveness, partly because at last she's acted on it. And finally James is forced to recognize his responsibility *to* as well as *for* everybody else. He has to face up to the fascist element in every well-meaning Gilgamesh or Oedipus. Hero gives way to tragic hero. It's hard to express except in the way I've tried to express it in the novel.

HZ Could you say that the three kinds of freedom collide, releasing a higher freedom, as soon as you are forced to take responsibility?

JG Exactly. The thing about the three kinds of freedom is that they all work fine when you don't have to deal with other human beings. With robots — or with stick-figures in a trashy novel —you

can take any course you please. As soon as you deal with other
human beings then everybody has to face up to the same values —
or at least they all have to compromise their values. Ultimately it
comes to something beyond that, as it always does in my fiction, not
just responsibility for other people but responsibility for all of
nature, all of life — you know, bears, trees, cows, chipped bedroom
doors, the noises which, rightly organized, make music. What I
think happens at the end of the novel is that Sally gives up her fight
for good reasons rather than for bad ones. Always in the past she
has given up simply because she's given up; she just didn't want to
fight. Her fantasy identity has been enough for her. When she
comes out of her room at the end of the novel she comes out because
of something that has happened to Ginny and to James; she doesn't
even realize that she has come out of her room; she does it as a
spontaneous gesture, selflessly, *forgetting* herself. And, because
she sees that James is distraught, she sees everything from a new
point of view which, in a funny way, she learned from the
experience of reading her escapist novel. It's made her think of
other people as they really are, not as bad fiction presents them.

What happens in the world, it seems to me, is that people come
together in moments of crisis, and they all work by the same system
for a little while; then they can safely go back to their own systems.
Sally will still dream, maybe with the same touch of bitchiness, but
the novel's events will have their subtle effect. James can never go
back to quite the same bullying he was guilty of before, but you can
bet that if Sally talks too much on the telephone two weeks after the
end of the novel, James is going to yell like hell about the bill. His
character won't change, her character won't change, Lewis Hicks's
character won't change; but they at least know how to function with
one another now, behave like human beings. I guess what I mean is
that it doesn't matter too much what your individual road to
freedom is; individual roads to freedom are fine, and it's only when
you're with other people that values have to be agreed on. They
have to be shared, and they have to be shared emotionally; you
can't just decide intellectually. And I guess I think that the only way
that that can come about is that the values each person lives by have
to backfire badly, so that he recognizes that there has to be a higher
value. It's like nature versus super-nature, you know — or raw
nature, jungle nature, versus civilization. Ultimately what
civilization does, it seems to me, is to protect nature — individual
natures. When civilization is doing its work, everything becomes
part of everything, but itself is still *part*.

HZ   Would you say, then, that your liberalism amounts to a desire to reconcile opposites, to work towards harmony in social and political affairs? In *The Sunlight Dialogues* Congressman Hodge *worries* about the *E pluribus unum* principle; he assumes that, in the modern world, the differences in culture and opinion have become so great that any unifying idea would be too simple, a sign of madness in fact. Do you agree that the belief in the process of unification may indeed also lead to its own apocalyptic perversion, to entropy or chaos, a notion which seems to be prevalent in much recent American fiction?

JG   It certainly is true that that has become prominent in American fiction. I think it's come about because, instinctively, unconsciously, a lot of American writers feel that the American ideal — as they understand it — is wrong-headed, or unrealistic. But I think those writers are mistaken. They oversimplify. They secretly want their individuality, and they think they're wrong to want it — antisocial — and so they lash out at the ideal of conciliation that seems to threaten them, claiming that, though we ought to admire it, it's a false hope; or else they misapprehend it, confusing it with such amoral levellers as the international corporation. Some conciliation does occur, after all, and it needn't wreck individuality. I think you have to keep your merely social values to some extent. They give identity. Security. But you must recognize that they're not universally shared. You've simply recognized that we have to have a balance of private values and public values, and that, in the realm of public values, we have to compromise; we have to try to dismiss what our own fraction of the culture calls 'bad manners' and ask only for humane goodness. But if we do that privately, if we abandon all we've come from, what we get is — nothing. We poison our emotions.

The people who write nihilistic books in America, I believe, are pretty often people who have given up their private values and have carelessly thrown out their secure belief in universal values with the same bathwater, believing that all values are nothing but the manners of the brainless herd. What they're really saying —not consciously, of course — is, 'If I can't have my home group's values, nobody can have values.' They declare themselves Nietzschean supermen and strike superior poses — and they feel a great loss, which they then can't help but whine about.

I think the important thing — the thing that I tried to work out in *The Sunlight Dialogues* — is that you have to cling to your rituals, yet develop a powerful sense of empathy for other people through particular relationships with other people. In doing that you get a clear sense of what the universal values are without abandoning your own personal supports, the rituals that differently express the universals. Clumly, at the end of *The Sunlight Dialogues*, still wants law and order, which is mostly ritual, given the stupidity of the laws he enforces; but he knows that law and order doesn't lead to justice, and he wants justice even more. All he can really do at the end of the novel is cry, because he hasn't yet resolved the demands of written law and the demands of love. Nevertheless, Clumly's situation is focal. At the end of the novel, everybody understands everybody else better, except for Benson/Boyle who has lost everything; his failure to resolve the conflict is total, because from the beginning he faked both sides of it.

In other novels, I go past Clumly's position. But basically, all I wanted to do in *The Sunlight Dialogues* was to dramatize — not really 'dramatize', because I didn't know what I'd be forced to say until I finished the novel; I mean I had to think it out in the process of writing it; but what I think I came to by the time I had finished writing was the notion that whatever values you most prize must come from a deep empathetic sense of what makes other people precious (in the old sense). Whatever values you hold to, you have to hold to because they hold for other people, and whatever values you're inclined to enforce, you have to enforce knowing that you may be doing somebody damage, so you have to think hard about those values. Clumly is in a position where he can't enforce anything because the whole dialogue has broken down. Clumly's state is like that of the nihilists among contemporary American writers except in one important respect: he still feels compassion. And to reach that point is to come to the next step, which is working out the new morality for mankind. At the beginning of *The Sunlight Dialogues*, which of course takes place at the end — that is, it's a moment long after the action of the novel, a moment that serves as a prologue — Clumly is talking to the old judge who doesn't remember people who have died, doesn't remember what happened to Clumly's wife and to Miller and so on. Clumly remembers everything. At the beginning of the novel, the point beyond the end, Clumly is a sort of mass, like a planet, like a physical force resisting entropy, resisting everything's dribbling off. He remembers; he knows what happened. I think what I wanted to do in the process of writing the novel was to get him to that point. The opening value in that book, in other words, is simply knowing what's happening and remembering it — clinging to it; not passing it off and not going off in any crazy direction. From that stage, one can go to further stages. But Clumly is the recorder. In an earlier draft I had a line which I then took out: 'And I only am escaped alone to tell thee' — you know, a Biblical line that Melville had used; but I decided that there was enough quotation of other people quoting other people, and I cut it. Anyway, that's the position that Clumly is in. Clumly is the Muse; he's the voice of memory, epic song, whatever. The next stage of civilization has to deal with that knowledge and make a whole new morality. This is the big thing that I'm always working at — in all my fiction. All the codes we have available to us now seem to me too narrow. We have religious codes: the Jews have a code, the Christians have a code, the Muslims have a code; but they aren't the same code and, as long as they aren't the same code, they can't be right. They are only good as long as the groups don't meet. We have all kinds of ethnocentric codes. We have the Anglo-Saxon versus the Italian, Arabian against Jewish, and so on. The code that we have to get to is one that knows what the universal values are, what's good for people, what's healthy for them, what makes them able to live as individuals and as members of society. The first books I wrote all dealt with the limitations of the codes. In my later books I got more and more to mulling over what might be the right way, the new morality, a morality which would be every bit as palatable to a Hindu or Jew or Muslim as to a Christian, as palatable to a black as to a white, and so on. But I suspect that the only way for cultures to come together, the only way two opposite people come together, is through hurting each other so badly that they stop and cry.

HZ   Susan Sontag, in a recent three-part article, 'Images of Disease', in *The New York Review of Books*, warns against what she calls 'sublimated spiritualism, a secular, ostensibly scientific way of affirming the primacy of "spirit" over matter'. Out of what seems to me to be a similar attitude, you state in *The King's Indian* that 'it's never required enduring forms to make the world Platonic; it requires only inescapable pain'. But should the belief in a spiritual ideal really be abandoned altogether for a pragmatic notion of morality? Perhaps the Platonic forms do reduce man and his actions to imperfect shadows, but they also make it possible to think of progress positively — as a moral approximation to an ideal — rather than negatively — as merely behavioural avoidance of pain.

JG   What I mean when I said that 'it's never required enduring forms to make the world Platonic' — that is to say, it doesn't require deism or Plato's museum in the sky — is that you don't have to have eternal verities or images or forms, all you have to have is successive generations of human beings who always hurt the same way when you hit them the same way. As long as some particular mode of behaviour causes you pain, generation after generation through the centuries, that mode of behaviour is unhealthy, unfit for survival. As long as people pay attention to their pain and to other people's pain, they can try to avoid it — try not to do the things that cause pain to individuals or sickness to individuals and to the society as a whole. So that, obviously, you don't have to have fixed ideas, you don't have to have concepts of good; all you have to have is a sense of self-preservation which recognizes the importance of the preservation of other people's welfare so that they won't hurt you — the golden rule, except it's a negative version of it. It seems to me that the only eternal verity there is for human beings is what works to make you physically and spiritually well, and the main business of civilization should be trying to figure out what are the healthiest ways of doing things to keep everybody going.

HZ   But might it not sound rather too optimistic when you say that the only thing we have to do is find a new morality? And that you can simply get to it through the experience of pain which, although bad in itself, leads to a better understanding of other human beings?

JG   Yes, I suppose my general argument on the probability of humanity does sound optimistic. But I think it's a matter of evidence that the world does get improved. I think that the present behavior of policemen in America is a result of learning through pain. That is to say, we went through the sixties and the cops beat up the kids, and half a century before that it used to be quite normal for a policeman to shoot. But it's top priority in police departments everywhere now, or everywhere but Philadelphia, that you don't kill — even a crazed sharpshooter you try to take alive. We have to find out what works. I mean we can't solve the problems of the world sentimentally; that would be grotesque. We just have to find out what works. The survival of the fittest is a law without heart, but my bet is that the fittest are the gentle people, the just ones.

I'm not after the spiritualism Susan Sontag objects to. What happens at the end of *The King's Indian* is that they get to the point where they see the world of the spirit clearly and they turn back; I mean they move away from it as fast as they can, back to safety.

What Jonathan Upchurch wants at the beginning of the novel — his idea of perfect happiness — is to get to southern Illinois, which is his symbol of the world completely visible: Indians and bluffs and the Mississippi River and complete immersion with the physical and no nonsense of intellect, which he has gotten a bad view of through the minister he works for, and spirit, which he's got a bad view of, and poetry, which he's got a bad view of because his father tells all these lies. He wants to get out of all that. But, by the nature of chance, he's thrown into a world where the conflict is over spiritual matters. (They turn out to be fake spiritual matters — and real also, but a hoax.) But ultimately, when he knows where spirit leads, when he knows the value of spirit and he knows the danger of spirit, he turns the ship around. What he wants is to be in the middle of the world, where you are solidly in touch with the physical and you know the spirit is there.

HZ   This leaves us with the impression that mind and matter are not only opposites but irreconcilable opposites, right? Therefore, does the notion in *The King's Indian* that God may be unparticled matter disregard the question of truth? Or does it mean wanting to have things both ways?

JG   Right. The idea that God is unparticled matter is Poe's, of course, not mine — though one of my characters maintains the point of view. I think that finally what I'd say is that it doesn't matter if it's true or not. There may indeed be no God; the only undetermined thing we know by direct experience is consciousness; the rest is none of our business, it's irrelevant; the whole spiritual world is an irrelevant kind of thing except as a metaphor for values, and those we can get at empirically. The only thing that's fundamentally important in 'the spiritual world' is the notion — perhaps metaphoric, but valid for all that — that every life is one life — you know, the Hindu business — that is to say, the notion that there is one life force that is in everything, that pushes up wherever it can, in an insect or a daisy, in a black or a white or an Indian or a Chinese — it's all one same thing. From the time I was writing the first novel I ever wrote, that has been the metaphysical promise or metaphor behind all my things — as it is, by the way — or so it seems to me — with Joyce Carol Oates and a lot of contemporary American writers.

If it's all one life force, and if you can get the experiential sense of that, if you can really experience what Jonathan Upchurch experiences with his beloved in *The King's Indian*, that they really are the same person, then it becomes possible to behave in a different way from the devouring wolf. As soon as you know that, as soon as you know that there is this one spirit in everything, that's enough; that's all you have to know. You don't go beyond that, kill yourself to get to heaven, you know, which is what would happen if Upchurch and his ship continue toward that maelstrom at the end of that book. What happens in Poe — in *The Narrative of Arthur Gordon Pym*, which is the base of my novella — is that the events form a progression, from the beginning of the novel to the end, of people disobeying rules. The novel opens with two kids going out in a boat into a storm, disobeying their father, and each later event is a further disobedience or mutiny, one kind of disobedience after the other until finally the great white law consumes them, they get swallowed. I don't think that way; I think the world is much more chancy than that, more balanced, more lucky. But I think that it is certainly true that there *is* a kind of great white law out there that is very dangerous, that is to say, that can kill you. A law of spiritual fitness which means destruction of the unfit. I do have a Collingwoodian notion of history; I think Greece fell because it had a built-in mistake; the Romans corrected that mistake. That is, the Romans were not ethnocentric to the same degree that the Greeks were. The Romans went to Ethiopia and didn't notice the Ethiopians were black, and married them; they went to Jerusalem and married the Jews. They were just, but also Laodycean. That's why Virgil is so sad — Virgil's idea is that only one or two things can happen to such a civilization, a civilization which holds itself up to judgement and which is reasonable and responsible as the Romans were trying to be, I mean to everybody — accepting the gods of everybody, accepting the morals and customs and everything else. They would have to end up either orgiastic — exploding into moral anarchy —or else (he didn't know the word Stoic) they would end up nobly suicidal. *Sunt lachrymae rerum.* His intuition was right; there was a mistake built into the Roman Empire. An emotional mistake, also a moral one. And I think that that mistake got corrected by what started out as the Christian Middle Ages, and then they too made their mistake, too much code instead of too little.

And so I think that there are mistakes we make, both individually and in our religions and social systems, and those mistakes are absolute. They're like Platonic absolutes. That is to say, an individual or a civilization can't work if he or it does so and so, violates the terrible white law. And so, step by step, we survive toward a better way of working or else we perish. It may be that we will make the wrong turn before we find it; you know, a technological society could be the wrong turn and end everything; I hope not.

HZ For me, the question still remains whether the life force you are talking about — apparently a force that drives rather than leads — can, after all, be sufficient. If every civilization has its built-in mistake and if these mistakes arise from having either too much code or too little code, isn't that the result of the spiritual and the physical possessing different degrees of gravity? I mean, human consciousness is defined by spiritual needs and goals derived from them as well as by life force, isn't it?

JG Not if it's wise, I think. Consciousness loves only itself, ideally. Except for happiness — the timeless happiness of a child lost in play — all the goals of consciousness are secondary. Consciousness makes up goals for each game it plays, but the real goal is always the same, not essentially spiritual but existential: everybody wants to be happy. From particular experiences of happiness we abstract forms of happiness (being just, being rich, being admired for our looks); and if we're careless we confuse the secondary goal with the primary one. When a whole civilization does that, we get neurotic displacement on a grand scale.

Every civilization that's ever been built has had an idea of what the perfect life would be, what happiness is — always an inadequate idea. The civilization's members arrange their lives —or their lives fall into a half-accidental pattern — in pursuit of that goal. And insofar as they've forgotten something, insofar as they've gotten the idea of happiness wrong (for instance, if they think it's happiness for me but not for my neighbor, or if they think it's a static condition rather than a mode of action), then that mistake destroys them. The member of the self-centered civilization can't keep his happiness because his neighbor is trying to keep happiness too, and pretty soon he comes out with a machete because the first citizen is in the way of the second's happiness. The mistakes are always of the same kind: a failure to define happiness wisely. Definitions of happiness are always pretty largely unconscious, unfortunately. Philosophy comes along when it's needed to justify what everybody is doing already or else to figure out what's wrong. Existentialism was around for a long time, but it was only when the French underground was living an impossible life in which the odds were overwhelmingly against it that suddenly existentialism came in as a persuasive philosophy. Because existentialism tells you a wonderful lie — which is that you can do something today that violates all history; that you can reverse your own momentum; that your own past has nothing to do with what you decide to do today or tomorrow; you can change it all. Or the history of the world has nothing to do with what tomorrow will give the world. That's a wonderful theory — if you are a French existentialist in the underground, where because of history's momentum — the odds — you haven't got a chance. If you believe, you die happy. But it's a lousy theory except in that situation. Well, all the philosophies that we have developed have developed out of real-life situations. Plato comes after the events which bring him about; he's a necessary response.

I think what really happens in a civilization — since civilizations do go a long time and do make a lot of adjustments and do narrowly escape a lot of dooms — I think what happens is that all civilizations have a pretty good idea of what they want — what will bring happiness. They almost make it; and philosophy helps. Americans, for instance — I don't know if they're right, I think it's a kind of silly idea, but, basically, when Americans speak of happiness they generally mean the freedom to have material comforts. They go after that happiness and gradually things begin to go wrong. They don't see that they are going wrong; they're too busy looking at the grindstone and its benefits. But they feel an increasing vague distress. The philosopher thinks it over and at last he says, 'Wait! The thing that is wrong is this: we've got to stop throwing away styrofoam', or whatever. When things get bad enough, the commoners grab his idea and maybe it helps them; maybe not. Perhaps I shouldn't say philosophers make the discovery. Maybe it's the crazies. People push toward happiness and they begin to make errors, and the errors become fairly radical before they notice them; then a few people, usually the crazies on the fringe of society, say, 'Look, this is what is wrong', and they try to lay out, in public demonstrations, in philosophy books or in bills which at first fail to become law, what ought to be done. When the situation gets really horrible, people grab those ideas. They're the only ones at hand. Reason is not very reasonable, as a rule. It arises out of the same roar lions are born of.

HZ   I'd like to change direction somewhat by asking about your concept of parody in *The King's Indian*. It seems to me that your use of parody is specific. Normally, I think, parody is understood as a literary device oscillating between imitation, regarding form, and play, regarding content. Now, you seem to substitute exaggeration for imitation (John Hunter, for example, in 'The Ravages of Spring', is resurrected in *three* little children; or Captain Dirge in 'The King's Indian', who is modelled after Captain Ahab, is literally propelled by coils and springs); and you seem to substitute seriousness for play (for example, when you say at the end of the book that it is not 'one more bad joke of exhausted art' but that 'you are real, reader, and so am I, John Gardner'). Thus what you seem to do is shift the play element in parody towards form, the imitation element towards content. Do you thereby mean to signify that we are supposed to take the content of your literary model seriously?

JG Yes, I do. But first I should say that the American idea of parody is in general very different from the European. Most of the great American writers were conscious parodists in the same way I am. Edgar Allan Poe in 'The Devil in the Belfry' writes a parody of 'The Legend of Sleepy Hollow' by Washington Irving. Washington Irving tells the story about this intellectual, gangly guy, Ichabod Crane, who comes to this Dutch town and, since Washington Irving was fundamentally a philistine — maybe that's too strong, but he was a trifle anti-intellectual, loved the common people, didn't trust intellectuals, and so on — Irving makes Ichabod a comic, grotesque figure who is chased out, scared to death, driven away from the community by an apple-cheeked, beefy Dutchman. Poe brings back Ichabod Crane; he doesn't give his name but he has the same red-cheeked Dutch characters, smoking their pipes, listening to rigidly timed martial music, and so on, and Poe's Ichabod, sawing away *rubato* on his violin, goes up in the belfry and beats up the bell-ringer. Poe uses the style of Washington Irving because he wants the reader to be thinking about what Irving said — notice how wrong it was. If Poe's imitation of Ichabod Crane is clear enough, then the reader who's been reading Washington Irving will catch all the connections, and Poe doesn't have to spell them out; so Poe cannot only flat-out disagree with Irving, he can make a fool of him, in the beloved style of nineteenth-century American politicians. Poe imitated all the time, he loved parody. He even parodied painting in 'Landor's Cottage', this time for a serious and noble effect. Melville used parody again and again. The most obvious example — kind of horrifying, in a way — is in *The Confidence-Man* where he has this terrible action, you know, where the devil is personally perverting the world towards his murderous doctrine of materialistic capitalism. Awful things are happening, in Melville's tale, and the characters are for the most part missing it because they're responding in a sweet, mindless, so-to-speak Dickensian way. And so Melville uses the style of Dickens to give you the horror of what's happening. The effect is striking — chilling. It makes him seem a quite nasty man if you happen to love Dickens — but that's the point! Melville knows Dickens's virtues as well as anyone does. In the opening of 'Pierre', Melville parodies Byron among others, because he's attacking self-regarding romantic ideals, and the whole book is a bitter, horrible sort of excoriation of the romantic — especially the Byronic way of thinking. Stephen Crane — his first works were literally parodies, and then he became a parodist in the higher sense ... The critic Eric Solomon has a wonderful book on the subject. So! I'm in an American tradition in doing what I do.

What I was doing in *The King's Indian*, sort of, or at least what I was consciously doing, was setting up — well, I started out, in the first of the book's three parts, with a set of notions which are common among contemporary writers, basically gloomy notions that the world is a terrible place, doomed. Then I used one after another of the styles of well-known English and American writers, finally bringing them all together, in the book's third part, into a sort of fancy orchestration of several major American styles plus the main person behind the American tradition, or so it seems to me, Samuel Taylor Coleridge, one of the main inspirations of Emerson and others, a poet whose vision, for better or worse, is still set deep in the American psyche. I think 'The Ancient Mariner' really influenced an awful lot of the work of Poe and Melville: *Arthur Gordon Pym, Benito Cereno, Moby Dick* ... What I wanted to do was set up a group of stories in which you take the blackest view you can — the typical contemporary American writer's, intellectual writer's, dark view of things — and then analyse it, taking the style and basic premises of some great writer — a technique which gives you a kind of triangulation. I'm saying, in effect, 'This is how it used to seem in the nineteenth century on these issues; and this is how it seems now.' I didn't stick only to American writers — obviously I used Browning, Kafka, and other Europeans — but basically, especially in the novella, I focus on American writers and American positions. And then I wanted to move toward the second section, from the notion that things are really terrible and that we can only make the best we can of them as forlorn individuals — which is what happens in the early stories — to the pivotal story, 'John Napper Sailing Through the Universe', where John Napper, a real painter who spent some time in this country, says, 'Yes, it's awful, we will just have to make up a different world and make it a possibility, a model for the future.' Then I offer, in the book's second part, a set of stories which are fantasy, a better world made up by fiat, in a kind of existentialist way — the Queen Louisa stories — in which you simply make a better world by denying the world that exists. That's what Queen Louisa does essentially. Her daughter has died. She can't face it, so in fact she doesn't face it, she changes the world for the better by a mad program, a fantasy she happens to have the power to enforce. But that's not really enough, of course. That's the second movement of the collection. It's a bad option, but it's better, you know, than staring at the abyss and groaning. And then the final section is the novella, in which all of these things get a positive restatement, a positive program which is not existential fantasy — oh, I obviously play a lot with fantasy, and I imitate and echo just about everybody I've ever read. It's a book about literature and life, sort of.

A novel — any work of literature — can be just about life, can be just about literature, as Donald Barthelme's things are, or can be about both, can be about the interplay of literature and life. I was fascinated with the whole metafictionist business at the time I wrote this collection. All the things that I was working on then, *The King's Indian*, the beginnings of *October Light*, and the beginnings of the new *Suicide Mountains*, in all of those I was constantly playing literature against life, looking for the answers literature gives, or so we're told. Contemporary writers are over-concerned about the whole business, but the questions are interesting ... The Heisenberg principle as it applies to literature: if you're trying to tell the truth and if the way you tell the story changes the truth, does literature ever get to the truth at all? What I obviously think is that every element in a piece of fiction, that is to say, every element of plot, every element of character — fatness, thinness, meanness, stinginess, whatever — every single element, discrete as a tree or a mountain in a painting or whatever, is a word, the complex language of literary art. You put the elements together in a way that expresses yourself, your intuition of truth, and I don't think you're talking nonsense, you know. If it's true that you can write a description of how to make a bomb and somebody else can read your description and make a bomb that will explode, then language has some relation to reality and those who deny the relation are wrong. And if literature or the arts are a very, very sophisticated language; if the kidnap plot, you know, the archetypal kidnap plot, already means something inherently, well, then writer after writer will understand what it means, however unconscious the understanding may be. Take *ordinary* language. Most Americans don't know what *matrix* means, right? They know what it does, how to use it in a sentence, but they don't know that it has anything to do with the womb. Nevertheless they use the word. In the same way, I think, a writer who doesn't know exactly what kidnapping means, inherently or fundamentally, as a piece of artistic language, an element — that writer nonetheless, when he writes a kidnapping story, feels out the essential meaning and works out what he believes to be the truth; that is, he makes the characters do what they really would do and doesn't force them, bully them. He ends up saying something, something very complicated about the treatment of people as objects, the theft of personality, the general idea of psychological tyranny. The more unconscious he is the better, in a way — the better he uses his literary language. Anyway, given that premise that every element in fiction, including literary style, has a meaning, it becomes interesting to play one against the other. In the 'King's Indian' novella, the two root styles are those of Edgar Allen Poe and Herman Melville; and then, of course, Twain and Coleridge play through it; and then minor writers, other people down to, say, William Dean Howells.

Poe and Melville offer an interesting contrast on basic American values. Poe was a Southerner and a very self-conscious Southerner, thought of himself as a Southerner, wanted to be a southern gentleman. He believed in slavery, or so he says, because he thought the alternative to human slavery was slavery to the machine, which had, he thought, more terrible implications. He thought that with human slavery, you would eventually get civilization evolved properly: humane treatment of slaves, eventually a situation where the people who were slaves would be the least intelligent, least sensitive, least hurt. The Man with the Hoe kept from harming us, that sort of thing. Melville, on the other hand, was a Yankee through and through and believed very much in big industry. He had his criticisms, God knows; nevertheless, he thinks slavery to that super machine, the whaler, is preferable to human slavery. He introduces speeches against slavery — all kinds of human slavery — again and again. The opposition of the two views is one of the deep oppositions in the American spirit, and so I copy the way Poe writes and the way Melville writes in my attempt to get at the basic ideas, the

American 'problem'. By using parody, by using Poe against Melville and then commenting on the two of them with the help of Mark Twain, the great literary exponent of the flim-flam man — Jonathan Upchurch as trickster — you get the whole spectrum of American opinion on freedom and responsibility. So the answer is: Yes, I certainly am using parody very seriously and I definitely want the voices to be heard.

It's important that one knows, as one reads, apropos the sense of the novel or whatever it is, who is talking, what style it's in, because, particularly in parody, the style is part of the meaning. I think that is probably more true of American than it is of European forms of parody because Americans started out as thieves, that is, the American literary tradition begins as a pirating tradition. The great books in America in the nineteenth century are mostly the ones they stole from England and elsewhere, lots of translations, all kinds of things. Americans imitated those pirated books. That was the easiest way to sell a book for one thing, because American literature itself had no prestige. It wasn't until Poe and Hawthorne that people really began to take American literature seriously, and even that came mainly in France and Germany and England — not in this country. You almost had to be a parodist. It was the same with the Romans, of course, who imitated the Greeks.

HZ So parody establishes, if I understand you correctly, a connection between aesthetics and morals, literature and life — by constantly playing one against the other. And as you imply, you again dramatize this connection in your latest book, *In the Suicide Mountains*. Here you seem to twist the Aristotelian notion that art imitates life by maintaining that after a while life will begin to imitate art. 'The mimic is doomed to become what he mimics.' The abbot who expounds this theory and who is a masked incorporation of evil therefore becomes his own 'victim': by imitating the saintly abbot whom he has killed, he himself has to become saintly. This notion that life imitates art certainly attributes a great importance, even power to the artist. But doesn't the ensuing responsibility weigh him down too much?

JG I don't think so, because I think it is what serious artists have always assumed, whether or not the society around them assumed it; I think that when Homer wrote, he very consciously attempted to build a certain kind of society. The reason he puts all the different dialects in, the reason he uses all the gods even when he knows perfectly well that some of them are doubles — different pronunciations of the same goddess's name and so on — was that he believed that, by powerfully presenting a model for life, he could make it happen. He wanted the world to be a better place in specific ways. I think that every great artist does this. Wilde's image of the artist as indifferent to morality is merely a reaction —disingenuous, I think — to pretentiously moralistic Victorian art. I think that Shakespeare talks about the things he talks about because they were the most important questions in Elizabethan England. He names them and he offers you ways of living, gives you possibilities of a future, sometimes in a tragic way — 'Don't do this', as in *Macbeth*, and sometimes in a direct, almost preacherly way, as in *The Tempest*. I wouldn't really want to call that a sermon but he does tell you: 'This is how to live, this is what to do.' I think artists have always taken the position — particularly literary artists — that they are telling the world how it should behave. It's also true of musicians, obviously, people like Beethoven very clearly saying, in emotional terms, 'This is what I am for, this is what I am against.' It's also true of certain kinds of painters, though perhaps not of all painters; painters are much more mystical and private in dealing with individual sensation. But I think every artist starts out wanting to tell the world how to be, how to feel, how to avoid insincerity and falsehood. I think there really is a basic relationship between the priest and the poet. The difference between the two is that the priest gives you fables and insists that they are true, and if you don't believe they are true, he kills you — at least the old-fashioned priest did that. He slaughters you, sacrifices you to the hungry gods because you're wicked. But the artist gives you metaphors and says, 'Yes, I know they're metaphors but nevertheless, listen to this; it's true.' And I think that's what he wants.

Bad artists do the same thing; Harold Robbins — well, not a bad artist — a slick entertainer. To take better examples, John Hersey or James Michener are very much preachers — good ones, understand. They wouldn't sacrifice anybody. Michener wrote *Tales of the South Pacific* because he was horrified by the treatment of Hawaiians in America at the time, and he had enormous effect. After *South Pacific*, the musical, came out (it was much more popular than the book, I think) people just couldn't look at Hawaiians the same way they had before. I mean, they really had looked at them as animals. Every time a James Baldwin comes along, he changes the world. I think it has always been true that art leads life, not the other way around. That whole notion of the self-transcendent, you know: you cast ahead into a future what you want and then you try to create it; that is the fundamental process of real art. Real artists make up a world that would be worth living in, recognizing the faults in our world, the faults that in theirs will no longer exist. Every generation of artists talks about, I think, the same old values but applies them each time to a new group. In Homer's day it seemed perfectly obvious that the individual should have dignity, that if he doesn't get his due, he should yell. But Homer didn't stop to notice that that should apply not just to kings but to the woman or to the slave or to the barbarian. Generation after generation we have applied the ancient universals more broadly. In every generation, there is always somebody who is getting screwed. The person whose business it is to notice that is the artist. I think there are artists now who don't do that. I mean serious artists do a lot of things. One of the things that legitimate artists do is to describe the way the world is right now; just getting a good image of it, a good photograph, is sufficient for them — and that's fine; that's realism. But the kind of art I particularly value doesn't do that. The kind I like sets up visions of what is possible and helps to move humanity toward them.

HZ   *In the Suicide Mountains* is subtitled: *A Tale*, and the tale — the fairy tale, the gothic tale, the epic tale — tends to reappear in your fiction. It is almost as though the tale had a certain redeeming quality for you. It seems to be able to transcend the nature of evil, as expressed by the old priest in *Grendel*: the two facts that 'Things fade' and that 'Alternatives exclude.' Regarding the first issue, the tale has a timelessness which is not inhuman as is the timelessness of the dragon in *Grendel*, who knows past, present, and future; it is, rather, a timelessness which rests upon the possibility of repetition. Regarding the second issue, in the tale nothing is lost, that is, every part retains its meaning throughout the tale; not in the way that nothing is lost for the dragon in *In the Suicide Mountains*, who 'embraces good, evil, and indifference', but in the way that, within a tale, evil can turn into good or vice versa and yet coexist with the good or the evil respectively.

JG   Yes. That's true. I love the form of the tale. When I was starting to write, I wrote nonrealistic fiction and it was at a time when realistic fiction was very popular in this country. The most published writer in America was John O'Hara, a realist, a sort of bitter realist — I guess, that is rather common in that tradition. But everything New York was publishing was realistic. All the books on understanding fiction included only realistic short stories. And I was writing these things about dragons and so on, and everybody said, 'No, you can't write that for grown-ups, this is ridiculous, John.' It took me a long time to get stuff published because I kept insisting on doing these non-realistic things. In fact, one of the reasons that I wrote *Nickle Mountain* was that I wanted to write a pseudo-realistic piece. It feels like solid realism and yet there are ghosts in it and talking windows and all kinds of things like that. It seems to me that what is wonderful about the tale is that it goes right straight for the moral universe, which is what I am interested in — a universe in which you are responsible for what you do. If the universe is orderly, then your behaviour has to be orderly, and if it isn't — trouble.

There are all kinds of things about tales that are wonderful though. The fact that tales are always in their pure form set in some remote place, old buildings, characters larger than life — the whole remoteness and oldness of the tale implies values which hold on and which curse you if you go against them. The problem in the tale is to find out what are true values and what are false values; what works and what doesn't. In an ordinary piece of fiction, in a realistic piece of fiction, what happens is whatever is causally likely — plausible. In a tale, what happens is what morally has to happen. And so without any pussyfooting, without lots and lots of pages proving that this story takes place in St Louis, you know, where you fill in all the kinds of ethnics and you name the streets — instead of that, you go right to the heart of what you're talking about. Even in my seemingly realistic stuff I do that. In *Sunlight Dialogues,* I have a veneer of realism all the time but underneath that realism, things are bubbling to the surface. Quite literally in one case. An old car in which two people have been murdered comes bubbling up to the surface of a creek. Nobody knows who they are or were, but what you know when you read that scene is that these policemen, Clumly and his friend, who are trying to make a just world, are doing it in a world where there are old evils, crimes which aren't understood and will never be explained, and they have to make some sense of a moral universe in spite of the mysteries that come from the past. So that I have always inclined in that direction rather than in the direction of realism — merely because I want to talk about what I want to talk about: responsibility. What goes wrong when you get the rules wrong, through selfishness or through a notion that you are right and everybody else is wrong or whatever, is that you begin to do things which destroy yourself and other people. The tale is an efficient way of getting at that.

HZ   Is that why the dragons of your tales are the real horror? Because for them there is no distinction between good and evil, no boundaries between past, present, and future; because the dragon is a metaphor for entropy?

JG   Yes, the thing about dragons — and I think it's traditionally true — the reason they are the way they are is that they're practically invulnerable; there's hardly anything you can do to a dragon. If you're not vulnerable, and if nothing you love is vulnerable, there's no reason to be good, no reason to be orderly. It's mortality that makes morality. The dragon is a classic symbol of all that's beyond that rule. But it's nice to have dragons around, to keep us honest.

William H. Gass

William Howard Gass was born in Fargo, North Dakota, on 30 July 1924, but his family almost immediately moved to Warren, Ohio, where he grew up. He began college at Kenyon and briefly attended Ohio Wesleyan before serving as an ensign in the navy in the Second World War. After the war, he returned to Kenyon College, where he majored in philosophy and took a BA in 1947. He attended Cornell University as a philosophy graduate student and received his PhD in 1954. His dissertation, 'A Philosophical Investigation of Metaphor', develops many of the concepts and concerns which were to surface in Gass's later critical and literary works. In 1955 he began teaching at Purdue University, and since 1969 he has taught in both the philosophy and English departments at Washington University in St Louis. In 1979 Gass received a gold medal of merit from the American Academy and Institute of Arts and Letters for his work as a novelist.

In his essay 'The Artist and Society', Gass contends that 'reality is not a matter of fact, it is an achievement'. And reality, for Gass, includes fictions. Gass the philosopher may pose the epistemological question: what is the ontological status of fiction as compared with that of reality? But for Gass the novelist the question already predicts the answer: works of art, like other real things, are ultimately surrounded by silence. Therefore their essential task is to talk, even at the risk that such attempts remain perpetually futile. James Joyce meant to demonstrate with his concept of epiphany that the essence of a thing is identical with the observer's experience of its 'whatness'. Similarly, Gass wants the reader to be arrested, not by the novelist's subject or concern but by his language — fiction's essence. In other words, the question concerning the ontological status of fiction will be tentatively solved as soon as fiction becomes self-reflective, self-referential, and thereby self-sufficient.

The problem implicit in this concept, which strives continuously to replace traditional with innovative aesthetics, is that it has to be proved or dramatized again and again. Thus Gass's critical essays, collected in *Fiction and the Figures of Life* (1970) and more recently in *The World Within the Word* (1978), attempt to show that the void — the certainty of annihilation — gives meaning not only to ethical values or philosophical ideas but most of all to the realm of fiction. Important in this context is what Gass affectionately refers to as a 'certain poetry to the logic of limits'. The rigorous observance of an appropriate periphery — a concept, abstraction — forces the mere quantity of any given assemblage of words into the limits of meaning — or quality.

The notion that fictional language ought to be an expression of the writer's consciousness of quality as opposed to that of quantity is most clearly stated in the philosophical essay *On Being Blue* (1976), but it also pervades the stories put together as *In the Heart of the Heart of the Country* (1968). In the title story of this collection, place or space, initially the pure embodiment of quantity, is gradually infused with quality through a unifying concept: lost love. In a similar fashion the surface realism in the story 'The Pedersen Kid' eventually yields the mystery of ungraspable evil.

For Gass this quest for quality makes language sensual, even sexual. In the novella *Willie Masters' Lonesome Wife* (1968) the juxtaposition of text and the image of a nude — sometimes the superimposition of the one on the other — serves as a graphic metaphor for the existentialization of the narrative perspective: Willie Masters's — or every author's — lonesome wife is the language of his imagination. Moreover, the confinement of disparate collages within the text demonstrates the tendency of metaphor in postmodern fiction to become self-referential. Thus, the final passage of *Willie Masters' Lonesome Wife*, which invokes the saving vision of a new language, offers the provocative dictum regarding that new language: 'Metaphor must be its god now gods are metaphors.' Gods having become obsolete, metaphor is no longer responsible to any other force than its own inherent tension.

In Gass's only longer novel to date, *Omensetter's Luck* (1966), the action centres on the change of heart of the vindictive Reverend Jethro Furber toward the hapless Brackett Omensetter, but at first glance the ultimate narrative 'triumph' seems to go to Israbestis Tott for whom the past has metamorphosed into stories, told and retold endlessly. Only in the listener's or reader's mind does any fictional action come into existence: it grows in reality in that it is not made to refer to any other extant reality. Yet Tott, because he is incapable of understanding the concept at the centre of his stories (he fails to grasp, for instance, that not Omensetter's luck but the love he and his wife share for one another constitutes Omensetter's charisma), ultimately cannot hold the various parts of them together. Instead of flowing from him, they rather seem to flow through him. Thus Israbestis Tott seems to stand for Gass's indictment of carelessness towards the word, for a lack of intellectual insight and, even more important, for emotional failure to face up to the void, the void without which any story becomes devoid of meaning.

Interview with William H. Gass

Munich, 11 June 1979

HZ   In your early fiction, you seem to be concerned with the relation between reality and the imagination, and with the dangerous necessity of symbols in that relation. In *Omensetter's Luck*, for example, Jethro Furber has a contrived and fanciful personal vision of the interpenetrations of reality and imagination, a vision he is anxious to maintain because it serves his manipulative ends. But the very presence of Omensetter is — if I may indulge in the obvious pun — ominous: he is a kind of unreflective, prelapsarian presence who seems to threaten others; who assumes fearful symbolic dimensions for the likes of a Jethro Furber. Might one say that this unreflective, natural, threatening character is a symbol for the concrete moment when all reflection breaks down, when those who reflect on different levels of consciousness can no longer communicate? Does Omensetter represent the opacity of the relation between reality and the imagination?

WHG   Yes, I think that's true. It starts, of course, with a traditional American theme — the theme of the naïve, the innocent, the natural man. Its commonness is one reason I chose it. Then I interpreted that theme, in part, in terms of myth in general — the tendency of people to make myths, turn people into symbols, project on to them their wishes, fears, etc. Omensetter strikes various people in town as a sort of reflector, precisely receptive to symbolizing because he appears not to do so. So each character in the novel is busy turning Omensetter into a kind of material for the symbols they wish to make. For Furber, at a certain point, Omensetter appears to be the kind of person who doesn't have to interpret the world. For Pimber, the freedom that Omensetter has is a different sort of freedom; he seems to have a kind of fine and harmonious relation with nature. Furber sees this as a freedom *from* having to symbolize, from having to interpret. But, of course, that, for Furber, is in a sense the worst possible condition, a threatening condition. Pimber interprets Omensetter as the kind of person he would like to be; Furber finds him a threat, a threat to his whole way of looking at things.

HZ   When you said at the annual meeting of the *Deutsche Gesellschaft für Amerikastudien* at the University of Tübingen last week that the difference between *Willie Masters' Lonesome Wife* and *In the Heart of the Heart of the Country* was, mostly, that in the former the author is speaking whereas in the latter the respective narrator is the centre of each story, it came to my mind that, in a sense, Furber transcends his role as character in the direction of both narrator and author. For instance, when he says: 'The great moral question, gentlemen, ... is not the evidence of freedom ... but the very possibility of law itself,' then he seems to describe not only his own belief but the conditions of conceiving of a character like himself as such. Therefore, doesn't he transcend his role as character and mirror the concerns of the author?

WHG   Well, he becomes a content for himself. I have constructed him in the act of constructing, so what he reflects is also one of *my* interests as an author. The whole investigation of the ground, as Kant would say, of the imagination, the conditions of the imagination as such — quite apart from any *specific* imagined thing — leads to (for me) a theory of fiction, and then finally to a theory of art in general. First I imagine a man. That man is imagining himself, making himself up, fictioneering. And he knows this. We all construct ourselves to some degree, but Furber is a student of the activity. Eventually, that's what he makes himself up to be — a character concerned with the collision between order and dream, wish and reality. Kant's effort, of course, is ultimately to make a kind of harmony hold between the categories of the understanding and the ideas and the ideals of reason. Finally, the ground of the imagination in Kant rests upon the very possibility of order. I agree with Kant, but I'm not so sure it can be done. So I'm interested in the tension, in the almost successful, possibly failing, *attempt*. Is the imagination, in a sense, based upon unification, or is it in a certain fundamental way disruptive? Is there a real harmony possible or is there not? That goes quite far away from Furber as such but he's engaged in that problem, I think.

For me, of course, characters are fundamentally built in two ways. Either as the object of modification of language in a text —you have focal centers just as you have subjects in sentences, and then you notice that the sentence is organized by the fact that ultimately every phrase, every clause modifies or is attached to that subject. So, say, in a certain section of the book most of the language modifies or is about Pimber — someone else or something else. The character could also be, as in *Under the Volcano,* a mountain; it could be an idea; whatever the main series of language is about. And then you build up large units; you might have one whole section of the novel, or some other novel, basically modify, let's say, first Israbestis Tott, and then, through Tott, some other idea which is the real character of the first section, namely the character or narrative of history. So history is really the character of the first section of the novel, in my point of view. That then is what the language modifies, what it moves toward and disappears into.

The other way of thinking of character, is, for me, the source of language: where does it come from? In a sense, then, there are two kinds of characters: characters as sources from which the language comes, and aims or ends towards which the language flows. Sometimes they turn out to be the same. For example, when a Dickens character speaks, we know that the language — the conversation — is coming from that character and has its source in that character. But it also, in function, is primarily designed to reveal that character, is more *about* that character, though ostensibly it may be about getting a job or dodging the cops. Often, conversations are that way: *you* are talking, and so the source of the language is your character, your voice, but perhaps you are also talking about yourself — as I might say, 'I feel a little dizzy today.' The language comes from me and it is about me. But it also might be that I am just talking to a waiter or somebody else or am talking about something else. But the way I order my dinner reveals, as Dickens's characters always do, *my* nature. So Dickens's dialogue is almost invariably about, or revealing and modifying, the character who utters it. So, in the novel I'm working on now, *The Tunnel,* the source of the language is the narrator. His language is constantly about something, but it is really building and constructing the consciousness of the narrator. So that there is really only one character in this book, and the source of language and the object of language turn out to be ultimately identical. The language is not going from A to B; it's all staying in the same place. I am not thinking of the novel as concerned with characters in the old sense, as describing people, but of a broader linguistic problem in which what we call character is just one more linguistic source of energy — where the language comes from and where it is going.

HZ   Does that affect the epistemological premises of fiction as such? You distinguish between source and aim or end as aspects of character, and one could probably say that the source from which language comes is connected with the idea of subjectivity and that the aim towards which it flows is, in a sense, objective. Now, I am wondering how to describe the epistemology of language in, for instance, *Willie Masters' Lonesome Wife*. In that novella, is language objective, a cultural tradition outside of yourself that you have to make contact with, that you have to grasp and understand before you can use it, or is it subjective, flowing from the imagination as from a source?

WHG   I think you've brought up a very interesting philosophical issue. The problem parallels the distinction, for instance, that Saussure makes, between a language as such and blind speech acts of various sorts. Or, Chomsky's notion of competency in a language. It is a different, but parallel distinction. One's language is indeed outside oneself. English exists quite apart from me and will exist when I have stopped talking. In that sense language and the whole tradition of language and all the objects that have been made of language, etc., are quite outside, and I have to become familiar with them; I learn the language; I take in the tradition, etc. In another sense, of course, language is so inherent to my nature that it is, for me, the deepest and most fundamental expression of the self. It is possible to distinguish between an individual voice, an individual soul, so to speak, and that kind of collective speech that human beings as a whole have had. Each individual is a series of special personal speech acts within the larger gabble. This is, I think, the most essential and most interesting way in which human beings are alike, especially if they share the same language. To share the same language is not simply to have some external piece of equipment you can both use. For Beckett, I think, the last resort of the self is this internal speaking voice. It's not just audible speaking, but the talk which we have with ourselves, which he renders, in effect, so magnificently; and that last continuous voice — if it is silenced, that's all there is. So one is reduced, really, to the *logos*. This *logos* is a personal *logos*, the *logos* of the individual, but it is shared, it is taken from the whole tradition of speakers. So we have a nice, I think, almost epistemological problem concerning the relationship of the internal speaking voice to the external speaking voice and then to the collective tongue. That little silent inner squeak — that's all that's left in our world of the soul.

HZ Does linking 'the internal speaking voice to the external speaking voice and then to the collective tongue' imply the notion of gradual loss? In the new preface to *In the Heart of the Heart of the Country,* you say at one point that 'a sense of resonant universality arises in literature whenever some mute and otherwise trivial particularity is experienced with an intensely passionate particularity — through a ring of likeness which defines for each object its land of unlikeness, too ...' That is, if I understand you correctly: the intensely passionate experience of particularity is like the stone you throw into a lake, and as the rings created by the stone spread, the particular experience extends into the world of the other until it becomes universal — covers the whole lake. I think there is a paradox involved here because any such extreme subjective experience, while it assumes universality through language, becomes less intense as it is gradually objectified: when it achieves its aim, intensity and passion might be gone altogether.

WHG Well, again, that is a parallel of the problem I was talking about. That's exactly the issue, I think. The particularity of experience is rendered by the writer (or by anyone) in language which is again universal, and all the concepts are universals. The words you want to use, which might have to do with the sun or the weather or something, are universal and may be used by anybody; so if the particularity of the event is to be captured, it means that you have not only to render the event in language, but in *a* particular language. As regards your subjectivity in perceiving, let's say, a stone falling into a lake — and you are going to use a universal means to render that — that rendering must be as particular as the stone's dropping into the lake. Your style has to be distinctly yours; and then it has to be a style that captures that event. So for me, again, style is an indication that a speech act, which is made up of universals, is a particular. Again, to return to the Beckett problem (this is also an argument about computers), how do you show that a particular answer that might be given to a question is an answer that a human being has made? Or is it an answer that a programmed computer might make — simulated schizophrenia or whatever? A similar issue arises when we talk about the collision of cliché with the artistic vision: one of the reasons writers like to use clichés is because they are indeed the enemy; they are anybody's; they are thoughtless counters; they don't reflect the particular. For example, when James is describing a scene, or Beckett is describing a scene, or Günter Grass, we know that it is Günter Grass or it is Beckett doing it. No one else perceives events in this way. That's individuality, particularity, at the level of language. So, what has happened here is that the particularity of experience has now, through style, been transformed into the particularity of language. They are not the same particularities, of course, they are parallel. I think that's what gives, and the only thing that can give, particularity to the page. My feeling about writers frequently is that they don't care enough about the particularity of the experience; they let it get washed away in universals. They don't care enough about the particularity of that experience to make sure that their rendering is equally particular, equally thing-like. So, a great description of a table is as physical and particular and solid as the table itself. That means that you have got to observe. But you are observing (not in this descriptive sense in which the description disappears and you are looking at some universalized table, seeing some particular table through universals) in order to replace the object with your description.

HZ You say that many writers don't care enough for the particularity of their experience and the particular rendering of this experience. Does this result, perhaps, from a desire on the writer's part to create something that will immediately take its place within human literary history? Perhaps the idea of capturing one particular experience seems too trivial, too ephemeral to such writers; so they attempt to arrive immediately at a universal value; or they mistake universals for universality. I was wondering whether the fact that you write both fiction and literary criticism supplies you with the opportunity to concentrate, in your fiction, on the particular experience while reflecting, in your literary criticism, on general tendencies or theories of fiction.

WHG Yes, except that in my criticism, one of the things I try to do — that I am interested in — is to respond to a particular work with the same kind of particularity that I would to some experience, and to write about it in such a way that I can get a bit of that particularity across. Not so much to explicate a text (that's sometimes needed because of the job I have, doing reviews or making judgements about this or that) but to render some of the particularity of the artist's vision. I'm interested in the writer's style, basically. That's a problem, then, for me, in *my* style — trying to give a feel for the nature of that special vision, that special style the writer has. For that reason, very frequently, when I'm writing about Henry James, my language will be Jamesian —not in an attempt to give a pastiche or parody it, but rather to try to show, within my own sentences, some of the qualities of James's style or language or his way of approaching matters. Style seems to me to be the ultimately important thing about a writer, and what distinguishes him from anybody else.

Related to that is this sense of the solidity of language. William Carlos Williams said: 'No poetry but in things.' I think what he meant to stress was the close observation of things themselves, the same kind of thing we find in Rilke's poems. He is beginning to look at the world, but why? So that he can make another thing; so that the poems become things; so that you have two kinds of very concrete objects. The problem with literature, I think, is this two-fold tendency, often seen in certain German writers, in, let's say, Schiller — too quick a flight to the abstract, too great a readiness to move from experience to the moral, to the general, 'What does it mean?' What I would like to see done is to pack that meaning into the thing. This is why Rilke was for me the most important writer. He does it, I think, better than any writer I've ever read. In his work, you really have a rival of the object, because the poem is an object with those universal qualities built in. There is a constant tension in language between the physically arbitrary sound and its slowly built-up senses. Rilke really allows us to establish a hierarchy of things; and in our world, as he perceived it himself, we are creating, furthermore, more and more physical objects which are really not things at all. Take plastic cups, all alike, indistinguishable from one another, made to be indistinguishable, to be used, to disappear into their function and be thrown away. No history is allowed to accumulate in a plastic cup, no dent is made by the person who uses it. Those are really terrifying objects. But that is what most prose is, it disappears, it's nothing, makes no dent in the world and is not dentable. Whereas, suppose you have a beautiful cup or something like that, the whole history of a life can be put into it, as a person's use molds it and responds to it, until we see a history in it. That's what happens with really great literature and great critics. If, for instance, I'm reading Wordsworth, I'm not just reading Wordsworth anymore, I'm reading Wordsworth and I see where Coleridge has held and drunk from Wordsworth. So now I have these two things — Wordsworth and Coleridge — and that doesn't spoil Wordsworth. It's like picking up an ancient cup and saying, 'Well, here my great-grandfather also ... And we see here where it was cracked when they carried it by wagon ...' You know, all of those things. So, now when I pick it up, I am picking up a tradition of reading a writer who has been loved, whose work has been molded without being destroyed. Good critics do that. Bad work simply will not receive that kind of activity without being used up, broken, destroyed. And it's meant to be consumed. Most literature being produced in America, for example, is simply meant to be used up. Then you move on to the next little excitement. There's a new genius, a new miracle, every month. The press, the publishers, the public demand it. I happen to like things that have been around for a long time, I like literature to be like the ancient castles we've been going into, the old churches. You look up and things are a little blurry in this text, and you see dimly the figures and the shapes. But what you see also is a history of use, of humanity within the work. But you can't have that unless you've turned it into an object and unless everybody is allowed to leave his mark in that object without destroying it. That means that the work has got to have great resiliency, and has to evoke care. Just as with some beautiful churches — the church is beautiful enough that it evokes the love and care of people. So, they use it, they leave a mark, but they also preserve it. A work like that, if you are reading Dante or Goethe, for instance, is not only Dante or Goethe — it is like entering a great cathedral which has been around for a long time, and all kinds of people have left their marks, their interpretations, their responses, their lives in it. And that's when works get to be really great. It's very thing-like — that state of affairs. It's to make objects that people participate in.

HZ   You say that the great work of fiction assumes an historical dimension. But what happens if a fiction strives for nothing but self-referentiality? Again, I would like to refer to Willie Masters' Lonesome Wife, who is supposed to be the language of the imagination. This is the guiding metaphor of the text, and one could probably say that the rest of the text is subsumed under this one metaphor, that the different parts of the text constitute a fugue of metaphors subservient to the idea of the whole. Now, if a work of fiction thus becomes self-sufficient, self-referring ...

WHG   Oh yes, it is self-referring, that's the idea! Again, that's an object, an independent entity. The more an object is independent, in a philosophical sense, the less contingent. God is, of course, the purely necessary being. He doesn't depend for existence on anything else. That would be the ideal condition. What you are doing is taking language and making something that is fundamentally referential into an object which is entirely internal. There is nothing unusual about this. A chess board is such an internalized field. Now, of course, a work may have these other references outside itself as well, like a doll's house, which may be full of miniaturized history; but the aesthetic experience, just as in the church, is of the church as a building of a certain kind. Its Christianity doesn't make it beautiful. As you look at the church, you recognize the parts, and the symbolism, etc. You recognize those references, and they are part of the meaning, but you hold them within the frame of the system. If you don't, then you lose sight of the aesthetic quality. The worshipper is interested in the presumed reality of the event which the crucifixion refers to, for instance, but, then, he doesn't need a beautiful object — any crucifixion will do as a reminder. That's why I think the iconoclasts were wise in a peculiar sense, because the more beautiful the object, the more the worshipper is returned to the actual structure of the object itself and doesn't pass through the symbol to its presumed reference beyond. Churches need to be beautiful only for those who aren't believers. That, again, is why the Puritans knew that a beautiful church was dangerous to the faith. Beauty always brings things back to itself. So you use wide references. That is why a comparative unbeliever, for example like Corbusier, is challenged by the idea of building a church, and can do so very powerfully. But of course it's terrible for worshiping, because you worship the church. So, then, there is that kind of constant opposition.

Again I would have to go to Rilke. Take the poem — now I am using the poem as a referential object, not as a beautiful object —the poem on the archaic torso of Apollo, where the poet, in describing a mutilated torso, depicts an object, a thing which, though mutilated, is so beautiful that what its beauty says (and by that beauty one means its being, its reality, its presence, its independence from other things, its refusal to refer) is that its existence in the world is so powerful that what it says to an observer is: 'I am more real with all my mutilation (I don't have a head, arm, legs, genitals; I just have a torso) than you are', more real than the observer who presumably has all of these things. And of course you have a nice moral conclusion: you must change your life. Now what's powerful about that very injunction, that very command, is that it is within the poem. If it were not within the poem, it would just be another little moral thing that wouldn't have any power at all. What one can see is that a work of art has more being, in a philosophical sense of value and independent existence, than most people who disappear into their dependencies and relationships and meanings. So I think what Rilke is saying is that yes, we want to make things, but real *things*. The tape recorder that is taping us — what existence does it have beyond what it does? Well, my typewriter happens to have been picked as a design triumph by the Museum of Modern Art, and so when I go into that museum I look into a case and see my typewriter. It's got enough of these qualities that they put it into a case. It isn't *that* nice, but what's happened to the model means that it has already begun to escape its function. Then, suppose you had a typewriter for a long time and you have only been using it —just like some ideal spouse you are merely using, using, using — then, at a certain point, it doesn't really function well any more. But if you continue to like it, it will *be* because it has had so much poured into it — of yourself, your past, etc. But now it is dependent for its existence on what it has nearly become. It's like a pair of stone steps that have been worn by the pilgrims. That's not beautiful, but it has the mark of the passage of the world. I think what I am concerned to do, or would like to do, is to make an object which will sustain itself independently. But that, of course, is philosophically under great tension. The question is whether it is possible to create at all. If you can't solve that problem, God couldn't create either, and the large philosophical issue remains: how could it have been done?

HZ   So by continuously shedding its function and by striving to become more and more self-referential, fiction parallels the things of the Creation? And even if a work of fiction cannot become truly self-referential because all kinds of outside references remain, we can still see the unfolding of an ideal in the process of its shedding these references and assuming its own structure?

WHG   Or if not shedding, then taking them in — like a Proustian novel just takes the whole world in and makes it. Again, in the moral sphere (I'm a Kantian, I'm afraid), to be an end in itself, not a mere means, seems to be a very beautiful expression of an important moral relation. But it is an important value relation. To evaluate anything is always to evaluate it as an end in itself, and not as a mere means. Therefore I like to think that the relation of the ideal reader to a work is that of a love relationship. When you are in love with somebody, you are not just involved with them as a mere means, but as an end in themselves. You don't say of someone you love 'What is your meaning? What is your significance?', though, of course, they are not without significance. I think one of the persistent themes in Henry James is this sense of human manipulation in which people are reduced to a function. Particularly, because, say, a woman is rich, she is married; or because she has a high social status; or she shows off the taste of somebody because she is beautiful; or ... whatever. Now individuals might be rich and they might have social status, and they might be physically beautiful, etc., but your question seems to me to be the question of being, of becoming an end in itself. Well, works of literature are like that, works of art. At that point, interpretation is a violation. You don't say to the work, 'What do you mean?'

HZ Your preoccupation with the independence of works of literature makes me wonder about the function which, in your opinion, the comic and the tragic might still retain in a fictional context. For, usually, the comic and the tragic seem to require, as their foil, a special value horizon, as it has been established in a certain society, in order to become effective. However, I would like to suggest that, in your fiction, the *pun* is used to substitute for the effects of the comic and the tragic. Do you think it's true that, through the ambivalence of the pun, you capture the tension between the particular and the universal: the dual nature of the comic and the tragic?

WHG Yes. I think that's a very good description of it, of what one is trying to do. But again, as everyone is aware, the conditions under which ordinary tragedy and comedy were in the past made, may no longer exist. But that very fact leads to the kind of persistent mode that we now have in almost all writers. I think you can speak of comic writers and tragic writers still, but what you mean is that the so-called Shakespearean and tragicomical thing is connected now in all writers in a very ambiguous sense. The question is: Which direction does the turn go? Is one opening the pun, in this case, or closing it? Our laughter, nowadays, has very little basic humor in it; it's not Good Humor. Sterne, for example, is basically good-humored when he's poking fun. When you get humor, however, like the jokes, let's say, in Stanley Elkin, that's not good-humored fun at all. I think that most of the fine writers — again, like Beckett — are funny in a fundamental sense. You may smile or even laugh, but that laughter has as its object a quite different condition: you are now laughing at the condition of man — a condition which is not a happy one. When you are in misery, laughter is the noise of a necessary illusion. My work tends to be much more in the old-fashioned mode than most writers' now. I'm not basically a comic writer in a fundamental sense — in the way one would say that Stanley Elkin is. Stanley gets to his grotesque world through that mode, while I make jokes that cut around the edges of the paper like a decoration. Basically, I am aiming at tragedy. *Omensetter's Luck* was conceived by me as a tragic book, but it is not tragic in the old sense; it's just the other side of that coin. For example, *The Floating Opera* is the other kind; it's a comic novel, but dark; mine is a tragic novel, but light. These are just two slices from the same cheese — only my side is all rind.

There are writers who still have some old faith; and it is still possible to write brilliantly with beliefs like Singer's, or Mauriac's. Such people, however, are professional naïves, even if they are ultimately sophisticated. You cannot exist, I think, with any kind of awareness of the nature of the world today and have that kind of unambiguous stance. Now, some people can do it; there are still many people running around believing things of all sorts. But I think it is a very risky and dangerous thing now, because there are too many matters you must avoid noticing if you are going to hold traditional beliefs. It's just not possible for sensible people, except for a few peculiar throwbacks. Take the great tension in a poet like Claudel: the pull between his commitment to Catholicism and his real knowledge as an artist and person in the world — he's somebody who has really got great knowledge. So he has got to hold what he knows within this compartment of his dogma, and that allows Claudel (because he *was* a great artist) to let his superior understanding of the world, which should have led him to disbelief right away (as Gide saw in that marvellous correspondence between the two), flow out through this marvellous interpretation of the religious tradition that he was working with, and it fills that tradition with resonance and tension. A great deal of that tradition is about to come apart at any moment. And so, a highly religious work like Claudel's becomes very much the nature of the present day because it is belief at the point of bursting — exciting stuff. That is increasingly difficult to do, however. So, if you're going to build a tragedy, let's say, which has to do at least with the loss of value, the irreparable loss of value, then you have to build that value up in your world; you have to establish it within the work, so that you give the reader a sense of what is valuable. It has to be verified, justified within the borders of the work.

Now for me, of course, art seems the only objective thing left whose value can be reasonably justified, but I have great skepticism even about that in my wiser days. I have to be careful not to make my belief in art into a blind superstition. So, when I am thinking carefully about it, I realize, of course, that the world can do without all of these productions of mine or anybody else. The world will survive without it, ninety-nine percent of the world's population will. Ninety-eight percent of the population of the world has never even heard of Shakespeare — billions of people don't know the name Shakespeare. So we are dealing with a very little frothy tip of human experience. One must be skeptical. That's one of the reasons I disagree with some writers who still want to believe that there are easily demonstrable truths or easily demonstrable moral systems. I don't think that it's impossible that they are all false. It's not that all moral systems deserve to go down, but I have had enough philosophy to realize that all philosophical systems are very shaky. Kant builds up a whole scheme of what constitutes morality within his system. There are many *people* who believe it, but the *world* needn't believe Kant, and doesn't, and won't. Or, if I am reading St Thomas — a writer I admire enormously because he was a great philosopher — I don't share any of his views; yet, within his world, you can see what's right and wrong and why, etc. He imagined a fiction which once seemed real. A novel has to build its own system. So within Camus I can be a sort of crude existentialist. I'm not an existentialist; I think it's a lot of baloney; but in Camus I accept it. In the properly detached mood I can read Aristotle, for instance, when he is giving me this picture of the magnanimous man, and I can say, 'Oh yes, the great-souled man, what a wonderful man!' But, of course, if you met the great-souled man in the street, you wouldn't like him. And he wouldn't speak to *you*.

HZ   You say that art itself is the only objective thing left which you find valuable, and if I understand you correctly, this value needn't be elusive. For instance, when you say, in *On Being Blue*, that 'paradoxically, every loving act of definition reverses the retreat of attention to the word and returns it to the world', then you seem to be saying, implicitly, that the very act of writing is its own justification.

WHG Yes, but a very fragile one. I mean that this justification, within the context of the needs and problems of the world, becomes rather slim. It's very problematic, although I would personally hold such values to be the whole point of existing at all. I have a great respect for science, philosophy, etc., as intrinsically valuable activities. The sum of their instrumental contributions is hard to ascertain — the good and bad are so mixed. There are even many false philosophical views which are worthy of the greatest respect. The same is true of religious systems. Really, it is nice to cleanse yourself of beliefs. It is positively pleasant to find out that you don't need to believe nearly as many things as you thought you had to believe. It's a catharsis of the mind. A lot of contemporary writers are trying to kill beliefs off, step on them, finish them off. But, of course, you can't; they spring up again. In 'Night-Sea Journey' Barth establishes a beautiful tension between the spermatozoa, which say 'No', and the finale, which, like Molly Bloom, says 'Yes!' But, I think, Barth means the *no*, far more than the *yes*.

HZ But, then, the *yes* is necessary to go on.

WHG Of course! It's like Beckett saying 'I can't go on, I must go on, I will go on.' But he's down to the barest essentials. Now, I am not as pessimistic as Beckett, and therefore certainly not as comic. I find so much positive quality in art itself, possibly because I have done work with philosophy for such a long time, that I find the falsehoods that one is constantly dealing with in philosophy so appealing, so genuinely fictional. Yes, I'm annoyed that people should be taken in so readily. On the other hand, there is a certain great magnificence about this. One can be taken in for a time and within a scheme, a system — the willing suspension of disbelief again — and that's what teaching philosophy is all about. You enter these various systems believing they are beautiful. I am teaching Plotinus, and I think: it is so magnificent; there is nothing I believe about it; yet this is a work of great art. And indeed it moves to a triumphant conclusion when Plotinus is ending the *Enneads* and you have gone through all of this elaborate system and he is describing the fountain pouring out the soul trying to move back up toward the highest levels like a stream swimming upstream; and when he ends with that magnificent section with the soul's flight from the alone to the alone then you say, 'Well, I'm a Neo-Platonist here and now.' So, I'm caught between the beauties of belief and the knowledge that most of this is, indeed, false and, indeed, pernicious. So there is a sense in which you can say 'This is wrong! And that's not true! Look at this! And look at that!' But you can also say, 'It's wrong, but look at how glorious it is that someone ever thought of this.' Philosophy is full of such aesthetic moments, of moments when you shift into the only gear that really succeeds, and that is an aesthetic mode. (Kierkegaard would hate this.) You want to stay away from the moral at all costs in that sense, for suddenly you'd be in the stiff-necked position of being unable to appreciate a Romanesque church and only liking Gothic. They are different styles and express different kinds of things, but there is a traditional link; they are not totally opposed; there are grounds of connection. One then can move from one quality to another quality without having to sacrifice. I think that is very important to an adequate philosophical theory of art because an adequate philosophical theory must account for the data. An aesthetic theory which is really forced to throw out this and throw out that — whole areas — just won't do. You must be able to justify, let's say, the greatness of Wallace Stevens as a poet and Whitman as a poet: the same theory has to accommodate both. That means that you must have a theory of sufficient generality that it understands the grounds of aesthetic experience itself. It should not exist just to be a partisan for a particular mode.

The same is true for philosophy. You can criticize philosophical views, but ultimately you must have a point from which you are able to see that Hume and Kant are both great philosophers, even when opposed. What makes them great? It can't be merely truth because they can't both be right. Milton and Goethe can't both be great if art depends at least fundamentally on truth, or Dante —because they contradict. Thus, as far as value is concerned — in Dante's world or Goethe's world — we are in different worlds. So, when I'm in Goethe's world — this great pagan world I am very sympathetic with — it's beautiful and I love it; but in Dante's world the beauty is every bit as great, although I am much more personally sympathetic with Goethe. Each establishes his world, and inside that world you are, for a time, possessed of, and by, those values. What you can say of Dante is that he gives almost the greatest expression to those values possible. Then you put the book down, and the next day you are reading *Paradise Lost*. Outside the poem I find Milton's Puritan or Protestant position very unappetizing, whereas Goethe's I would find appealing. But within their respective poems, they are equal: they have sustained those values, and that is the only place I think that is left to sustain them. Pure philosophy can't, because objectively they have no grounds; but within the novels, plays, and poems, they make sense and are strangely, radiantly beautiful.

John Hawkes

John Clendennin Burne Hawkes, Jr, was born in Stamford, Connecticut, on 17 August 1925. His studies at Harvard were interrupted near the end of the Second World War by his work with the American Field Service, for whom he drove an ambulance in Italy. After spending some time in Belgium and Germany, he returned to Harvard, enrolled in Albert J. Guerard's creative writing class, and took his undergraduate degree in 1949. Hawkes has been a teacher at Harvard, writer-in-residence at the University of Virginia in 1965, a visiting lecturer at Stanford University in 1966-67, and Visiting Professor at the City College of New York in 1971-72. He is currently a professor of English at Brown University. Hawkes has earned fellowships from the National Institute of Arts and Letters and from the Rockefeller, Ford, and Guggenheim Foundations. In 1973 he won the French Prix du Meilleur Livre Etranger for *The Blood Oranges (Les oranges de sang),* and in 1980 he was elected to the National Institute of Arts and Letters.

For Hawkes paradox lies at the centre of life and art — not the paradox of logic, but the experiential and reflective dilemma of striking the necessary yet impossible balance between the inevitably opposed forces of Eros and Thanatos. The task of the artist consists in pointing to this paradox and, in doing so, striving to overcome it. He incessantly attempts to create clarity out of incongruity, to reveal beauty and innocence within acts of hate, violence, and humiliation. Paradoxically, the initial situation which demands fictionalization must be destructive in order that vision or structure ('verbal and psychological coherence'), which provide the basic stimuli in the struggle of Eros against Thanatos, may become paramount. Thanatos must be overbearing if the eventual victory of Eros is to appear both delicate and poignant.

In Hawkes's early novels vision or structure can find expression only through the impact of metaphorical language. Only through authorial device are the outbursts of love and compassion on the one hand and hate and violence on the other forced into a pattern of keen correspondences, which conform to the imaginative leaps required by metaphor. Hawkes withdraws behind language and strives not to identify with the narrator or the characters in order not to individualize and thereby belittle the impact of either Eros or Thanatos. Thus in *The Cannibal* (1949), Hawkes's brilliant first novel, even the first-person narrator is so remote, so hidden among incongruous events and narrative passages of apparent authorial objectivity as to be no more than a faint silhouette, the symbolic shadow of evil order rising again from the ruins of post-Second World War Germany. On the other hand, in Hawkes's latest novel, *The Passion Artist* (1979), which is, in a sense, the counterpart of *The Cannibal,* the psyche of the protagonist himself has become the battlefield of Eros and Thanatos. Yet again, the protagonist is less individualized than typological, for he represents everyone's ability to become an artist in the 'willed erotic union', overcoming the paradox of death-in-life through an act of aesthetic transcendence.

Through artistic consciousness, the Eros-Thanatos paradox is transmuted into the opposition of design and debris. In other words, through the workings of the imagination, decay and ruin can be tricked into revealing an intricate pattern which may then serve as a new standard — if not for moral action then for beauty. The novel *Travesty* (1976) is an epitome of this aesthetic conception, where the very act of combined suicide and murder develops into the willed expression of joyfully embraced artistic design, because the process of narrating, paralleling the workings of the imagination, creates constant meaning out of impending destruction.

If, therefore, Hawkes's protagonists increasingly evolve into the mouthpiece of their author's aesthetic concerns, appearing more and more involved with the implications of the Eros-Thanatos paradox, they must become both more pronounced as characters and at the same time less concerned with standardized moral values. In the early novel, *The Beetle Leg* (1951), Hawkes still challenges the American dream and turns it into nightmare in order to expose the negation and duplicity which debase the national experience. And even in *The Lime Twig* (1961), a novel of Gothic horror, moral values are still asserted — though only through tragedy.

But after *The Lime Twig* the absorption of traditional ethics into the realm of Hawkes's aesthetics becomes more obvious from novel to novel. Thus the protagonist of *Second Skin* (1963) can only achieve his final redemptive status as a person by continuously shedding the traits of his former guilty self. In *The Blood Oranges* (1971), the confrontation between conventional moral convictions and aesthetic imagination is recast as the agon between Thanatos and Eros — as narrated from the perspective of the artist-lover. And in *Death, Sleep and the Traveler* (1974) the narrator may deny his guilt for having killed the young woman he loves, because no man can be expected to bear the combination of perfect beauty and devotion. Thus, for Hawkes, any failure in his characters— and by implication in all human beings — has its source in the constrictive landscape of the unconscious and can be redeemed only through the creative energies of the imagination.

Interviews with John Hawkes

Providence, 4 October 1978

HZ It seems to me that there is a change of attitude in your fiction after *The Lime Twig*. Most critics, in fact, agree that a change has taken place, but they generally locate it around the year 1960, that is, before *The Lime Twig,* and they define it as a shift in accent from Thanatos to Eros, or from a darkly pessimistic to a more affirmative view of life. I don't necessarily agree with that opinion, but neither do I quite agree with someone like John Kuehl, who claims that your fiction is deterministic from beginning to end. It seems to me there is a shift, and that it has to do with the opposition between world and self: with your concentration, in the earlier novels, on the world — the world seen as an incongruous mixture of things and psychic states — and, in the later novels, on the self — when the world seems to become an extension of the self rather than subsuming it.

JH I'm not much versed in criticism of my work, but I think there are those who would say not only that my fiction has become more affirmative, starting with *Second Skin,* but also more conventional. I would argue that my fiction is 'affirmative' from beginning to end, that the most destructive elements in my work are associated with comedy, and that my shift toward a more conventional fiction hasn't lessened the power of the nightmarish aspects of my work. But when you refer to 'self', are you thinking of a character's self or the author's self?

HZ I would say that the use of a first-person narrator, beginning with *Second Skin,* suggests the expanding importance of the self.

JH   What did John Kuehl mean by deterministic?

HZ   He means, if I understand him correctly, that your fiction is dominated by a cause-and-effect relation and that every novel, even *The Cannibal* — which at first sight seems to defy the notion of cause and effect, because it starts in 1945, then goes back to 1914, then continues the 1945 section — can eventually be seen as deterministic if the events are put in chronological order.

JH   I haven't thought about determinism in my fiction. But I remember that when I was writing *The Cannibal* I had the clear notion that the landscape of that novel would be an equivalent of the unconscious. I had no thought of projecting my own personal self into the fiction, and didn't think of the unconscious as being my own. Nonetheless I knew that the world of *The Cannibal* would be a configuration of unconscious life. That was my private view of *The Cannibal*. At the time I wasn't thinking of the reader.

The curious thing is that the unconscious coheres totally, yet not because of cause and effect. *The Cannibal* does in fact cohere in this fashion, and such total coherence may indeed amount to determinism. But this quality in *The Cannibal* actually has nothing to do with chronology, or cause and effect. As you probably know, *The Cannibal* was written in alternating time sequences, commencing with 1945, and as I alternated between 1945 and 1914, I was thinking not of cause and effect but of parallelism. Or rather I had a notion of parallelism in mind, and wasn't much interested, consciously, in the structure or form of the fiction. It was at the suggestion of my friend and teacher Albert Guerard that I grouped the 1914 sections together in the middle of the novel when the first draft was completed. I still can't quite account for my final gesture, which was to go through the manuscript changing the third-person pronoun to the first-person, thus identifying myself with the neo-Nazi leader, Zizendorf. At any rate, that gesture led to my increasing use of the first-person narrator in my fiction after *The Cannibal* until, with *Second Skin,* I was able to write a novel from beginning to end in the first person.

But what were we talking about?

HZ   The opposition between world and self ...

JH   Which means, I suppose, the opposition between world and the authorial self or between world and character. I still think that most of my fiction is a configuration of the unconscious, though with *The Lime Twig* it's true that for the first time two characters stand at the center of the fiction. In this sense *The Lime Twig* became more conventional, at least on the surface. I didn't know it at the time, but these two central characters, Michael and Margaret Banks, were versions of the two characters in the first fiction I wrote. That is, my first short novel *Charivari* is about a middle-aged couple who are naïve and childlike. *The Lime Twig* is about a naïve and childlike young couple who behave in every way as if middle-aged. From this distance in time (*Charivari* was published in 1949, *The Lime Twig* in 1961) it's easy to see that both couples are not only inversions of each other but are, quite obviously, projections of the authorial self. *Charivari* is a much disguised youthful satire on my own childhood and early days. The butt of its satire is innocence, and the same holds true for *The Lime Twig*. That is, in *Charivari* sexual fear is organized around the efforts of the middle-aged childless couple to adjust themselves to the woman's fearsome discovery that she is pregnant. After considerable anxiety and horror the pregnancy turns out to be false and all ends well. In *The Lime Twig*, Michael and Margaret Banks are also childless and, to all appearances, sexless as well. But in this novel sexual fear becomes explicit so that Michael's erotic yearnings are gratified, but in such a way as to cause the deaths of both Michael and Margaret. The landscape of *The Lime Twig*, though it is that of post-World War II London, is just as charged with destructive sexuality as *The Cannibal* and, to a lesser extent, *The Beetle Leg*. The obvious point is that in *The Lime Twig* my comic 'dark vision' is spent as much on the central characters as on the landscape.

As I've said elsewhere, *Second Skin* was a deliberate attempt to use the first-person narrator throughout a novel, and to write a novel that could not be mistaken for anything other than comic. *Charivari, The Cannibal, The Beetle Leg, The Lime Twig*, all were to me quite obviously comic. But reviewers tended to insist on the nightmare quality of these works, thus overlooking a central aspect of my work and limiting its readership. When I was ready to begin *Second Skin*, in the West Indies, I had the pleasure of telling an overly curious American tourist that I had brought my wife and family to an isolated tropical island in order to write a comic novel about suicide, and that's what the novel became. But its narrator is undeniably 'real' and his imperceptions involved me as never before in the conventions of fiction. For the first time, with this narrator, Skipper, I allowed innocence to win out. In many ways, then, the change between *Second Skin* and the earlier novels was considerable. But I don't think this change denies what I'm insisting on: that the 'dark constants' are evident in my work from first to last.

HZ However, don't you agree that this change is radical enough to imply a modification of whatever sense of fatality was dominant in your earlier fiction? I think this becomes obvious when one compares the way you treat 'things' in the novels before *Second Skin* and the later novels. For example, *The Cannibal* contains description after description of things, which sometimes seem to resemble mere enumerations or catalogues. The reader tries to find some dark pattern or ominous mood underlying this obsession or necessity to assemble things. But if one would hope with Kuehl that Section Two of the novel supplies the explanation — that the events of 1914 or the world of 1914 had to lead to the world of 1945 — then one would have to be disappointed: the incongruity then was as great as it is now. However, when one compares *The Cannibal* to, for instance, *The Blood Oranges*, one can immediately perceive a change in the way you treat things. They don't appear incongruous any more. They are ordered; everything in *The Blood Oranges* as it is perceived by Cyril's mind has to be read as a sign, a symbol. Thus, it seems that in the earlier novels, individuals are completely dominated by things; in the later novels, they gradually learn to master things and to put them into perspective. Perhaps this could even be called a shift from determinism to freedom.

JH But aren't we merely talking about the difference between a 'fatality' that is the result of authorial omniscience, and the power a first-person narrator appears to exert over his narrative? I think we could argue that Cyril is a kind of magician of things, but also that things in my fiction are always coherent, no matter how chaotic my earlier treatment of concrete objects may have seemed. I think there is an obsessive quality in my treatment of things throughout my fiction. I am sure that Albert Guerard would say that the obsessive quality of my earlier fiction gives way to conscious control and conscious manipulation after *The Lime Twig*. He may be right. But I see my work as a continuum of recurrent images, obsessive thematic concerns, repeated form. We might say that *The Cannibal* is a history of cataclysm self-contained, hermetically sealed. *The Cannibal* ends with the success of the neo-Nazi uprising, with the inmates returned to the institution, with one child dead, a victim of cannibalism, and another child assigned, finally, to sleep. Cataclysm seems ended, order restored. But the sleeping child is the carrier of history, and when she awakes cataclysm will again erupt. This form and meaning is evident in my novels from *The Cannibal* to *Travesty*: in each there is a sense of closure and then a sudden suggestion of expansion toward nothingness that will once again or soon again be filled with chaos.

HZ   But don't you think that there is a change in how this is shown?

JH   It's certainly true that the first-person narrator creates an impression of order and perhaps a more conventional or believable kind of 'reality'. But I would insist that *The Cannibal* determined my subject matter and even my method for whatever was to follow it. Eros is only the obverse of Thanatos.

HZ   Would it be more apposite, perhaps, to say that this shift in perspective is a movement from the absurd to the romantic impulse? You do, as I recall, say in an interview that, for you, both of these impulses are present in your work all the time. But I would like to suggest that the accent is on romance in the later novels and on the absurd — or maybe the grotesque — in the earlier novels.

JH   I'd like to know what you mean by 'absurd' and 'romance'.

HZ   May I begin with the notion of the absurd and its relation to the grotesque? The absurd, as an existentialist concept, is a metaphysical concept — a negative metaphysical concept, to be sure, because it involves the meaninglessness of the world against which — with Camus — man can either rebel or which — with Sartre — he must embrace. The grotesque differs insofar as the force that victimizes man is not a larger-than-life force, but society, a society that dehumanizes man. From this perspective, it might be appropriate to describe *The Cannibal* as grotesque rather than as absurd.

JH   If I had to choose I would say that it is more profitable to look at *The Cannibal* in terms of existentialism than in terms of the grotesque. In *The Cannibal* what is ordinarily thought of as catastrophe gives rise to the simple value of existence. Despair and hopelessness are rendered concretely in a way that is shocking, exhilarating, comic. Behind all the wreckage and distortion in *The Cannibal* is evident the severe distance of the envisioning writer. But perhaps you can tell me in greater detail what you mean by 'grotesque'. To me the word suggests no emotional or intellectual commitment to the derangement which, in my work, might be called grotesque. But in my fiction destruction or derangement are not gratuitously offered up as rare specimens of perverse thinking.

They constitute, for me, the only serious condition there is, the constant inversion of the ideal.

HZ   I think I can tell you why your work is often associated with the grotesque. The grotesque means the paradoxical combination of the terrible and the ludicrous. The irreconcilability of these two sentiments is thought to give rise to grotesque laughter, laughter that sticks in your throat. However, I believe that the grotesque has to be modified in the direction of the absurd if applied to your work. For the grotesque distortion of man — a distortion which, in your fiction, *is* both terrible and ludicrous — is not brought about by society; it is a given.

JH   That's right. My work is not socially oriented. I have a sense of Camus's hero, the figure in heroic struggle against meaninglessness, but to me what's important is the first recognition of meaninglessness, or the sheer insistence on meaninglessness, which lies at the center of my work. If we may move on to the third term you mentioned, romance, I would say that it means to me nothing more than the desire to create something out of nothing and all the attendant images and emotions that that impulse carries with it. But we seem to be moving towards the claim that the more conventional my fiction is, the freer the characters are. Whereas I think that the sense of a confining world is just as evident in my later novels as in the earlier.

HZ   I don't think that your fiction has become more conventional.

JH   Is *The Fall* conventional? Or *The Stranger?* What do you mean by a conventional novel?

HZ   One which employs fictional devices that can be found in most other fiction at a given time. I would like to believe that your novels are innovative. I think that the idea of growing conventionality in much of the criticism of your work arises when your novels are seen as a sequence, not because of their similarity to other novels.

JH   That's a nice thought. What about the romantic impulse?

HZ   I would define it as a mood of extension and reflexivity. The characters in your fiction not only start to dominate things, but their vacillating moods come, in turn, to be mirrored in the change of situations, the prevailing features of nature, and so on.

JH   Is there really much difference between landscape as mirror of everyman's unconscious, and landscape as mirror of a character's unconscious?

HZ What I suppose I really want to suggest is that your characters take on the role of author in a much more comprehensive way than the average first-person narrator does. I would define the perspective of your first-person narrator as an omniscient perspective within the limits of character. I am talking about the sympathy with which the first-person narrator regards himself. The best example, again, seems to be Cyril in *The Blood Oranges*, who is openly in love with himself. This appears to me to be different from the fact that many authors become more involved with their characters as they write about them. For Cyril as first-person narrator has to remain detached from himself in order to be able to sympathize with himself. Therefore, starting from this concept of omniscient narcissistic narrator, I would argue that the romantic impulse entails extension as narrative device and that its correlative in terms of character consists in the mood of persistent tolerance.

JH That's a splendid idea, that 'romantic impulse entails extension as narrative device', and that you see my narrators mirroring the authorial self. In this way Skipper, Cyril, Allert and the nameless narrator of *Travesty* aren't merely conventional. For some time now I've insisted that the subject of my work after *The Lime Twig* has been the imagination itself, and your view of my narrators gives more substance to the idea. Skipper is the *artificial* inseminator, Cyril is the sex-singer, Allert is the pornographer, the narrator of *Travesty* is the true poet. In each case these figures embody both the victim and, more important, the victimizer; each narrator is both creator and destroyer, and each seems to suffer in one way or another the power he exerts. Each narrator both exalts and punishes that which cannot be tolerated in a banal pragmatic world, namely his innocence. For me the poles of the authorial self, or of that self that creates something out of nothing, are precisely these: cruelty, or ultimate power, and innocence. I think you're the only person so far to bring up this idea of doubling between author and narrator in my fiction, and to associate this narrative device, as you call it, with romantic impulse. But do you see any connection between romantic impulse and tragic irony?

HZ Yes, there is a connection, I think, at least in your work. It seems to me that you are not giving free rein to the romantic impulse; that what I would like to call the tragic irony of your fiction consists in a constriction of the romantic impulse. This impulse is put under pressure in *The Cannibal*, *The Beetle Leg*, *The Lime Twig*, and, again, in *Travesty*, but it is not put under the same kind of pressure in *The Blood Oranges*, *Second Skin*, or *Death, Sleep and the Traveler*. The pressure in these latter novels seems to be more involuntary, a psychic pressure within the character, like Skipper's unacknowledged desires or Allert's haunting dreams.

JH   Again it's a splendid idea, that tragic irony is romantic impulse constricted or put under pressure. I should think that the romantic impulse is in itself a duality, or holds in balance the power of unlimited possibility and the nothingness that is the context of all creativity. The phrase 'romantic impulse' makes me think of André Breton's locomotive in the forest. The vine-covered rusted engine that's forever inert, forever immobile, dead, somehow conveys more of 'locomotive' than the enormous slick black machine roaring down the track. So that the destructive image posits the ideal, while the romantic impulse is always in a sense self-threatening. At any rate, if we generally find constriction or pressure in the destructive image and metaphor, then it seems to me that *The Blood Oranges*, *Second Skin*, and *Death, Sleep and the Traveler* are not so very different from the earlier novels. The chateau dream in *Death, Sleep and the Traveler* was one of my own dreams and was immediately recognizable as a more explicit version of the sharkskin trunk metaphor in *The Cannibal*. The abandoned lighthouse and severed fingers of Fernandez in *Second Skin*, the split knuckles of the xylophone player in *Death, Sleep and the Traveler*, for me these are examples of constriction or pressure. Perhaps in *The Blood Oranges* these same materials are less pressured since the chastity belt and fortress, as well as Hugh's amputated arm, for example, are all conscious renderings of the similar content of *Second Skin*.

HZ   Can you tell me why you think of *The Blood Oranges*, *Death, Sleep and the Traveler*, and *Travesty* as a triad, as opposed to *Second Skin*?

JH   Because after *Second Skin* I was explicitly and consciously interested in the relationship between sex and the imagination. When I began writing *Travesty* I recognized it as the last in a triad of novels which I hoped would eventually appear together under the title of *Humors of the Blood and Skin*. I thought of *The Blood Oranges* as the lyric sung by the sex-singer; *Death, Sleep and the Traveler* was the poet's descent into the underworld or into the unconscious in search of the self; *Travesty* was a portrait of the poet as both murderer and suicide. The epigraph most appropriate to this triad is by Georges Braque: 'The vase gives shape to emptiness, music to silence.' Incidentally, after my American Field Service days in World War II (as an ambulance driver) I underwent a form of psychiatric treatment known as insulin shock therapy. Only when I had completed *Death, Sleep and the Traveler*, about twenty years later, did I learn from a friend, who was a psychiatrist, that in the insulin coma the patient is brought as close as possible to death. My friend also told me that, because of its dangerous aspects, the treatment has been long abandoned. Clearly this is the treatment Allert dimly remembers in *Death, Sleep and the Traveler*. It bears out my notion that annihilation is the twin of the imagination.

I might also mention that when I finished *Travesty* I thought that I couldn't go beyond the orgasmic closure of the end of *Travesty*, that I could not improve on the form of that short novel, which is as close as I've come to perfection. I felt that I had nothing to write. But then I thought of the brief scene in *The Cannibal* when the townswomen attempt to put down a riot in the mental institution for men. I remembered the anecdote that originally prompted the scene in *The Cannibal*: my father's story of how as a young man in the National Guard he had helped to quell a riot in a women's prison. I decided to attempt a novel that would deal in a much longer way with what had been confined to a page or so almost thirty years before. The result was my new novel, which is about a man who becomes a hostage in a prison for women. If the imagination fails, the best thing is simply to start over.

HZ Actually, the fascinating idea in *Travesty,* as I see it, is the idea of paradoxically paralyzing life through the creative act. The narrator's planning of the combined murder and suicide creates a situation where his friend is forced to give up real experience for imagined experience, as can be seen when the narrator repeats his words: 'Can I have heard you correctly? *Imagined life is more exhilarating than remembered life.*'

JH I must say that I enjoy the comic irony of that particular formulation of the romantic impulse. The narrator of *Travesty* offers his friend and poet Henri only two choices: *imagined* life and *remembered* life. He omits the most obvious choice of actual life as it's lived, partly because the occupants of the car have only moments more to live, and partly because he thinks that life as it is lived isn't even worth comparing with imagined or remembered life. When the narrator insists that imagined life is the more exhilarating of the two, a part of me agrees.

HZ Isn't this because the narrator forces the artist to be absolutely true to his art? Henri had to give up reality and choose imagination instead; he has to commit himself to his own murder as if he were committing suicide. And I think that when you insist on the creative power and the destructive power as both being present in your fiction all the time — death incorporating the seeds of life and vice versa — then this had to lead, eventually, to the idea that an act of real destruction can be parallel to the creative act. I think that, in a sense, *Travesty* foreshadows *The Passion Artist*.

JH I'm grateful for your view of it. I wish I had had such a perspective during the eighteen months or so of depression and paralysis between the end of *Travesty* and the beginning of *The Passion Artist*. I think I felt especially bereft of imagination after *Travesty* since it was probably the most conscious fiction I've written and so tended to be doubly exhausting. *Travesty* seemed conclusive, unconsciously and consciously as well.

The irony is that *Travesty*, like *The Passion Artist*, also came out of a prolonged period of creative paralysis and in the same way was prompted by fortuitous circumstance. Sophie and I and the children were in Brittany, at the start of a year off from teaching, when I happened to read Camus's *The Fall* and, within the week, saw the worst head-on collision imaginable between the cars of two vacationing families. The crash was so violent and in its own way perfect that there was almost nothing left of the cars, the families, the picnic gear, etc. Between the reading of *The Fall* and the sight of the crash I had my novel. I recalled Camus's idea that we can't really live without first answering the question, 'Why not suicide?' A dim version of Camus's own death came to mind. (My memory was quite mistaken; I thought erroneously that Camus himself had been driving the car in which he died and that in the car with him was only one passenger. After finishing *Travesty* I learned that my own imagined situation, that of driver, best friend, and daughter riding together in the speeding car, was oddly close to the real situation in which Camus died.) I more or less followed the pattern of *The Fall* but subverted Camus's question so that it became, not 'Why not suicide?', but *how* suicide, *when*, and *where*. I was interested not in how to live but in what could be most taxing to the imagination. It came to me that cessation was the only thing unimaginable. Cessation and the 'existence of that which exists no longer' are the only concerns of my narrator. Like Jean-Baptiste Clamence in *The Fall,* whose listener, a fellow lawyer, is actually Clamence's double, so too my narrator and Henri the poet are versions of each other. But whereas *The Fall* is about the 'prison' of Christian guilt, *Travesty* is about a nameless man who sheds guilt, turns perversity into an act of courage, and experiences what it is to be a poet.

One further irony is that immediately after the war, perhaps before I began writing *Charivari* and *The Cannibal,* I read *The Stranger.* No novel has ever touched me so personally. Its recognition of desolation became for me the purest kind of exhilaration. It's no wonder that I thought of my own short 'French' novel as a travesty, and acknowledged it as such in the title. Before we left France last summer, Sophie and I finally visited Camus's grave in Lourmarin.

HZ   As regards the title and underlying idea of *Travesty* — the linking of design and debris and the idea that, if a design is intense enough, conscious enough, it must lead to a debris which originates a new design — this idea seems to be a very positive commentary on Camus.

JH   Thanks. But now I think our discussion has left me a romantic existentialist, which is surely an anachronism in this postmodern world of ours. But perhaps we can just say I'm an original ...

Providence, 6 August 1979

HZ   I would like to begin by suggesting that *The Passion Artist,* like some of your other fictions, carries picaresque elements, but it seems to me that these elements tend to be tragic rather than comic. If you were to ask me how I understand the term 'picaresque', I would answer that to me the picaresque describes the quest of a hero by relating separate yet comparable events of his life to form a series, a series which perhaps gains meaning through repetition. If the hero does not change during the course of events, this repetition will be comic; if he does, as in *The Passion Artist,* tragic or pathetic or grotesque.

JH   I am trying to think of what elements in my fiction would be picaresque, because to me picaresque is always comic, but comic in a special way — hurtful comic, or gallows humor, the cliché of picaresque fiction. I don't know of any picaresque fiction that isn't comic distortion. I am not so interested in the picaro and the journey, the quest and all of that; I am only interested in the extreme detachment and the comic cruelty that's usually in it. The picaresque has to do, usually, with somebody who is, maybe innocent, maybe not, but who is extremely vulnerable: homeless, a pauper, a child ... . Maybe it's the picaro I am talking about, who is often the innocent little boy and who then works for a cruel master. The picaresque novel, as I understand it, is usually a kind of horrendous attack on society through a lot of horrors that befall somebody who doesn't deserve the horrors. Or maybe they do deserve the horrors! The only picaresque novel I am at all familiar with is Quevedo y Villegas's *Buscón*, and it has an old school teacher who is starving to death, and his nose is so long it hangs down to his mouth, and his mouth is always trying to eat the nose. It's a kind of cannibalistic treatment, autocannibalism — because he is so hungry. The hero is always poking terrifying fun at this ludicrous, pathetic school teacher. There is a group of novels, all of which are the same in tone, all of which are the same in their devilishly brutal, very detached, very witty assault on reality. They are in a sense realistic in that they are filled with concrete detail but they always have to do with deception, trickery. (The little boy who leads a blind man up to a stone wall and says, 'Now, master, we have come to a stream, now you must jump as hard as you can.' The hero who starts to enter his home town and discovers his father's dismembered body on posts at the four corners of the town.) This is my only concept of picaresque: a fiction that goes beyond social criticism, lays bare our inner horrors and does so in a comic way, always through some totally unexpected, totally unjustified event. And the language is always extremely detached, cold, witty, full of brutal similies.

HZ   How about *Don Quixote*?

JH   *Don Quixote* uses so much the tone of the romances it is parodying, and is, after all, so tender, generally speaking, so sweet, that I don't think of *Don Quixote* as picaresque at all. I mean the brutalities of it are psychological, not rendered physically. Don Quixote will never fear for his life, will never be dismembered, will never lose a hand, will never starve to the extent that his mouth will be trying to eat his nose. I would think that *Don Quixote* stands alone in the history of literature. A picaresque novel is savage, marvelous, but marvelous in a different way from *Don Quixote*. I think the ideal is never very visible in the conventional Spanish picaresque novel.

Now, in my own work, the instances of the grotesque (to use your word), of violence and comic violence (and what are some of these instances: the man who operates the motion picture theater in *The*

Cannibal and has only one leg, and bounces down the stairs like a duck — there's a comic metaphor, in effect making fun of his disability; the old people lying dead in the fields like punched cows), these instances suggest picaresque fiction. When I first read some Spanish picaresque work, I recognized immediately that there was, indeed, a kind of literary starting place for me that I had known nothing about.

HZ You say that you are not interested in the idea of the quest. But it seems, to me, that *The Passion Artist* does, in fact, show Konrad Vost's inner and outer quests, both of which amount to his search for woman. For example, the childhood scenes in the third section reveal his desperate, but futile, attempts to gain the love of his mother. And his aborted encounter with the mother-like Kristel cruelly ends this inner quest. So we see Konrad Vost the adult walking along the railroad tracks into the marshes surrounding the city, thrice meeting women (three stations, three adventures) on a now necessary outer quest back towards the unconscious.

JH The novel starts as a quest of his daughter. That treatment of the schoolgirl section, the sex section, is perhaps a mixture of comic treatment of pain or the unknown plus a kind of romantic poeticizing. There is a lot of ironic imagery in this scene, but Vost himself is like a survivor at sea lying on a beam of a wrecked ship. There is a comic treatment of pain which seems to me to be fundamental to picaresque fiction. He is questing, in effect, for the innocence of his daughter and he discovers the opposite. Then in the middle section, where he is looking for women in general, escaped women, he frightens the old woman to death, which suggests a picaresque mind. In the last scene he is passive but I suppose he is still questing: for his mother or *the* mother and, at the same time, searching for — without knowing it — the nature of sexual love. All the small women in the fiction, whether they are girls or women, are, to my mind, versions of the mother — true enough: the schoolgirl and Kristel and the small woman in the unconscious trial-like scene, the judge penitent-like scene, the mother herself and more. There are at least five. There is also the small woman in the riot scene who comes after Vost with a jagged piece of glass who is, perhaps, Gagnon's daughter. All of these, paradoxically, seem to be versions of the mother and he is destroying all of them or suffering at the hands of all of them. But the interesting question would be: what was the real nature of the Kristel episode, how did this episode relate to the final initiation or

embrace in the prison between Hania and Konrad Vost? Vost
seems to be a man who, on the surface, wanted nothing to do with
women. At least he seems that way as the novel begins. But isn't
there a line that says he wanted to live in a world of women?

HZ   You say right on the first page that women compose the
garden in which Konrad Vost is cultivated like a plant.

JH   And, of course, he is a bad plant! So without knowing it,
he seems to be pursuing that which he knows nothing about, that
which he fears, that which he probably loathes, and finally loves.
My notion is that he is an ordinary middle-aged man: repressed,
apparently self-confident, rational in a petty kind of way,
ultimately uninteresting. He is the rationalist, the bourgeois, the
clerk, the man of arrogance (but who wouldn't admit to such) who
is forced into a quest back over his life, back over his relationship
with woman, coming full circle to the mother and then beyond,
until he arrives, though dead (and it's interesting to me that he is
dying inexplicably, dying before he is shot; it's perfectly obvious,
he is getting colder and colder and withering away; and exactly
why he must die at the moment of experiencing normal life is the
whole purpose of the novel) — until he arrives at a moment of
sexual normalcy, which belongs to everyone but is the life's
moment of true poetry. It is a paradox that Vost, who is ordinary,
has been self-excluded from such experience and that he should
discover such experience through a quest he didn't mean to take,
didn't want to take, and that reveals all of his ignorance and
barbarous pseudo-masculinity. These traits break down as he dies
and are gone when he is finally engaged in sexual life. The man
who didn't know what he had never experienced, experiences
love, and that's the point of the fiction. Well, anyway, you're
right. My first impulse was to say: *The Passion Artist* picaresque?
Not at all! Now I've changed my mind. However, it's not because
of the questing, it's because of what *happens* during the quest,
which is a quest into the unconscious again. It exemplifies a kind of
cruelly comic envisioning of very serious material.

HZ   And the quest into the unconscious relates to the idea of
'the stationary traveler', right? Because you say at some point in
The Passion Artist that the stationary traveler is he who is
'traveling inside himself'.

JH   The idea comes from a little postcard we found in a
bookshop in France. It's a marvelous little picture (the work of
Topor, I think) showing a man in a suit and a fedora hat, chained
to a tree and carrying two suitcases — a stationary traveler! Of

course, the stationary traveler is the man who goes nowhere, which, in a sense, is the vision of life in *The Passion Artist* and, in a sense, is my own vision of life. We take literal journeys, travel all over the place, but in a sense are always stationary within the self. I like the paradox of going nowhere and everywhere.

HZ I was trying to figure out what the stationary traveler meant in the context of *The Passion Artist*. I think the idea could be related to Konrad Vost's belief that the storehouse of memory is like a railway station, that nothing of your conscious life is ever discarded, that, in fact, every image, sensation, concept has its 'own invisible track'.

JH Of course, those tracks relate to the railway tracks, and the railway tracks in the marsh relate to *The Cannibal*, to those blasted rails that are curling up at the edge of the town, and in the marsh vestiges of Spitzen-on-the-Dein, are supposed to be evident. We are archaeologically on top of the buried city of Spitzen-on-the-Dein, and ironically, the new world is bleaker, deader than the world of *The Cannibal*. The neo-Nazi politics of *The Cannibal* have been transformed in *The Passion Artist* to the political life of imprisoned women or of women achieving liberation. The absurdity and pathetic quality of *The Passion Artist* is that its most brutal character is its most innocent — Konrad Vost, who is an adult version of the little boy in *The Cannibal*. Slovotkin, the *alter ego* of Konrad Vost, is scientist as oppressor and is a comical, satirical version of the woman-hater — who is not exactly a woman-hater either by the time he dies: he too learns something about the sameness between man and woman.

HZ Which is the same sense of equality between man and woman that Konrad Vost achieves with Hania at the end of the novel, right? On the other hand, Konrad Vost, instead of trying to dominate women as had Slovotkin, has submitted to them throughout his life. As you say, Slovotkin is his *alter ego*. Now, it seems to me that the dominance of women over Konrad Vost follows a complicated pattern of substitution. In Konrad Vost's childhood, his mother is supplanted by Anna Kossowski, a kind of anti-mother, who is then, in fact, supplanted by Anna Kossowski the horse. Later on in his life the schoolgirl substitutes for his daughter Mirabelle, and even when his mother's love finally reaches him before he dies, her words come to him, so to speak, on the tongue of Hania. It appears that only when his mother willingly leaves Konrad Vost to Hania in the end can he finally become himself. Paradoxically, she seems to give birth to him for a second time just as he is about to die. So am I correct in assuming that the dominance women exert over Konrad Vost is dependent on this order of substitution — initiated and terminated by his mother?

JH   Exactly. But for me the question is still what to make of Konrad Vost's interest in his own daughter. He is unaware of his erotic feelings for Mirabelle, yet, in effect, experiences sexual life with a daughter substitute. He doesn't understand the situation, but since Konrad Vost is the most repressed character I have created, the fiction causes him to experience precisely, literally, emotionally, vividly, textually, the erotic side of a father-daughter relationship; and that trauma of a totally repressed area, acted out on him, in a sense, is both a beauty and a horror that he can hardly bear. The guilt drives him back into his masculine loathing self that is fated to fight against women. No doubt his fear of woman must have something to do with his powerful attraction to the mother and the fear or hostility toward the mother for having such power over him, or for being inaccessible, or both. These are the psychic materials which he re-experiences in the form of his journey. Each substitute is either a benign or malign version of the mother until we get to Hania, who is beyond the mother, and the simple way we know that is that the mother disappears and leaves Hania behind. Not as a substitute any longer, but as a unique woman. In most of his relationships with women, Vost's role is one of passivity and guilt. He is always subservient to woman. But by the end, the mother, again paradoxically, is the bringer of light, just as Psyche's initial use of light brings about her darkness out of which she achieves light or clarity. In *The Passion Artist* the mother's initial use of light brings about her imprisonment, brings about her son's 'blindness' throughout his entire life until, at the end, the mother becomes the light-bringer herself to clarify his life and to dramatize her own consistency of self. So that imprisonment has not minimized her existence, maimed her life. She has remained herself even in the worst of all possible conditions, and she loves someone and is in turn loved by that person — Hania. I'm really talking in the context of Angela Carter's *The Sadeian Woman*, a splendid book about the politicizing of gender or sexual definition. I, too, am interested in the demystification of woman. Of course, Angela Carter's whole vision is aimed at that, in an effort to help us see man and woman in their unmythical states — especially woman. It is essential to demystify woman and at the same time to overcome ignorance. We must have knowledge of both the male and female and destroy their mythological roles in order to experience what is in fact their mystery.

HZ   In the introduction to her book, Angela Carter says that, in her opinion, the problem between the sexes ought to be an historical issue and that the relationship between man and woman appears to be mythical only because it was established in its present form centuries ago and has remained unchanged since. Now, when you say near the end of *The Passion Artist* that Konrad Vost, in making love to Hania, at last knows the 'transports of that singular experience which makes every man an artist', do you mean that the artist is someone who is not caught in the contrast between male dominance and female submission — regardless of whether this contrast is either historical or mythical?

JH   I hadn't thought of that, to tell you the truth, but I certainly agree. I meant every man as artist simply in the sense that sexuality necessitates a free exercising of the imagination. In the sexual union every person knows the sublimity of art. For me the imagination is always and inevitably erotic; eroticism or sexual experience is inevitably and always artistic. To paraphrase Nabokov (a bit crudely, perhaps): art comes first, sex second; there can *be* no sex without what we can only call artistic consciousness …

Doris Lessing

Doris Lessing was born in Kermanshah, in what was then Persia, in 1919. In 1924 she moved with her family to Rhodesia and was educated at the Girl's High School in Salisbury. She married twice while in Rhodesia, her second husband bearing the name Gottfried Lessing. In 1949 she was divorced for the second time and settled in London. She has three children.

Doris Lessing is a recipient of the Maugham Award. She is an Honorary Fellow of the Modern Language Association and an Associate Member of the American Academy of Arts and Letters. She now lives in London. She has always been and felt an expatriate. And this fact has been of significance both on a thematic and a moral level. It has afforded her a perspective from which barriers of national identity, race, class, and even sex seem deeply suspect, destructive of a unity which she feels to have existed in a distant past and towards which she looks with some hope. She also feels that her expatriation is in some sense a modern condition, conferring an insight which is at the same time privileged and increasingly likely to be that of the individual cut adrift from cultural, political, social, and moral traditions which have become suspect.

When she first appeared she was seen primarily as an African writer and her first works were indeed set in Africa, though she was in England by the time her first book, *The Grass is Singing* (1950), was published. An account of the destructive myths generated by social divisiveness, *The Grass is Singing* established the tone for the *Children of Violence,* a sequence of five novels which examined the relationship between the individual and the group, a subject which had engaged her directly through her activities with an unofficial and visionary communist party. This sequence of novels, was, however, interrupted by *The Golden Notebook* (1962), whose concern with a crisis in the personal and artistic life of a woman writer was both an expression of a deeply personal experience and a radical reconsideration of the form of the novel and the direction of her own career.

The shift from a realistic tradition of writing was vital for her career and the final volume of 'The Children of Violence', *The Four-Gated City* (1969), showed signs of a new interest both in the possibilities represented by projecting the action into the future and in pressing the novel towards myth and prophecy. An increasingly apocalyptic tone typified works like *Briefing for a Descent into Hell* (1971) and *The Summer Before the Dark* (1973). Breakdown and catastrophe were seen as the key to personal and social reconstruction. The nightmare vision was balanced, or at least mitigated, by a utopianism, a growing belief in the ability of man to regenerate or evolve, if necessary through the violent agency of a cataclysm whose inevitability human imperfection ensured. Perhaps in some degree these ideas owed something to Sufi thought, which began to engage her attention, but Doris Lessing resists too mechanical a connection between her work and her spiritual and philosophical concerns.

More recently her work has taken a new direction. Always fascinated by space fiction she has come to feel that it offers her the opportunity to combine experimentalism with tradition. In *Shikasta* (1978) she attempts a version of world history as seen from the perspective of a distant star system whose interventions in human affairs account for both human history and for the various religious myths common to the holy texts with which man has attempted to account for himself. *Shikasta* turns myth into history and history into myth. Once again it foresees catastrophe but beyond that the possibility of rebirth.

The Marriages of Zones Three, Four and Five (1980) is a more lyrical work. Somewhat akin to a medieval story shifted into the future it describes that collapse of boundaries which has always been her concern. Her paradigmatic male and female worlds come together. It is a humorous, even a gentle, work. It was followed, in 1981, by the third volume, *The Syrian Experiments*, which concerns itself with the plight of a female bureaucrat on a distant planet.

Doris Lessing has written plays, short stories and poetry as well as novels. She not only has an international reputation, she has an international perspective. The range and depth of her work is considerable. She has constantly concerned herself with testing the potential of the forms which she has used and if literature is indeed, as one of her characters remarks, 'analysis after the event', then she has now moved to a concern with analysis before the event. She is, in other words, part historian, part spinner of legends, and part prophet and seer.

Interview with Doris Lessing

London, 23 April 1980

CB   You once said there was a great deal that George Eliot didn't understand because she was moral. What did you mean by that?

DL   Well I think she was a victim, like many of the women of that time, of Victorian morality. Because she was 'living in sin' with George Lewis there was a great pressure on her to be good. The reason why I think this is because I noticed the same pressure on myself when I wrote *The Golden Notebook*. I am not being paranoid; you have got no idea of the kind of attack I got. It was really quite barbarous. They said I was a man hater, a balls cutter, particularly Americans. I noticed enormous pressure on me to be feminine and to be good and to be kind and sweet. Quite nauseating it was. I notice that other women who have gone through the same pressure confess to the same; they suddenly find themselves thinking 'Oh God, I mustn't do that because they will say I am a balls cutter.' Well this has already gone because Women's Lib has achieved so much. But to go back to George Eliot, I would be very surprised — let's put it this way — if she wasn't falling over backwards to be good because of the pressure on her. I mean it was no joke living in that society. It must have been dreadful.

CB   You mention that you were alarmed or surprised by the reaction you got from men with respect to *The Golden Notebook*. Were you equally alarmed by the reaction you got from women?

DL   Oh, you are quite wrong in thinking that I only got attacks from men. I got a lot of support from men, from a few men, and the most vicious attacks from women, on the lines that I was letting the side down by revealing the kind of things that were said. I had never thought on those lines at all. Not only had I not thought that I was writing a women's book but it had never crossed my mind to think anything of writing the kind of things down that I was writing. Women talk like this. Men talk about women, letting off steam in locker rooms and so on, but they don't necessarily mean it. And when women sit around and say these things they don't necessarily mean it either; it is letting off steam. It never crossed my mind when I wrote all that down, that it hadn't really been done before. It's true that I can't remember that kind of conversation ever having been written down. I simply didn't think of that until I got the reactions I did. I thought, how was it that I am getting these violent reactions? What have I done? What have I said? And when I started to look around I couldn't think of any novels voicing the kind of criticisms women have of men. Almost like breathing you know, so deep rooted.

CB In an essay called 'A Small Personal Voice', which, admittedly, you wrote quite a long time ago now, you said that the highest point of literature was the novel of the nineteenth century, the work of the great realists. You also said that the realist novel was the highest form of prose writing. What led you to say that then and why did you move away from that position with *The Golden Notebook* and with most of your subsequent work?

DL I was wondering myself not long ago why I reacted so strongly — something must have happened to make me react. I do remember having that set of thoughts about the nineteenth-century novel. I mean it was magnificent wasn't it? What they had was a kind of self-assurance which I don't think any one of us have got, we don't have it. Why don't we have it?

CB Well you did say that part of your admiration came from the fact that they shared what you called a climate of ethical judgement.

DL That's right. Well they did. We don't have anything like that.

CB On the other hand, you said of George Eliot that she didn't understand certain things *because* she was moral.

DL Well, there was a kind of womanly certitude in George Eliot which you would not find let's say in Chekhov. There's something tight there in judgement. I admire George Eliot enormously, I am not saying I don't. But there is something too cushioned in her judgements.

CB In talking about a climate of ethical judgement were you suggesting that there is a necessary relationship between art and morality, or that there should be, that art is a moral force in some way?

DL I don't know if there should be. But if you write a book which you don't see as moral believe me your readers do, and that's something that I can't ever quite come to terms with. Now *The Marriages of Zones Three, Four and Five* I almost regard as outside judgement because it's a legend. It is full of forgiveness, that book. Wouldn't you say it was full of forgiveness? An old warrior of the sex war simply shrugs his shoulders and gives up and laughs, I mean that is something ...

CB   Yes I think it is, but reverting to this question of why you admire the nineteenth-century novel, why did you yourself move away from that tradition which you wanted to claim early on?

DL   Because it's too narrow, that's why, because we have gone beyond it. Let's take *Anna Karenina,* what a marvellous book. It is all about the social problem which existed in a very narrow bigoted society and which was completely unnecessary. In fact a good deal of Victorian fiction can be classified like that. Look at Hardy, for example. These tragedies are mini-tragedies because they derive from fairly arbitrary social conditions; they are not rooted in any human nature. When you finish reading *Anna Karenina* you think, my God, here is this woman ruined and destroyed because of this stupid bloody society and it does make it a smaller novel in my opinion, it does. Because it is Tolstoy it is full of the most marvellous things but in actual fact the basic story is a story about nothing, about a local society, a very local, temporary set of social circumstances. My train of thought was that we now live with our head in the middle of exploding galaxies and thinking about quasers and quarks and black holes and alternative universes and so on, so that you cannot any more get comfort from old moral certainties because something new is happening. All our standards of values have been turned upside down, I think. Not that I don't think life doesn't do that for you anyway because it seems to me there is a process of losing more and more conviction all the time. I really did have very firm opinions about all kinds of things even 15 years ago, which I am unable to have now because the world has got too big, everything is too relative. What's true in one society isn't true in another. What is true for one time isn't true five years later.

CB   So in fact there are no fixed moral standards.

DL   No, I don't think there can be any fixed moral standards. I mean you can pay lip service to a fixed moral standard because it saves you trouble, which I am perfectly prepared to do. I have got a different attitude towards hypocrisy, perhaps.

CB   Yet isn't there a strong moral drive in your work, a sense of trying to stop a headlong rush towards disaster by deflecting your reader away from a dangerous path.

DL   When you say that it sounds as though I believe I can do it.

CB   I half think you do.

DL   I think in the past I have had some such thoughts, that if enough writers write this, which God knows we do, if enough writers say 'For God's sake look out at what is happening', things might change. But I have gone back to a thought I had in the *Children of Violence* series right at the beginning. I reread *Martha Quest* recently. Do you remember, the passage when she stands at the door and watches the prisoners walk past in handcuffs and thinks that this has been described now in literature for so long and nothing has changed. Well you know this is a very terrible thought for a writer to have, and this is another of these complexes I live with because with one half of myself I think I don't see the point of it, I don't think we change anything.

CB   That is the function of art then, is it, to change reality or to change the way people perceive reality?

DL   I think the function of real art, which I don't aspire to, is to change how people see themselves. I wonder if we do. If we do it is very temporary. Let's go back to the Russians, you can say that Turgenev and Tolstoy and all that crowd of giants in fact changed how people saw themselves. They did, but to what end? Because look at the Russians now. I have just finished reading a book called *The Russians,* by an American correspondent in Russia, and it is very clear there is very little difference between a communist society and a capitalist society. I think perhaps the communist society is worse, but there isn't very much difference; they have got a new ruling class, a differently-based class, but it is a highly privileged class that has got every intention of hanging on to its privileges, and a whole mass of serfs who get very little. And, as for freedom, there is as little of it as there was under the Czars. So you ask yourself, I ask myself, if you can have a blaze of marvellous writers, which they had, all shouting the same thing, which they did, in one way or another, and yet they have so little effect, what then?

Now it so happens that I am a writing animal and I can't imagine myself not writing; I literally get quite ill if I don't write a bit. Perhaps that is my problem and not anyone else's.

CB   But I wonder if in a sense you don't compound that determinism. Take a book like *Shikasta.* Contained in it is a version of world history, history as pathology, as degeneration, as movement towards catastrophe. But we discover that that movement is not chance, it is not arbitrary, it is actually the result of interventions, of manipulations by various distant star systems.

That being so, aren't you proposing a determinism in which it is impossible to resist this onward movement because it derives from outside of humanity?

DL   Well you see this is what I think I think, or what I think now. I don't know what I will think in ten year's time. I think in fact that we do not have much influence on events, but we think we do, we imagine we do. There is a marvellous Sufi story about the mouse who, through a series of accidents, becomes the owner of a cow. It has the end of a rope which goes around the cow's neck in its mouth and as the cow wanders out across the countryside it cannot control the cow. But as the cow stops to eat some grass it shouts 'that's right eat up some grass' and when the cow turns left it shouts 'that's right, turn left'. Well this is what I think we're like because it seems to me self evident. I know that is arrogant, but just look at the course of events. We are continually, and by 'we' I am now talking about politicians, are continually suggesting decisions to cope with the results of other decisions which have turned out quite differently from what was expected. We do not plan, we do not say what is going to happen.

CB   And is there a governing manipulative force behind this?

DL   No, I don't think so. But I do not see humanity as the great crown of all creation. Let's put it this way, we are sending rockets at this moment around Jupiter. Why do we assume that we are the only people with technological knowhow when the astronomers and physicists talk in terms of planets, many many hundreds of thousands of inhabited planets. I mean it is not some lunatic novelist who is talking. The novelist now cannot keep up with the physicists in what they say.

CB   Isn't there a danger, though, that if you accept this view you are in fact advising people that there is no point in playing a role in the social world or indeed in attempting to intervene in history at all? You are inviting them to be supine in the face of violence.

DL   No, I am not. Certainly I would never have anything to do with politics again unless I was forced at the point of a gun, having seen what happens.

CB   Early on in your work you were interested in the problem of the individual's relationship to the group, that is you had a conception of the individual as apart from the group and then negotiating his or her relationship with it. But isn't individuality without meaning once you acknowledge sheer determinism?

DL No, I don't see that at all. I mean this is a very ancient philosophical debate. Can you have free will if God has planned everything? Well the answers to that, as you know, have been going on for centuries, particularly in the West.

CB But your view has changed, hasn't it, because even in the 'Children of Violence' series at the beginning Martha Quest is very much the focus of the book: things are filtered through her sensibility. But in the last volume, which I presume you hadn't actually predicted when you started writing the sequence, we move through catastrophe to a situation in which Martha Quest disappears from the centre of the novel, and she disappears because the situation has changed fundamentally and she exists only insofar as she serves the perpetuation of the race in some sense. It is the sheer survival of the group that becomes the important thing at that stage. The individual has been reduced by the impact of history.

DL But she has lived her life and has influenced events and individuals.

CB Yes, but in the context of a deterministic move towards catastrophe. In your later books individuals seem to be admired to the extent that they realize that their chief function is to submerge themselves in a generality. You talk about moving from 'I' to 'we', as though a state of being 'I' were in some sense undesirable, something to be transcended.

DL I am really not chopping logic. I think that the individual is extremely important. I think the individual is more and more important in what we are going into, which is horrific. I do think that what matters is evolution. I think that the human race is evolving probably into something better through its usual path of horror and mistakes because when have we ever done anything else, when has history ever shown anything different?

CB So history isn't pure pathology; it reaches some kind of critical point of regeneration.

DL I don't think like this. I find it very difficult. You keep saying things are different from each other. You see it as either/or. While there is something in me which I recognize is uniquely me, and which obviously interests me more than other things and which I am responsible for, at the same time I have a view of myself in history, as something which has been created by the past and conditioned by the present. And when I die I will have left something, for good or for bad, not because I am a writer but because I am alive. I wrote that essay in *Declaration* in the mid-fifties but this was at a time when I was preoccupied with the relationship between an individual and political groups because all the people I knew at that time, or nearly all of them, were political in one way of another; they were either communists, or ex-communists, or Labour Party. Also, don't forget it was just after McCarthy in America and I had a lot of American friends and they were very preoccupied with the way they had either given evidence to the Committee or had refused to give evidence. This whole problem of the individual and the group was very strong at that time and in that particular form.

CB   And particularly with you because you had yourself been involved in one form or another with the Communist Party for some time and left it in 1956, but not because of Hungary.

DL   No, it wasn't. I decided to leave a long time before. What had happened was that I joined informally in 1953 and I think it was a fairly crazy act, actually, looking back, and also pretty unimportant because I was very little involved with the British Communist Party. And it was only because of conditions at that time inside the Party that it was possible for someone literally not to go to meetings, because I said I wouldn't go to meetings. The morale of the Communist Party was at an extremely low ebb of course. These were called the black years in the communist world; these were the last few years of Stalin when absolute mayhem was going on anyway in the Communist Party. I was very much involved with people who knew what was going on and they were my friends and it was another example of how difficult it was to stand out as an individual against groups. People who are so involved in events were my friends and that is why I thought it an act of solidarity joining something that I thought was awful. I think it was a fairly pathological action. It is one of those things I regret really. But I didn't have any part in the day-to-day communist movement, though there was a thing called the Communist Party Writers' Group which met irregularly and casually in a way I've got a feeling that King Street would not have approved of.

And I was emotionally a communist in Rhodesia, where there was no communist party because the then legal system wouldn't have accommodated one. We created a highly romantic, idealistic, rather marvellous thing which had no connection at all with anything around us; it had no connection with the Africans, very little with the white people, who regarded us as completely crazy, because everything about us was alien, chiefly because we were interested in ideas. I don't know what Zimbabwe is like now but at that time Salisbury was an extremely philistine town where people were interested in sport and sundowner parties. And what happened was that there was an invasion of refugees and the Air Force. Many of the former were intellectuals from various parts of Europe who were appalled at what they found themselves in. And those in the Air Force had been educated in ways that most Rhodesians were not, so what we created was really, looking back on it, a combination of a social group and a kind of intellectual refuge for a lot of people who were very displaced. And it was extremely exciting and I learned a very great deal from it. The amount of work we got through no one would ever believe. For two or three years there was a hardcore of I suppose about 20, and perhaps in Bulawayo and Salisbury it didn't add up to more than 40 or perhaps 50 in all. We ran all kinds of societies and clubs, the Left Club and debating clubs and the Beveridge Club, anything you could mention we were in. We had to read a lot of things, we had to do lunatic things like sell the local communist paper around Salisbury. Can you imagine a couple of earnest females on bicycles turning up outside a villa in a Salisbury suburb with the communist rag approaching the white Mrs and saying, 'Excuse me'. Never had this occurred. And they just looked at us. Well the other thing that we did, I described this actually in *A Proper Marriage*, I think, was, when selling the *Guardian* down the coloured quarters, we got involved, we became social workers in fact.

CB But you are saying that really there was never an involvement with the Communist Party as such, or never a kind of passionate commitment to the Communist Party. You either had your own idealistic group which you called 'communist' or you joined in London but didn't actually involve yourself in its day-to-day activities. Does that mean that you didn't subsequently feel either the sense of guilt or the sense of bitterness that usually came to people who left the Party at that time?

DL Well you see I wasn't emotionally committed to it in the way some of the people I knew were; it was their family, their God, their life. I was never that much a part of it, so what I missed, at that particular time when I left, was being out of the company of people who knew what was going on and talked about it because a barrier came down. You instantly became a baddy, well not so severely then because things had softened considerably. I wasn't a traitor so much as a lost sheep. I did miss that but the thing was that everybody, in quotes, then left the Communist Party. Another interesting thing that has happened is that ideas which, when I was young, were the most seditious, impossible ideas which you were hounded for, and people wouldn't speak to you because of, have now become such a commonplace on all levels, that you find them in the leaders of *The Times*; this is the spread of ideas.

CB   There was a time when you accused Beckett and others of making what you called 'despairing statements of emotional anarchy' and you said that 'the pleasurable luxury of despair, the acceptance of disgust, is as much a betrayal of what a writer should be as the acceptance of the simple economic view of man', and you identified both of these approaches as a kind of false innocence. Is that a view that you would hold now, and what exactly is the writer's function then if that isn't his function?

DL   Well, I don't hold those views now. About the simple economic view of man, of course I hold that, that was a specific statement about a communist view of literature. About the other I don't remember. You see I don't remember the emotion that made me write that, I don't remember why I said those things about writers that I admire. So that has gone. But about what the writer should be, I think what any writer should do is to write as truthfully as possible about himself or herself as an individual because you do not write about an individual, you can only write about a lot of other people because we are not unique and remarkable people. And over and over again I have had the experience of writing sorts of themes that I thought were quite way out and I have discovered, simply by the letters I get, or because ideas that hadn't before surfaced then surface all around you, that I have been on a fairly low-class common wavelength. Over and over again I have written ideas down that shortly afterwards have become commonplace. I am saying it exactly like that because I don't want to make it sound something high class, I don't think that. But I do think I have sometimes a sensitivity to what is going to come in five years time, and it happened with *The Golden Notebook,* for example, when I didn't know I was writing what I was writing.

CB   When you made that comment about Beckett you also said that the writer must become a humanist, feel himself an instrument for change, for good or bad: 'it is not merely a question of preventing an evil but strengthening a vision of good that will defeat evil'. That puts enormous weight on art; art becomes an instrument for good in some way.

DL   You see I wouldn't say that at all now because I don't know what good and evil is. But the way I think now is that if writers write truthfully, write really truthfully (it is very hard you know to be truthful, actually) you will find that you are expressing other people. I do believe that to be true.

CB   You have had a sense, and you were mentioning it earlier, that the human mind in some sense is changing, or the way that we perceive reality is changing; you were suggesting that this might be a result in part of advances in physics. Does that really filter down to the individual, or in what other ways is our sense of reality different now, being perceived differently?

DL   Well, I don't think it is filtering down as fast as it ought, and I think the reason why it doesn't is a fault in the education system. I am not talking so much about the discoveries in physics, the new ideas in physics, but sociological ideas, some of which are quite shattering in their implications. And they should be taught to children. I think the child should be taught that you may easily find yourself in your life in a situation where you can behave as Eichmann did — I am using Eichmann simply because he is a symbol for mindless obedience. Eighty-five per cent of all people, it has been proved, can be expected to behave like this. You may find yourself in such a situation and you must now think about it and prepare yourself for such a choice. In other words, give children choice, don't let them be precipitated into situations that might arise. And then there is this whole business about thinking and acting as an individual instead of as a member of a group because we now know that very very few people, a negligible number, are prepared to stand up against a group they are a part of. This has been proved over and over again, by all kinds of experiments; if you put a certain number of people together, people will do anything rather than stand out against it. And it explains, for example, why certain advances of knowledge get accepted with such reluctance. We have discovered a whole armoury of facts about human nature since the Second World War. Because of the events of the Second World War and the horror of the Second World War and what we discovered human nature was capable of, research has been going on in universities all over the world into this field. We now know what we are really like. There is also a great deal of knowledge about how groups function.

CB   It seems to me actually that that is a running theme in your work, the need to escape the definition that has been offered to you as a member of a particular group, a race or a country, or in some sense as a sex — the need to escape the type that is offered to you.

DL   Yes, well I think it is prison, we live in a series of prisons called race, class, male and female. There are always those classifications.

CB   But equally, I think, in the most recent books, you seem to be urging the breakdown of divisions within the sensibility as well, divisions between the mind and the imagination, the body and the spirit. Intuition, for example, which is usually treated with scepticism, becomes a real force. To feel something is not presented in your work as in some sense reductive, it actually has meaning. Feeling is a genuine response.

DL   It is interesting, you use the word feeling to cover both emotion and intuition. Because intuition has been banished from our culture emotions are spread to include it, whereas in actual fact I think there is thinking and there are emotions and there is intuition which is something quite different. It is fascinating, you see it on television for example, in God knows how many series. For example, *Startrek*. Mr Spock has no emotions and therefore he is handicapped, but the good earth people have emotions and therefore they are on a higher level. The word emotion has been spread to include intuition and this is how we get round it. Well I think intuition is not the property of women or of sensitives; I think everybody has intuition but, somewhere in the past, probably in the renaissance, there was an unspoken agreement to banish intuition. But none of us could operate for five minutes without it. I think we all use it all the time.

CB   When you talked about evolution did you mean the intensification of those abilities which have decayed. Are you actually anticipating the restoration of these abilities or the intensification of them?

DL   I think any human being can, if he watches and listens, use them now. It takes practice.

CB   Is that the appropriate moment to ask you about Sufi?

DL   Yes, it probably is. The reason I became interested in this was because I had to recognize that what I had experienced and what I was thinking and feeling had got nothing whatsoever to do with my philosophy. This happened when I was writing *The Golden Notebook*. Writing that book in the form I did forced me to examine myself in all kinds of ways. And, then, I was writing about things, experiences, that I had never had myself personally. I have had some of them since, let me tell you, but I had to recognize that the way I thought then, my philosophy, was absolutely inadequate. I either had to pretend that I didn't have the experiences I had, or thoughts I had, or admit them openly. I think enormous numbers of people do this. There comes a point where they have to make a choice and I think a lot of people

decide to forget it. Well, when I got to that point and I examined
how I was thinking, the whole progressive package (which is
shorthand for all the ideas the young people have now as if they
are programmed, which they are. They are all materialists, and
socialists and semi-Marxists or something of the kind and there is a
whole set of ideas that go together.) I decided I could no longer
live with it so I started looking around. Now the interesting thing
about that — I have described that in *The Four Gated City* — is
that I simply read extensively in areas which were regarded then as
quite cooky, though they are not so much now because in fact they
have got quite trendy. So I did an immense amount of reading and
I came up with certain basic facts. One basic fact was that our
education was extremely lacking informationwise. You could be
brought up in this culture and not know anything at all about the
ideas of other cultures. We are brought up with this appalling
Western arrogance, all of us. This is the reason I am glad I haven't
been educated because it seems to me almost impossible not to
have this arrogance if you are brought up inside the Western
education system. The other idea I came up with was that if I was
going to do this seriously, explore this area, it was a dangerous
thing to do it without a teacher; people go crazy and they go
wandering off, God knows what they don't do. They go off to
Katmandu etc. So I took a great deal of trouble. I am nothing if
not obsessive, perfectionist, and boring when I am faced with this
kind of situation, and I put a great deal of time and trouble into
looking for a teacher. I went through some experiences which
were quite interesting, making mistakes, and then I found Sufism
as taught by Shah, Idries Shah, which claims to be the
reintroduction of an ancient teaching suitable for this time and this
place. It is not some regurgitated stuff from the East or watered
down Islam or anything like that. And I read a book called *The
Sufis*, which I knew was on its way. I waited for it and read it and
thought simply, well fine, here we are, this is where I might find
what I am looking for because my ideas were there and no other
place; there was no other place for them. I did not want to become
a Christian mystic. I couldn't possibly be a Christian. I can't be
religious; I haven't got the religious temperament in the way it is
demanded of you. In parenthesis, again, Christianity is a very
emotional religion; that is its characteristic. In Hinduism you do
not have to be emotional. But Christianity demands an emotional
response and I couldn't do that. There are other things that
demand of you a totally intellectual response and I couldn't do

that. So what I have found is the beginnings of a way of looking at things which unfolds as you go on, and if that is an annoying phrase I can't help it. You discover all the time. It is very difficult, the thing is it is very hard, it is not easy, it is not an easy thing.

CB   You said that you couldn't be religious but is it pantheistic or does it posit some sort of ultimate being?

DL   Is it any help if I say, yes it believes in God? So what. Do you see the point I am making? Supposing I said it didn't believe in God? What then? I mean they are words. Supposing I said it believed in the Devil? These are words, they don't mean anything.

CB   But it does talk about oneness, doesn't it?

DL   Yes.

CB   Now is that oneness shared individuality. Is that the sense of the oneness, not actually a being external to the self but in a sense the aggregate of the selves. Is that what it means by unity?

DL   Perhaps I don't know either. I am still at the beginning of it. What you start off with is shedding prejudices and preconceptions. If I say 'mysticism 'or 'Sufism' I don't know what your particular set of associations is, but they are likely to be something like the Maharishi, Mantras, Yoga, chanting, dancing up and down and Islam, something like that, because that is the culture we live in. So you begin by shedding the ideas that you have, many of them unconscious. Let's take the word 'teacher', a teacher is someone who stands at the end of the room on a dais and he lectures to you; that is a teacher. But you see this is not a teacher as I have experienced it; it is something quite different, but it takes a long time, even when you have accepted that intellectually, to translate it into how you experience what is happening, because all the time, unconsciously, you are thinking 'Ah, one day the guru will announce to you, my child this is the truth.' Now I am caricaturing a very deeply-rooted psychological need and I was quite shocked to find how deep it is. One of the things that Shah says is that we are taught all the time in this culture that we are not conditioned, that we are free, that we have made up our own minds all through our lives about what we believe and that we are here as a product of various acts of will made throughout our life that we are going to be this and that. He will simply say I am sorry but this is not so and in actual fact you have been programmed to want authority, you want to be told what to do, you want a guru, you want something to belong to, you want rules. Now when he first says this to you, you say 'Oh come', but then you are put in a situation where you find out that it is true and very humiliating it is, because it is true, I did want all those things. Well, now, please God, I don't. But the thing is you learn to shed all the time, not through an intellectual process at all; all the time you are put into situations where you see the truth about yourself and it isn't at all pretty, actually. It is humiliating.

CB   It seems to me that *The Marriages of Zones Three, Four and Five* is actually suffused with this kind of thought. Isn't it about the breakdown of these kinds of assumptions, the recognition of a determinism?

DL   You keep talking about determinism. It is the opposite that I have experienced.

CB   Well, Al.Ith, the princess, receives a summons. It is a summons which really doesn't immediately operate on the conscious mind but on the subconscious mind. It is a summons which must be obeyed. There is no scope for denial. That is what I mean by determinism; her actions are determined quite apart from her own sensibility. Now isn't that what you were just talking about, the recognition of that determinism. And indeed the recognition becomes a kind of moral act; it is what you pay, it is what you owe, the recognition of an element of determinism?

DL   Well you see; in the first place I don't think that *Marriages* is a description of Sufi attitudes, I don't think it is unless what I have learnt has become very unconscious and has come out differently. But I am not at this moment qualified to judge, I really am not. One cannot judge the processes of sea change in yourself until later. In ten years time I might be able to say so but not now.

CB   But one thing that Al.Ith has to learn sounds very close to what you are describing. You are saying that the individual has to learn to see himself outside of the group, outside of that set of assumptions. This is what Al.Ith herself has to learn; she has to move outside the group in which she feels so much at home, and for whom she in a sense resonates. She has to move outside of that.

DL   I hadn't thought of it in those terms, but I suppose so.

CB   And the marriage which is contracted and the subsequent marriage, as there are two, isn't that the marriage of two people who are themselves being forced out of their set of presumptions? And presumably some kind of new quality is coming out of that, some third thing which pulls those zones together or breaks down the barriers between them.

DL   Yes, but let me do something different about this book. It was written out of this experience. When I was in my late thirties and early forties my love life was in a state of chaos and disarray and

generally no good to me or to anybody else and I was, in fact, and I
knew it, in a pretty bad way. Unconsciously I used a certain
therapeutic technique which just emerged from my unconscious.
What I did was I had a kind of imaginary landscape, which is not
identical to the one described, but I had an imaginary landscape in
which I had a male and female figure in various relationships. And
don't forget this was twenty years ago or so and this whole business
about what men are and what women are was a question of debate
and of course it still is. I made the man a man who was very strong
as a man, responsible for what he had to do and autonomous in
himself and I made the woman the same because I was very
broken down in various ways at that time, and this went on for
some years in fact. And then I read about it; it is a Jungian
technique. They tell you that if you have some area in yourself
which you can't cope with, to do this; you take some part of you
which is weak and deliberately fantasize it strong, make this part
different, make it as you would like it to be. So this book has come
out of years of the closest possible work of the imagination. Now
the fact that when I wrote it it turned out somewhat differently has
got nothing to do with it; this book goes right down into me pretty
deep. How and why I really don't know. This book is the result not
of any theories or ideas but of some pretty close work of the
imagination on my experience of the past.

CB   Why did you take so long to get round to writing it down if
it came out of that experience?

DL   I suppose it went underground and came out in this form.
It was marvellous to write this book, I really enjoyed writing it
because it was so easy and there is a level that I hit and I wrote it
out of that level. I knew perfectly well that I'd hit it and I enjoyed
it and I knew it wasn't going to last. It will never happen again.

CB   Can I revert to asking you a question about novel writing
and the structure of the novel? The 'Free Woman' section of *The
Golden Notebook* is a conventional novel but the book as a whole
is about the inadequacy of the conventional novel in that it is about
the complexity that has to be rendered down finally into a fixed
form. Isn't that reductiveness in a sense unavoidable, whatever
technique you are using? In that novel you were drawing attention
to the problem, but drawing attention to the problem doesn't solve
the problem. Is it a solvable problem? Isn't art always reductive?

DL   Yes, it is, but that is why we are all breaking the form, we
have to break it. The five-volume or three-volume realistic novel
seems to me dead, the family novel. Well, maybe it is not dead,

but I am not interested in it. I am much more interested in a bad novel that doesn't work but has got ideas or new things in it than I am to read yet again the perfect small novel. I read somewhere the other day that in 1912 in China when the civil war was all around they were still writing the most exquisite little poems about apple blossom and so on, and I have got nothing against exquisite little poems about apple blossom and I very much enjoy reading the small novel about emotions in the shires, but I do regard it as dead.

CB   Is that why you have responded so enthusiastically to science fiction. You said in the introductory note to *Shikasta* that it enables you to be both experimental and traditional, in a way that I suppose *Marriages* is because there is a recognizable traditional element there?

DL   I think that is a traditional book. I think it is almost a timeless sort of book where *Shikasta* is a mess, but at any rate it is a new mess.

CB   *Marriages* is, what, a sort of legend or myth?

DL   Well, yes. I have been fascinated with science fiction and space fiction because it is full of ideas. In science fiction the real scientist who writes it will produce some scientific idea and take it to its logical conclusion and say 'well, if you do this that will happen' and so on, which I find fascinating though very often I can't follow the science. And I am sure that this genre of science fiction has educated a whole generation of young people into thinking scientifically where they certainly don't get it where they are taught.

CB   In the prefatory note to *Shikasta* you seem to suggest that the novelist is driven beyond realism because reality itself has become more fantastic. I wonder if that is really the reason or whether, at least in your case, it isn't because you believe that reality is more dense, more profound, more various than we usually assume, in other words reality has not changed, reality has always been this. What has been failing is our perception of the fact that it has been this.

DL   This is true, of course, because our view of ourselves changes all the time, our views of ourselves, of humanity; we always have a different view. Sometimes this view is based on some kind of mythical framework, legendary framework, like people we describe as backward, or it can be based on fact. We like to think of ourselves as based on facts, but the facts are changing, are becoming so extraordinary.

CB   I don't know that they are any more extraordinary now than they used to be. For people who believed that the earth was flat it must have been quite a staggering thing to discover that it wasn't. I mean in a sense contemporary reality is much less extraordinary than that. We are now attuned to absorb almost anything within very rapid time. It becomes part of our world view. A few hundred years ago it would take a century to get people to accept things.

DL   Yes, that is true I suppose. Things have speeded up so fast, they have speeded up and I don't think that we can cope with it. There is a point I want to make about writing, or telling stories. It is a thought that I can't come to terms with, which is why do we tell stories? What is the function of the story-teller? We never stop telling ourselves stories, it is the way we structure reality; we tell stories all day don't we? And when we go to sleep we tell each other stories, we tell ourselves stories because a dream is a story, maybe sometimes very logical and straightforward and sometimes not, but there is something in us that needs stories. Well I heard someone on the radio the other night say that the dream is a way of reprogramming our minds. Well, this is a theory, it is not anything more yet. But when somebody sits down to write a novel, well what are we doing? We don't know what we are doing. Why do we have this need? Why does humanity have this need? We might just as well have a need to do something else, I don't know what, jump up and down, shout 'Eureka', but we don't. We tell stories all the time. It is a strange fact isn't it?

CB   In fact story-tellers play an important part in *Marriages* don't they? The narrator is a professional story-teller, that is, his cultural function is a story-teller isn't it? A singer of songs.

DL   I wanted one voice so I had to think who was likely to have that one voice. I couldn't have either Al.Ith or Ben Ata because they were too partial, or even my lovely servant, who I adore.

CB   You have an interest in the realm of the subconscious, do you not, and to some extent what is now called paranormal. Now that is not just as metaphor is it. You mean that literally?

DL   Yes, literally. Well I mean it is what I have experienced and what a lot of other people have experienced.

CB   Telepathy, for example.

DL   Yes, I have experienced telepathy but then I think a great many people do. I think we are probably at it all the time without knowing it. I think ideas flow through our minds like water all the time. But my interest in the paranormal is not as kicks. I used to be terribly fascinated but now I think more soberly about it. I try and use it in a very quiet, sober sort of way. For example, I keep a diary where I note down the odd events, like coincidences and things, that I think are going to happen whether they do or not. I am quite objective about that, I don't make things up. I use dreams all the time. I have done since I was a child. I use dreams in my work because I get ideas or I get warnings in my dreams about people or situations. I don't know if that goes under paranormal or not but humanity has been using dreams ever since it was born.

CB Moving to your more recent books, there are constant images of devastation, but on the other hand humanity seems to come out the other side of that devastation. It was true, of course, of *The Four Gated City*. But in the latest books you move towards, what, a simple faith isn't it, a kind of declaration of faith in something not fully perceived? Obedience to some sort of cosmic will?

DL I don't know about obedience, do you choose to have obedience?

CB But I think you use the word 'faith' yourself. That is what finally they are left with.

DL I thought a lot about putting that word in because it has got religious connotations.

CB What is it they are believing in, then?

DL Well, look, you see the thought that came out of was this, that never, since the history of man began, has there been anything else but disaster, plagues, miseries, wars, yet something has survived of it. Now our view is of course that we're onwards and upwards all the time. I just have an open mind about all that. I do wonder if it is true. But I do think that if we have survived so much in the past we are survivors if nothing else, and if nothing else we are extremely prolific. Has it ever occurred to you how prolific we are; we are worse than rabbits. We just breed; the world is full of babies. Well I like to think some of them will survive, perhaps even better. Also, is it possible that the radiation that we are going to inflict upon the world might make us mutate? We don't know. There is now a theory that the dinosaurs died out not because of a shift of climates, so that they couldn't stand the cold and the vegetation, but because of a different kind of radiation. I mean we are bombarded by different kinds of radiation. Neutrons pour through us as we sit here, did you know?

Well, you see, we don't know what else pours through us and how we might react to a different kind of medicine.

CB   So this is faith?

DL   Optimism.

Iris Murdoch

Iris Murdoch was born in 1919 and educated at Badminton School, Bristol, and Somerville College, Oxford, graduating in 1942. During the war she was Assistant Principal in the Treasury and an Administrative Officer with the United Nations Relief and Rehabilitation Administration in London, Belgium, and Austria. From 1948 to 1963 she was a Fellow of St Anne's College, Oxford and a university lecturer in Philosophy at Oxford. Since 1963 she has been an Honorary Fellow of St Anne's. Iris Murdoch is an honorary member of the American Academy of Arts and Letters and a member of the Irish Academy. She is a recipient of the Black Memorial Award and the Whitbread Literary Award. She is married to the writer and critic John Bailey and lives in Steeple Aston, Oxfordshire.

Iris Murdoch has called for a 'renewed sense of the difficulty and complexity of the moral life and the opacity of persons'. Her work attempts this particular task by balancing a realist account of character, milieu, and social relations against a sense of the mysterious, the deforming power of the imagination and a fascination with the plots which people create for themselves as an analogue for the real.

Her first novel, *Under the Net* (1954), which she herself is prone to undervalue, is concerned, among other things, with the space which opens up between the world of tangible realities and the conceptualization of those realities. She has repeatedly claimed that she is not a philosophical novelist despite her career as a teacher of philosophy, but the nature of reality and the means whereby it may be apprehended and verified remains a central concern of her work. Her characters are frequently shown as being trapped in a moral world from which they would willingly break free if only they could find the right mechanism, if only they did not grant some final authority to values which at times they affect to despise. And human relationships are the agents both of moral demand and release; they are the clue to a necessary definition of reality, public and private. In *The Red and the Green* (1965) the messy personal relationships parallel the confused political relationships in a novel set at the time of the 1916 Easter Rising in Dublin. Love, confused, at times humiliating and entrapping, nevertheless remains a central fact and primary moral agency in her novels.

Iris Murdoch is fully aware of the ironies involved in the processes of writing, of spinning fictions in the name of truth, trapping thought in language, sculpting contingency. Indeed at times this becomes her subject, as it is, in a sense, in *Under the Net*, and as it clearly is in *The Black Prince* (1973) and to some degree in *The Sea, The Sea* (1978). And this is not simply an expression of contemporary self-doubt, a concern with acknowledging the degree to which art is implicated in the contingent world which it describes. It is because the making of fiction is coeval with the making of history, the elaboration of private meaning, and the invention of a self.

Iris Murdoch is a prolific writer, producing twenty books in a quarter of a century. The range of subject, of approach, of style is considerable but there is an underlying continuity. She remains concerned with the struggle of her characters to deal with the dual problems of creating a life, constructing a coherent response to a world which presents itself in a series of tangible realities and moral dilemmas, while at the same time avoiding the facile consolations of simple fantasy and dream. The moral drive rests on her insistence on the primacy of the real and the obligation to distil its essence from the flux of events. In terms of personal identity it lies in the need to distinguish role from character. Sometimes the mechanism of release is humour, sometimes a commitment to values desperately invoked. The act of reconciliation may take place in the imagination, as in a sense it does in *A Word Child* (1975); sometimes in a gesture of resignation or self-abnegation. There is no single path to truth or the kind of integrity which on the whole her characters admire and long for. Their actions are hedged around with ironies, self-deceits and betrayals but the will remains alert if not quite intact, determined to make some sense of random experience. And if this image is not untouched by absurdity there is a certain dignity and even courage in a responsibility which can never wholly be discharged, a commitment which is often defeated because it is not wholly acknowledged for what it is.

Interview with Iris Murdoch

London, 5 December 1979

CB I want to start by asking about your philosophical position. You were once strongly influenced by existentialism — I think you said once that that was what drew you into a concern with philosophy — and also, to some extent, by Marxism. Why do you find those unsatisfactory now?

IM Well, they are very different cases. My Marxist phase, when I was an undergraduate, was really just part of a general political attitude. I didn't really regard Marxism as a philosophy and indeed it scarcely is one. And now, of course, my political position is quite different, and I am critical of Marxism in many fairly straightforward ways. If you regard it as a philosophy it is a very jumbled one, not at all without interest, and of course, not without importance. But that wasn't part of my philosophical life at all, really. I didn't originally intend to be a philosopher. It was the war that brought this about in my life because I wanted to go on studying at Oxford and I wanted to become an art historian or archaeologist; that was my ambition. But of course one was conscripted and one wasn't able to pursue one's studies. When I began to think, I didn't know what I was going to do, except that I wanted to be a writer. I was always quite clear about that. At the end of the war it was a very, very exciting time and existentialism was part of that time. I always loved France. I was very interested in France and getting back to contact with France for me was very much existentialism. I met Sartre actually in 1945 and I got hold of a copy of *L'Etre et le Néant* when hardly anybody else had managed to get one and things like this. So that was part of that excitement and then I'd studied philosophy at Oxford and then somehow I began to see myself as a philosopher. So it had that influence in that sense, but I don't think I ever was an existentialist. I think that my objections to existentialism went right back to my first meeting with it.

CB How would you characterize your philosophical position at the moment?

IM Well, it has developed a great deal I think. I mean it sounds rather grandiose to talk about one's philosophical position, and it is very difficult to have a philosophical position.

CB Not if you are a philosopher.

IM   Well it is, even for a philosopher it is difficult. But granted that this may sound over-important or not too clear or something, it is not easy to do this briefly, I think probably the major influence on me, philosophically speaking, when I was younger, was Wittgenstein. I was a graduate student in Cambridge — unfortunately I just missed being taught by Wittgenstein — but I met him and I lived, in terms of philosophy, in the aura of his work and I knew a great many of his disciples and this, I think, is a continuing influence. I am still within that world and I think the work of Wittgenstein has still got many things even to be discovered about it and I think that he was a great philosopher. So that travels with me, that particular sort of — I think it is misleading to call it linguistic philosophy because that has come to mean an awful lot of other different things since — that particular sort of philosophical attitude travels with me. Also, I think very slowly over the years I have become much more interested in religion, I have become interested in Buddhism, and I've once more become interested in Christianity, not in a dogmatic sense. I hold no dogmatic religious belief at all, but I feel now close to certain religious attitudes which are most easily expressed in Buddhist terms for me, though I am not a Buddhist. It is very difficult for Western people to be Buddhists, perhaps. But at any rate I wouldn't think of myself in those terms but it is expressed by Buddhism in a non-dogmatic, non-supernatural sense of spiritual life. That is something which is different from morality if one thinks of morality as excluding this sort of dimension, and of course many philosophers have spent a lot of time trying to define morality in terms which do exclude this dimension. I mean these are difficult questions but I think that Plato has meant a great deal to me, but I didn't understand Plato when I was an undergraduate and even when I started to teach Plato at Oxford — I taught Plato and Aristotle for quite a period — I didn't understand him. To pretend to understand him now is, of course, ridiculous because a great philosopher is never understood in that sense. He is always beyond one in a way. But I feel very close to certain aspects of his thought now and I did write a very short little book about him a while ago. I think that something to do with the aspiring and religious aspect of Plato's moral philosophy is very congenial to me.

CB   Is this a sense of reaching for some transcendent reality, reintroducing transcendence?

IM   Yes, it is to do, if you like, with reintroducing the concept of transcendence, and let me add here, if you don't mind me talking still about this, just to complete the picture, the other philosopher who has travelled with me, certainly since I was an undergraduate, is Kant. I feel again also extremely close to Kant's thoughts and Kant and Plato, of course, are in many ways contradictory to each other, or incompatible with each other. So that this is the sort of philosophical picture as far as I am concerned. My main interest is in moral philosophy and in explaining morality in a philosophical sense which I feel can't be done without the reintroduction of certain concepts which in the recent past have been regarded as metaphysical in some sense which made them impossible.

CB Does that mean that the character of James in *The Sea, The Sea* contains a position or represents a position that in a sense you would endorse?

IM Oh no, no. I mean James is a lost soul really and is too mystical ...

CB Too mystical?

IM ... In a precise sense, that he is pictured as a Buddhist and interested in the magical tradition. I mean he represents — this is a theme that I treat elsewhere in the books — somebody who has in a way sold out to magic. I think he is a spiritual being and as such, of course, he is incomprehensible to his cousin. Nobody understands James in the book, but he lives in a demonic world, he is a demonic figure and he has got the spirituality of somebody who can do good, but can also do harm.

CB So is that the distinction you make elsewhere between fantasy and imagination; he is a fantasist in some way?

IM Yes, one could say that. He is a complicated fantasist because he is a religious one. I mean he is not just fantasizing in an ordinary self-centred way, he is somebody who is really hooked on the absolute; he has got a religious passion but he is also in love with the magical aspect of religion which of course is anti-religious. This is one of the paradoxes of religion that it is partly magical, but that in a way magic is the greatest enemy of religion.

CB And yet in a sense in that book it is presented very ambiguously, that is the protagonist himself half believes in the magic, in fact half believes that he saw something that was indeed magical.

IM Oh, I think that something paranormal happens in the book, but I see no difficulty about that. I think that paranormal things do probably happen, particularly in Tibet. I think that this is just a fact that certain kinds of concentration can produce paranormal powers. The reader has to lend credulity to the writer I think in a quite harmless sense, about pulling him out of that pool and so forth. I mean whether any Tibetan could really do anything like that I really don't know, but I think one should think of it as having actually happened, that is that Charles is not mistaken in thinking that James hauled him out, and James did haul him out.

CB   By standing on the water?

IM   Yes, or something, yes.

CB   You've urged the novel itself as a place where freedom can be exercised, a house for free characters to live in. But isn't the novel in some ways an image of determinism, more even than the play, in that the play is available for some kind of modification which may be quite radical?

IM   Well, I think that the good artist builds indeterminism into his determinism. Of course in some sense any work of art is a closed object.

CB   Some are more closed than others.

IM   Some are more closed than others but if there isn't a closed object there isn't a work of art present, I mean there is a happening or some other kind of emotional disturbance. A work of art has got to have a form, it has got to have notation, it has got to have something which is fixed and authoritative, it must have authority over its victim, or client or whatever you can call the person who is meeting it. This of course is a principle which is now very much disputed and even attacked but in this sense I am an authoritarian. I want the work of art to stand and have authority and to be able to endure. Again the notion that it should endure is criticized by many now, and a character in my first novel raised this question long before it was raised elsewhere. I mean Hugo thought that one should make fireworks because they didn't endure. This was long before Barthes and Co. had ever appeared on the scene. But I don't hold this view; I think the work of art should have a very strong internal structure. This is a problem for every artist to decide how he does this but I think it is a problem he has got to solve artistically. On the other hand, the novel, particularly, is such that within this closed structure you can picture free beings. Look at Shakespeare, Shakespeare is the king of this whole business, I mean he is the king of the novel, he is the greatest writer that ever wrote and if one thinks how those plays combine an extraordinarily strong form with the cohabitation of these characters who are so independent that they were strolling around in real life as it were, they are strolling around in our minds as independent people.

CB   But where does that freedom come from?

IM   Well if you are raising the general question of whether any human action is ever free that is different kind of question isn't it?

CB   Yes, the reason I raise it is because you talked about free characters and I wondered in what sense they were free and where that freedom derived from.

IM   Well I am pointing out a distinction with which I think, if you see what I mean, you are bound to agree — I say confidently — that is between people that we think of as great novelists in the nineteenth century — and let's leave aside rubbishy, structuralist criticism of Dickens and so on, I mean I have heard such nonsense talked by structuralists. I'd better not say who this is, but one distinguished person said to me, 'I hope to make it impossible for my pupils to read Dickens.' Leaving aside nonsense of that sort and thinking in an open-minded way of the great writers of the past, say the nineteenth-century novelists, Shakespeare, one of the things that strikes one is the ability of these writers — say Tolstoy, Dickens, Shakespeare — to create characters who have got such inner strengths that they seem to be self-determined, they don't seem to be determined by the author. Contrast say Lawrence; Lawrence is a great writer and a genius but many of Lawrence's characters are not self-determined people, they are Lawrence-determined people and for this reason I think this is a fair criticism of Lawrence. I mean if you think of *Lady Chatterley's Lover*, for instance, where Mellors is Lawrence and Chatterley is wickedly treated by his author and made to look a figure of fun and so on all for the benefit of Mr Mellors. I think these are faults, these are aesthetic faults in the work. This is not a house of free characters; I mean this is not a novel where these people have any kind of self-determination. Whereas in *War and Peace*, for instance, or in a play by Shakespeare, or in the better plays by Shakespeare, because he didn't always write at his best, the characters are so substantial, they are so imaginatively created, this seems to me to be where the word imagination comes in. This is the work of imagination, to create things which are not just part of one's mind in a narrow sense; they are as if they were separate from one's mind, they are different, they are not projections of me, they are entities on their own and they relate to each other in a free way. Now Clifford Chatterley is not related to Mellors in a free way; he is related in a way which is entirely determined by Lawrence's cruel and ferocious prejudices.

CB   But even with Shakespeare they may be the embodiment of abstractions, say of evil, for example, with Iago.

IM Well, Iago is an interesting case. If Iago was just an embodiment of evil I think we wouldn't be so interested. But Iago's psychology can be very much argued about. I have heard people in Oxford arguing quite passionately about how one should see Iago. I mean he is so wicked. If you make somebody very wicked I think you do raise difficulties for yourself because I think it is hard to see what might seem to be wanton wickedness as personal. Iago's wickedness is not altogether wanton; I think there is a lot of psychology in it. If you really look at that play, if you really look at all the lines, if you really look at all the things that happen you can make quite an interesting argument about Iago's psychology.

CB But you could argue that the characters are trapped within a cosmology.

IM You mean the speculations about Shakespeare's religious beliefs and that kind of thing? It is remarkably hard to speculate about actually, isn't it? That is what is so great about Shakespeare. The same is true of Tolstoy at his best; it is very difficult to see exactly what the author is thinking. Shakespeare's plays are extraordinary in that they present a very strong moral world. This has been denied of course by, for instance, eighteenth-century writers who didn't see Shakespeare in this light. But they were wrong. There was a tremendous moral charge in these things. It is morality at its most refined, and at the same time it is not dogmatic, it has got an element of extraordinary openness in it. It gives this amazing atmosphere both of moral judgement and of poetic freedom.

CB You talked of yourself just now as an authoritarian but isn't *The Black Prince*, for example, an attempt to work against those authoritarian principles within a work?

IM The thing is *The Black Prince* has got its own inbuilt mode of explanation. It is made pretty clear in that book how you should interpret the wanderings and maunderings of a narrator and where you should believe him and where you should not believe him. I think this is true. The epilogue is just play. I mean it adds, pretty clearly, further comments on the characters of the people who were in the story but I think it is quite clear what you are supposed to think. In that sense the authority is there. But any novel contains this sort of mystification where the reader has to move with the author from perhaps a straightforward portrayal of character to a more indirect mode of narration where the character is giving himself away. I mean obviously any novel contains this device where the character is saying something which the reader is supposed not to believe.

CB So that you have a model of reality which is not problematic? There is a manifest reality which the reader will penetrate?

IM Yes, I think so. An author may leave certain things puzzling deliberately. These things are play, just play. Take an example from a novel I have just finished (this is terribly minor, it is not of the slightest importance), it just occurs to me as an example, there is a character who appears at intervals and it is never clear what the sex of this character is. If this was a main character this would be important, but it is a minor character so this is just a joke. Now if somebody said what sex was the character I can reasonably reply I don't know, in fact I have an idea what sex this character is but it doesn't matter. As far as the novel is concerned the character is of indeterminate sex. Jokes like this are one thing but deliberate and total mystification, a willingness to hand over the interpretation to the reader, is another thing and I don't want to do the latter.

CB You have written for the theatre as well as writing novels. Do you find that a play is a less authoritarian form in that it is available for mediation by directors, actors?

IM Yes, I don't want to let them do much. I want to have authority over them too. Well, I think I am better at writing novels, I know how to write novels now. It took me a long time to learn but in some sense I think I know how to write a novel. I don't know how to write a play and therefore of course it interests me because I like to learn. I think the reasons why people can't write plays are probably quite various. The thing is, in an abstract sense, it would seem that I ought to be able to write a play because I can invent plots and I can write dialogue. Now there is something else of course which a play has which isn't covered by these two headings and that is the thing which I can't get right, and I am not quite sure what it is. I think it is something to do with the structure of the play, though that would come into the question of plot but not altogether, it isn't quite plot, it is something about dramatic structure which I can't do. But the thing challenges me really because it is more like poetry. Now I am a poet manqué. I have been writing verse all my life and I think I have probably written about eight poems, I mean I constantly beaver away writing poetry and trying to get that right. But that is another question, that has nothing to do with the play thing except it is an analogy, that the charm of writing plays is like the charm of writing a poem for me.

CB   Because you have to condense?

IM   Yes, because it is a tremendously condensed object, it is a magical object. I mean a novel is a magical object, too, but a play is much more obviously a magical object. It is an enchantment, it has got to be a magical object or people aren't going to sit in a theatre three hours. There has got to be some immediate spellbinding quality which is more, in my mind, like writing a poem.

CB   The theatre seems important to you as an image, as well. I notice that in a number of your novels your characters have a theatrical background which perhaps is offered as a clue to the role-playing that is constantly going on. It is there in *Under the Net* and to some extent *The Black Prince*, and there in *The Sea, The Sea*.

IM   Yes, but I think it is different in these cases. I think in *Under the Net* it is a play really, it is part of the playful aspect of the book. In the *The Sea* it is perhaps more important because that is about *The Tempest* in a way, it is about Prospero and theatre is a great magical thing which you then have to give up and it is about giving up magic. And you see James and Charles are parallel cases of magic. I mean Charles has spent his life in magic in the theatre; James has spent his life in magic, in religion. They never, of course, understand each other and in a way James's problem can be seen as the same as Charles's. Charles's is an attempt to give up magic, to give up power and of course he doesn't succeed, he just gets himself into a complete mess because he is not a spiritual person. He is not even a particularly good person. He can't get things right. James, I think, has apprehended his own problem about giving up magic, that is that he wants to die, to die well, he wants to release himself from the wheel. But I think that he is deeply afraid that he has enmeshed himself too deeply in the magical side of religion. And then of course he has to do this thing for Charles which involves summoning all his magical power at a moment when he wanted to get rid of it. On the other hand, and this I think is a deep thing in the book, which no critic will ever see, but I will tell it to you, in a way I think James could be thought of as having saved himself because he goes on in the book, he says things to Charles, about how in order to be liberated you mustn't have any emotional attachments. Now the deep thing of course is that James has always been in love with Charles and this he more or less says at one point (and again nobody notices this kind of work in a book) and this is what is worrying James. This is why he comes to see Charles, he wants to get rid of his attachment to Charles and say goodbye in a friendly way, as it were. Then this thing happens where he has to save him and James — this isn't displayed I think in the book — he may have thought I really am done for because I have enmeshed myself again in this affection. But I think that the action itself sets James free, that having done this thing — remember he is very exhausted afterwards — I think he realizes that somehow or other the magic itself has broken its own spell or that he is going to be let off. This isn't a particularly Buddhist idea but one could imagine ...

CB It sounds more Christian.

IM It sounds more Christian in a way but I think that at any rate one should picture James as having escaped from the spells, that when he is sitting there dead and smiling he actually has escaped, and that he won't be in *bardo** being tormented by the demon. I think this is a terrible image of the nemesis of living a life of tormented anxiety and demonic imagining that this would go on. *Hamlet* picks up this idea: in this sleep of death what dreams may come, when we have shuffled off this mortal coil. This could be one's fate but I think that James escaped from that. And I think, incidentally, while we are talking about this book, one or two people wrote to me saying well of course James wasn't really dead was he? He really was in Tibet or something. No, I don't think one should think that. Now what were we talking about before I started off on this particular line? Oh, yes, roles, the theatre and role-playing. I don't believe I do think that people are constantly playing roles like that.

CB But they are trapped in fictions. Charles is trapped in his own fictions.

IM Oh yes, people are trapped in fictions. I think I would rather talk of this in terms of art rather than of theatre because theatre is just one kind of art and for me the role idea doesn't do very much. That is, as far as theatre comes into the novel it plays a different role in different books. Again you ask a philosophical question, you asked one earlier about the freedom of the will and now you ask one about the basis of morals.

CB You seem to equate moral sense with common sense. Is there a natural morality, which is instinctively perceived?

---

*A reference to states of being intermediary between this world and Nirvana as described in the *Tibetan Book of the Dead*.

IM   Well this is where this Kant-Plato contrast comes out. I don't think anybody knows the answer to this question really. Kant's moral philosophy rests on the idea of recognition of duty and the notion that this is a rational thing, that it is something which everybody can do, and that the unconditional nature of duty is something which is self-evident to every rational being, in fact to every human being if they are not mad or something. I am inclined to think this. This, of course, is a very unpopular view now; all kinds of ethical relativism are popular. So this would be a kind of common-sense idea and I think in a non-philosophical way some of the people in my books want to say this, that it is perfectly obvious what you want to do and if you fudge around and say well it is all very complicated and so on you are evading something. And, of course, the desire to evade what is obviously one's duty is a very deep human thing, I mean one is always being caught by this desire to evade something which in a way you also think is obvious because even the mind is so divided against itself. And this would be another Kantian image of the mind, absolutely divided against itself. This would be one way of looking at morality and one which would involve a metaphysical assumption, in a sense. I mean Kant's moral philosophy is metaphysical in that particular sense, it is one way of being metaphysical. You see another image which attracts me and which is rather different is a sort of platonic image, the notion that the good is very, very far away and that, this would be more of a religious picture, one's task is to transform oneself, to discard selfishness and to undergo a very long process of conversion.

CB   That is the process of many of your books in fact isn't it, discarding?

IM   Yes, though nobody in my books ever gets anywhere really, or gets very far with the process. It is extremely difficult, there aren't any saintly people — there is only one, to speak of another book — there is only one real saint as it were, or symbolic good religious figure in the books and that is Tallis, in *A Fairly Honourable Defeat*. This would be an image which isn't common sense but rather a religious image, that one has got to change oneself very fundamentally. It is an original sin kind of image, too, the notion that one is almost irredeemably selfish and must try to do something about it. Philosophically speaking these may be incompatible views, but I don't think really they are in ordinary life, and this is how we live. We live by these conceptions we have and in moral arguments you do come to these points where something is self-evident to one person and not to another. And it is very difficult to produce reasons. If you think about this ghastly business of the hostages* and so on, I mean there are things which seem to us self-evident, such as that you can't treat people like this, it is contrary to some natural law to do so. But this doesn't make any impression on the ...

CB   But doesn't that acknowledge that in some way values are culturally derived?

IM   Well of course they are culturally derived. You see one has to say all these things in a context. It is rather like the argument of freedom of the will in that one has to admit that, for instance, now a great many things which people do are excused because we know the psychological background to them which makes us regard them no longer as responsible actions. All the time one is balancing what one can find out about history and the human mind and all these things, these factual things, one is balancing these against these other factors which are to do with things which seem self-evident, with natural law, with a conception of human nature, with certain religious ideas, and so on. This is the human condition, there isn't any alternative to this as far as I can see. One is always fiddling around with these different elements both in philosophy, of course, and also in real life, which is much more important than philosophy.

CB   Doesn't this approach presuppose a continuous self, a self which is not subject to discontinuities, disjunctions?

IM   Don't we assume this?

CB   Well, I am asking you if you assume that to be so?

IM   Yes, I do. Again, problems arise about responsibility. 'I wasn't myself when I did it' could be something you said in a law court and somebody would let you off because you showed what you meant by this, that you were under the influence of drugs, or that you were tremendously under the influence of another person and so on. I mean these are things that we fiddle around with. In making a moral judgement you have to take into consideration a lot of things. A particular case is so particular. This is why novels are interesting objects; they explain particular cases in very great detail.

CB   But your sense of an absolute responsibility of the individual suggests that you haven't drifted very far away from existentialism.

IM   Oh, no. There are different kinds of existentialism but Sartrean existentialism, which is the kind I know most about, separates the individual so much from his context and from any sort

*A reference to the holding of American diplomats in the US Embassy in Iran.

of moral framework which is independent of his will that it either makes his responsibility absolute or it abolishes it. One could look at it either way. I never thought that it was a satisfactory notion to say each person invents his own values. There is some sense in the idea in some contexts but we enter a world where there are things which we discover and these things are discovered, not invented. It may be very hard to say what one means by the word discover, and this is where all these problems about transcendence and so on come in. This is very deep water, but I think the Sartrean picture is so simple and in so many ways seems to be so unrealistic and I think, morally wrong. You see one is also making moral judgements on philosophy. One rejects a philosophy because it seems to advocate things which one's own moral sense will not accept. I think that existentialism does advocate a sort of irresponsible self-centred kind of luciferian attitude to the world. It can also of course be useful as corrective against what Sartre called *mauvaise foi*. I mean Sartre is so — the same is true of Roland Barthes, incidentally — Sartre is so anxious to abolish bourgeois sanctimonious taking for grantedness of certain values and so on that he wants to suggest that everybody has always simply invented values. You see the word bourgeois crops up again in Barthes and I think it would be best to abolish the word bourgeois from this argument because it raises other problems — and to talk about people who just accept certain conventions which suit them and never criticize them. Such persons should be stirred up and made to realize that they don't have to believe these things; they choose to believe them, they ought to criticize what they are doing instinctively. But I don't think that this suggests the only possible philosophical image, that of somebody who is simply inventing his values, because discovery about the world is very closely connected with the evolution of the moral person and I think the word discovery is very much in place here. One is just not inventing it out of oneself, one is finding it out for instance by observing other people, and from art and from all sorts of sources.

CB   In 'Against Dryness' you rejected a particular model of liberalism but urged the creation of another kind which was a post-Kantean, unromantic liberalism with different images of freedom. Isn't that actually in a sense a description of your own work. Would you accept the label liberal?

IM   Yes, I mean 'yes' very roughly answers the question. I am not sure now, I can't remember that essay very much, it was a long time ago and I am not so sure that I'd put it like that now. I think it is very important that politics has got a complicated relationship to personal morality; they are not absolutely hand in glove, these systems as such. Most obviously, of course, it depends how you see personal morality, but looking at personal morality as I would look at it, I don't think this is far from what people actually believe anyway; there is nothing very eccentric about it. There is some very absolute demand which is made upon one in personal morality, that one has to think this thing out in one's own heart and there is a moral demand which won't go away, which is always there. This is what Kant would say, what Plato would say, and, I think, what the chap in the street would say, actually, if he hadn't been corrupted by some pseudo-philosophy.

CB But not what one of the writers whom you admire would say: Samuel Beckett?

IM I admire Beckett less than I used to, I confess, perhaps we will come to that in a minute. But politics has got to be a different game because governments are fighting for their own people and if a head of state gave up fighting for his own people and said I am going to fight for mankind so I don't care what happens to our fisheries policy, or whatever it might be, then he would be rightly told to go away. I think politics has got a built-in ruthlessness, an individualism, which is unavoidable and which does clash with certain moral views and this is one of these paradoxes. This is why liberalism is always in a fix because liberalism wants to combine the most high-minded sort of morality with a political ideal and this is absolutely OK in certain areas of thought; for instance, I would think, in everything to do with freedom and human rights. This is the glory of liberalism in that it puts this thing absolutely in the centre and makes it one of the compulsory aspects of any political policy. But also there are all these problems about what it is possible to achieve and whether you should cooperate with a state which has a wicked policy. It is all very well to say that Americans should never have cooperated with the Shah (the Shah incidentally was at least amenable to influence and change and so on — the regime improved, it was better about women for instance). Countries do have to support sometimes a wicked regime out of reasons of self-interest, and out of the kind of complicated reasoning that goes into politics. So that liberalism is a complicated creed in this sense and this thing that I said, about inventing a post-Kantean unromantic liberalism, I don't know how I thought this could be done. But to talk about literature for a moment, I think that I felt at that time that probably we had had enough of the romantic hero in the existentialist sense. I think part of this was directed against the existentialist romantic hero, the kind of rather dreary chap who is against society, who is a rebel and who is a solitary chap inventing his values every day and so on. He is rather idolized by certain kinds of literature and I think I was fed up with that hero and I don't like that hero, and I don't want him in my books. He might be said to be in the first novel and not in the next, I am not sure. But at any rate if that is a literary comment then it is about the existentialist hero.

CB   Does this mean that you see literature as having primarily a moral function?

IM   No, its function is art, forget about morality, its function is to be good art. This will of course involve morality absolutely one hundred per cent. If you are writing novels, you can't avoid morality. But if you are making a pot or something I can't see how morality comes into that.

CB   So a novel excluding a moral world is an impossibility?

IM   Well I think people have tried to write such novels, but I think the artist has got to decide this. I think his first duty is to his art and I think it probably is possible to write novels which exclude a moral world but this, in an odd way, can't help having a moral dimension, what you exclude. What are you thinking of for instance here, have you got any examples in mind, Beckett for instance?

CB   Or Robbe-Grillet.

IM   I don't think Robbe-Grillet excludes a moral world. I don't know, the only one that I have read lately, well I have only read two of his novels, I read *La Jalousie*, which I admired, and I read *Les Gommes* which I thought was a stunningly good novel. It is a detective story and it is very good. I mean somebody who wanted to make an exercise in literary criticism could try comparing it with *Edwin Drood*. It is totally different and yet not utterly different. *Edwin Drood*, of course, has a tremendous moral thing and evil and so on; the Robbe-Grillet thing has got morality in it actually but I can't think of an image here. It is like a picture where the things are made by very, very fine lines which you could hardly see; it looks as if the lines are doing something else, they are delineating something else when in fact they are actually delineating this thing so that morality is there in this book. He couldn't do it you see if there wasn't a moral background; the detective story wouldn't exist. I mean it is about the failure of the detective and then there is the suggestion, I don't know whether this is poor mystification, I couldn't understand this, or whether if one worked hard enough at it one would see what it meant, there was an implication of a connection of the detective with the story which isn't manifest. Somebody who is murdered is connected with him in a way which doesn't appear. This is a frightfully good novel but the thing is its the background of conventional morality which gives it its force. I mean it is absolutely electric with power, that book, but if you thought that the whole world was totally non-moral it wouldn't be interesting. You wouldn't be interested if somebody had been murdered for instance. Morality arises in the judgement of the reader on this work. He may think that this is so ...

CB   So it is moral because the reader exists in a moral world?

IM   Well it is moral because the writer exists in a moral world. If he uses his artistic ingenuity to deny this then the denial is of interest but it is of moral interest. I mean he can't escape from morality. It is a big thing to say that he can't escape from morality, but I don't think that is the mode of escape. There are people who recognize non-moral demands. You may say that Camus tried to do this but the force of Camus's book is that his hero of course is living in a world where people's moral responses are ordinary. All right you may say well let's have no ordinary people, let's just have these persons who are portrayed in terms of momentary figments, with no sense of continuity. Well I would think this would seem to be a morally eccentric person that is being portrayed, perhaps a morally wicked person or at any rate a morally unrealistic person, and the interest of this would be the moral judgement and I don't think that this would be just the reader's reaction. This would be something which the writer couldn't avoid delineating even negatively by what he writes. That is, what is he denying? Is it that he wants to deny something which other people want to assert? I think there could be a kind of poetic stuff, and I think Beckett sometimes comes close to this, which is sort of hygienically demoralized as it were, and if it is poetic enough ... I think that *Watt* might be thought of in this way. I don't like Beckett's later stuff, I have read some of the French stuff and I don't think this is very good.

CB   Are you talking about his prose or his drama?

IM   Prose. Drama is different, drama has got to be magic anyway and I have only seen *Waiting for Godot* and I think that works very well as theatre. The French stuff seemed to me to be rambling and just not good enough, just not bloody good enough, to do what he was trying to do, it wasn't poetic enough. I thought, and I think he should have gone on writing in English. I think he pays a penalty there. But if one takes *Murphy*, that is really an ordinary novel, an ordinary romantic novel written by some sort of very remarkable writer and very funny writer. The interest of it is partly the touchingness of the girl, the touchingness of the old man, the kite flying. Murphy's own character has got a sort of charm about it and one feels a kind of mixture of pity and exasperation in relation to him. And then, of course, the funniness which is frightfully important. *Watt* I think is an odd case; I haven't read *Watt* lately but if you are looking for an example of a novel which has really given up the ordinary world and yet still tells a story, I think it is possible there, partly because of a kind of metaphysical philosophical game which he plays in the book. I wouldn't deny that it is possible to do something like this. I don't think it is necessarily worth doing. I think it is frightfully difficult but I think certain curious geniuses would be drawn to it and I think that Beckett can write frightfully well. I don't think this is anything to do with what literature is about or anything of that sort.

CB   Why is story important to you?

IM   Well it is important to everybody. I am just an ordinary human being, I like stories, we all like stories. It would need a lot of explanation to suggest why there shouldn't be a story. I happen to like plots and also I think a novelist ought to have a plot. If he weakens his plot he has got to have something else. That is just an aesthetic judgement. I think plot is a very important part of novels and if one produces a lot of marvellous characters and a very shadowy plot, then OK jolly good luck. I think the average novel needs both plot and character, plot and character help each other along.

CB   A number of your protagonists are themselves plotters, that is to say they create coercive fictions, and that is true of *The Sea, The Sea*, which has a man who has an image of the world and then forces other people actually to inhabit those fictions and play them out.

IM   Yes, I think that is something which human beings do. This is an aspect of power which interests me. People force rules on other people and the other people like it. This is the important aspect of it very often that people want to admire somebody, people elect somebody to be their king and a group of people — I mean I have seen this happen quite a number of times — that somebody gets a kind of inflated reputation, they are given the role which they then play. For instance everybody is afraid of so and so or so and so is dictatorial and he suddenly says 'Look you have got to come and see me tomorrow' and you come however inconvenient it is. And people like this, they like to be bullied by some kind of quasi-fiction which they set going in their own environment.

CB Do you see any connection between the coercive plotters in the novel and yourself as a coercive plotter, a writer of fictions?

IM No, because it is quite different. I mean what the people in the novel are doing is working out their fantasy life in terms of some sort of pattern which suits them and I very much hope that I am not doing that. Of course any writer is tempted to — art comes out of the unconscious mind and there are bound to be personal obsessions and images which are around the place. If there isn't any force from the unconscious you haven't got a work of art so that the force is something you must thank the Gods for if it is there. The rational intellect is also involved. I have got no shortage of the stuff from the unconscious; it is rather a matter of sorting it out and preventing it from following patterns which it wants to follow. So the intellect comes in very much to prevent it, say, from being too coercive, to prevent the plot from being coerced by unconscious forces.

CB On the other hand, if it makes sense to talk like this, there is an element of coercion over the characters. You were talking earlier about Lawrence as, in effect, a coercer of his own characters. That presumably is a risk.

IM Yes, I think every novelist runs this risk and one hopes not to do it. I think some of my earlier novels do this. I hope I have improved; one likes to think this. Lots of people sometimes madden me by saying I thought *Under The Net* was quite your best novel, and of course it is not good news to a novelist. I hope I don't do this. I think perhaps I was unfair to Nan in *The Sandcastle*. I coerced Nan. And this is perfectly clear, it would have been a far better novel if I had spent more imaginative time detaching Nan from the story and not letting her just play the part of this rather tiresome wife but making her somebody with quite extraordinary ideas of her own, playing some quite different game perhaps, having some dream life of her own which is quite different from that of the other characters. This would have been an obvious way to mend this novel and make it better.

I think that one has just got to watch out and not to do this, not to belittle characters for instance.

CB   But you could, quite apart from characters, say that there is a kind of totalitarian element in art in that it commands the imagination and the attention of others. Without doing that it couldn't exist.

IM   Yes, it couldn't. If it didn't attract attention and maintain attention people wouldn't enjoy art. One terrible speculation about the future is that people will stop enjoying art, partly because they will be sitting looking at television all the time, partly because artists will destroy themselves. They are destroying themselves in front of our eyes, painters are destroying themselves, writers are destroying themselves.

CB   In what sense?

IM   Well they are stopping making authoritative objects; their desire to do it is weakening. I have noticed this with young people.

CB   That was the point in a sense I was getting at, that they are afraid of that totalitarian element in art because they are afraid of it in society.

IM   Well yes, totalitarianism is a nasty word, of course. Authoritarian is now a rather nasty word too but the old-fashioned art object, as it now perhaps begins to look from some points of view, is a creation of a strong mental impression of some sort, something that has got form and this form is art. Without some kind of strong form there isn't an art object present. If the reader or observer can do anything he likes with the thing then one result, of course, is that he becomes bored, he doesn't want to have it there. This is why in the Tate Gallery you have had these pictures which are just blank pieces of paint which for some reason are revered and people have paid money for. This is a degradation of art and it is a contemptible sort of thing which people support and respect and daren't say anything against.

CB   I suspect that one of the reasons why people claim the significance of *Under the Net* is that it anticipated a number of things that subsequently became fashionable, that are fashionable now, postmodernist doubts about the status of language, for example.

IM   Oh yes, all the stuff that Barthes and Co. think they invented. I knew all about that in the 1930s.

CB   However, I am interested in that because Hugo says language is a machine for making falsehoods and it seems to me that elsewhere in your work there is a kind of suspicion of articulateness, that is your articulate characters are often the most egotistical characters.

IM Yes, well the anti-art artist occurs here and there because he is an interesting figure. Bledyard is an anti-art artist in *The Sandcastle*. But this in my world is complicated by the emergence of religion as the competing factor, not anything social, not anything personal, but something religious. For, sometimes, for some people the religious claim runs counter to the artistic claim and counter to the claim of artistic form — like Charles giving up the theatre, giving up the world. Religious form is different from artistic form, and a certain sacrifice is involved. The idea of being a great artist I think is a great moral ideal but it needn't present itself so to everybody. The anti-art artist is an interesting figure to me because he becomes in the later novels a religious figure. I mean Tallis is a religious figure. Tallis of course is nothing to do with art, that is a religious allegory incidentally, *A Fairly Honourable Defeat*, and Julius King is the devil in person. Tallis is a high incarnation. It doesn't matter if nobody sees this but it is there, it is very much there in the dialogue actually if you look at it carefully. Julius doesn't at first see that Tallis is a high spiritual figure, he just sees him as a fool, then he suddenly recognizes that he is up against his own adversary here. Whereas Tallis recognizes Julius at once and this conflict then happens and even a sympathy between them because they are both spiritual beings in the middle of a non-spiritual world. Here in the figure of Tallis there is the religious thing which is nothing to do with art at all. Julius is an artist, he is a mathematician and he is interested in art, and he is an aesthetic figure, whereas Tallis is an absolutely non-aesthetic figure. This conflict just brings in this business about the status of art.

CB But there is, is there, that suspicion in your work of articulateness? I mean at another stage you say, or one of your characters in *The Black Prince* says, that being is acting, what redeems us is that speech is divine. So that on one hand speech is falsehood; on the other hand speech is a kind of redemptive force.

IM Yes, what interesting remarks I sometimes make. OK I suppose that means that speech is falsehood and art is falsehood and yet there is a religious way, as it were, to the divine which rests in these things. And one might ask the question is there any other way? I think there is another way in the sort of Tallis sense, in the sense that people who are simple, who are outside this refined business, are in the game of helping other human beings. But for people who have got mixed up in art very deeply, I think that this can be a kind of temptation to them, a moral difficulty.

CB   You commented on the tendency of art to console, in a sense a dangerous tendency, but isn't that exactly the function of your own novels, don't they move towards a kind of conciliatory resolution, a sense of balance at the end?

IM   Oh, I think art consoles, I don't see why not. The thing is to console without telling lies. One tries to be truthful — I think the word truth is very important here — art must be connected with truth, in some sense a truthful picture. Of course it is art, it is complicated, it is full of mystifications and it's funny, which I think is very important about the novel, it should never be forgotten. A novel is a comic form. A novel which isn't at all comic is a great danger, aesthetically speaking that is. It is very difficult to do this without losing something absolutely essential. If one thinks of the great novels, you may remember the tragic parts but my God how comic, for instance, Dostoevsky is, frightfully funny, how funny Tolstoy is too. But of course one is creating a work of art here and that has got its dangers. You have got to keep some sense of truth in the centre of the thing. Then you are also creating something which people will really like in some way. I am very pleased if people read my books and think what a good story, I want to know what is going to happen without bothering about any of the intellectual refinements which might be there, or the other things which might be there. I think to be consoled by art is absolutely OK. In a way it is the highest consolation, good art is the highest consolation — well it is not the highest, I think things to do with human love are the highest consolations — but it can be so high, that good consolation. It is not like watching television, it is different, it is high consolation, and that's all right.

Angus Wilson

Angus Wilson was born in Bexhill, Sussex, in 1913 and was educated at Westminster School and Merton College, Oxford, graduating in 1936 with a degree in medieval and modern history. He served in Intelligence during the war, this providing a brief hiatus in his career at the British Museum. Having worked in the Reading Room from 1937, he became Deputy Superintendent in 1955. He then became a freelance writer and lectured widely, being appointed Professor of English Literature at the new University of East Anglia in 1966.

Angus Wilson is the recipient of a number of awards, including the Black Memorial Prize and the Prix de Meilleur Roman Etranger. He is a Companion of Literature, a member of the Royal Society of Literature and a Commander of the British Empire. He was recently knighted. He lives in a small Suffolk village near Bury St Edmunds.

Angus Wilson was identified at the beginning of his career (which began when he was already in his forties) as a brilliant, if brittle, social observer — a witty satirist with a skill for mimicry which was both precise and malicious. It took some time for him to shake off this reputation which was built, essentially, on his early collections of short stories, *The Wrong Set* (1949) and *Such Darling Dodos* (1950). In fact, though he has never lost his incisive humour or his imitative capacity, his interests quickly broadened beyond a concern with placing his characters socially and morally with a precision which was part of the pleasure of writing.

The move from short story to novel invited a more engaged view of the human personality, a more humanist account. And though, as he explains in the following interview, he felt a profound suspicion of the manipulative intent and patronizing tone of the assertive liberal, his own 'gentleness' (his own word) balanced the occasional sadism of a portrait rendered so completely as to appal by the depth and extent of its revelations.

As many critics have observed there is a nineteenth-century feel

231

to his work. The plots are complex, dense with characters, events and meaning. The social world is so important to the task of locating his characters and identifying the moral dilemmas which they face that he feels obliged to elaborate that world. That he is highly selective in the tradition which he is prepared to acknowledge and claim is evidence both of his awareness of the nature and subtlety of that tradition and of his own sense of the literary world which he is constructing and thus in part validating.

There is clearly an extent to which Angus Wilson is a social realist who sees moral values as generated by the world which he describes. But he is also aware of the contingency of that world. The parodies of *No Laughing Matter* (1967) are a clear indication of his own awareness of the constraints which face the writer and the games which he plays in order to evade those constraints. If he is drawn to Dickens it is not because that writer is a reassuring piece of literary tradition, a witty observer of the public world. The Dickens whom he admires, and to some degree emulates, is Dickens the innovator, the experimentalist, the writer aware of the constant threat of deconstruction which confronts the author and his characters. And a certain self-doubt circles around Wilson's own liberal commitments. Clearly *Hemlock and After* (1952) presents the obverse side of the humanist commitment to individual freedom, to the liberation of the artist. The act of writing has a coercive quality which he suspects and which he thus exposes to view. And his liberalism is under pressure from another direction. The sheer density of his novels, the kaleidoscope of characters who parade before the reader, hint at a complexity of experience invulnerable to analysis, a perception of the real which, for all its apparent realism, hints at levels of experience just beyond the line of vision of the observer. The point of rest tends to lie in a moment of moral balance, of poise, deriving from an intimate connection between individuals, or, in a work like *The Old Men at the Zoo* (1961), a vital nexus between the individual and the natural world. The latter seems to offer both a resource and a principle of continuity. In the accompanying interview Wilson suggests that it may also be evidence of a growing misanthropy and certainly the social world is dramatized in that novel as being in a state of collapse. But against this must always be set his wit, his sense of the deep comedy of human affairs, which, if it can move moral seriousness to the point of collapse can equally redeem the bleak and the denatured.

The pressure is always on in his work; characters are placed under social and psychological stress of a kind which implies something about the nature of the culture which they inhabit. Their personal absurdity, portrayed, for example, in *The Middle Age of Mrs. Eliot* (1958), betokens a dislocation taking place on more fundamental levels. The spiritual vacuousness, sympathetically handled, of some of the characters in *Late Call* (1964) reflects that of the New Town in which they live. The personal and the public deceits of *Anglo-Saxon Attitudes* (1958) are proposed as in some ways paradigmatic. But then so is the urge to set things right.

Clearly Angus Wilson observes a society which is no longer homogeneous, as once it seemed to be, where barriers of class and sex are dissolving. And just as his early works observed individuals unable to rely on social position, money or a natural deference to find their way through life, so in a more recent book, *As If By Magic* (1973), he dramatizes the lives of other people trying to adjust to a sudden social viscosity, a world in which the rational and the irrational are no longer comfortingly held apart. The homosexual fantasies which play a central role in this book, constitute the release of energies formerly kept suppressed, or expressed only obliquely. But there remains a sense of moral behaviour, a sense of the need to act as though values survived even if the evidence for those values is not strong. And though he continues to doubt those who seek to impose their own moral certainties on others, to resist a patronizing insistence on redeeming the individual for ideals themselves only vaguely perceived, he remains liberal in his determination to locate freedoms which are not those assiduously prepared for him by others, in his respect for the distinctiveness of the individual, in a moral drive which continues to generate his fictions, in his commitment to possibility.

Interview with Angus Wilson

Bradford St George, Suffolk, 9 March 1979

CB   You have called yourself a liberal humanist. Could you say something about the evolution of your political and moral convictions.

AW   Well, I suppose I should begin with my family life. We lived in a kind of genteel poverty but my mother would never acknowledge it. And I suppose that as a young boy I thought of that as being what right-wing politics were, an attempt to assert we are genteel people, we are really a better class than you think we are. And so I came into school time ready for getting rid of this endless genteel phoniness which had surrounded my whole background. To use one example: we live in hotels so we must go abroad once a year otherwise people will think we aren't as well off as we would like to appear, though in fact we weren't well off at all. We'd go to Boulogne and on the boat back my mother would say to me, from the age of about twelve to about fifteen, she would say, 'I don't think there is any point in mentioning Boulogne, it doesn't interest people. You know that day, Angus, when we went over to Le Touquet, now that is a place people are interested in. You should say we were in Le Touquet.' And then she would look worried as to whether she had said something that might be morally wrong to teach a young one: 'It is not a lie you know, it is called a white lie. It is just making people realize the kind of people we are.' So this kind of perpetual thing made me, I suppose, look on the right as a pretense and something nothing to do with us anyway. Well then, of course, came the thirties, and this is the time, I think, nobody can understand. They must understand the degree to which I, at any rate, my friends at university and at school, supposed that this war would come and we would all be gassed and that there wasn't much time left and we must stop it. And so there was Abyssinia, and then there was Spain. There was involvement and I veered for a time towards pacificism. And then I decided this was no answer and I worked with the communists though I never was a communist. I don't say that just for self-protection; I just never was. But I belonged to the organization that Sir Stafford Cripps ran and so on. I was quite left wing and did a great deal of demonstrating. I did a lot of marching down in the East End to protest against the fascists coming there into the Jewish quarter and walked in processions saying 'Hitler's war on children' and 'Scholarships not Battleships' and other muddled things continuously. I was very active in the left and when I got to the British Museum my junior colleagues there were lefter than I was and I was brought into the act.

CB   But in a sense in the 1930s liberalism as such was out of vogue. It was a time dominated by deterministic philosophies.

AW   Indeed, indeed. I did history at the university and I suppose that I took it for granted that even though my teachers were Tories they taught us on what was a Marxist basis. They accepted this version of progress and this concept of class change, and so on, and I think I swallowed that pretty whole. I was, however, extremely suspicious of the role of the Communist Party in Spain, I will say that for myself, and so I was prepared for some kind of suspicion about this whole left-wing thing. However, I can literally say this is true, that when we got the Labour Party in power in 1945, I heaved a sigh of relief and thought well, I don't really need to do any more of this political work. We have done all we need to do; Utopia has arrived. And I have often said this, and it is true, that one of the reasons why I started writing was that my interests had been political, social, and amateur acting, but amateur acting seemed to me a disgusting thing to do when you were in the mid-thirties, and the political seemed to be over —we had got the Labour Government and social change. And at that time I was living out in the country and that is how I began to write. But ingrained inside there, (I suppose, it had grown up inside there since I had left behind the Christian Science my mother had brought me up in) was an ethic which was deeply connected with the importance of respecting human feeling and giving rights and concessions and acceptances to minorities, of being rid of patronage, a rejection of all the things by which my family had maintained their very precarious sense of gentility. This is deeply ingrained and I suppose also there is the sense that you ought to be on the side of the weak, the sense that power, and those who have it, are to be regarded with deep suspicion. This is still there in a novel like *No Laughing Matter,* or in *Magic* even. I am deeply suspicious of Lord Godmanchester in *The Old Men at the Zoo,* and people are rightly suspicious of those in authority and those in power. And you must remember again that throughout the thirties there had been this absolutely appalling national government, so-called, and, to we young people with leftish or liberal sympathies, it seemed somehow that it would never come to an end, and that is why it seemed like Utopia in 1945. And so, yes, I think there was this sense that one was on the side of the weak, on the side of the underprivileged, and so on and so on. But there was, along with this in my work, a deep suspicion of those who accepted their weakness. This has grown and grown, and it was there even then. I would say that a lot of the development of what you call liberal humanism has been something which begins with a satirical attack upon the whole false basis, as it seemed to me, of society, followed by an attempt to understand those who are weak or those who in some way or other have lost — Mrs Eliot and so on. And increasingly I would think a deep suspicion of those who live by being 'professionally a minority', those who go round with grudges. Perhaps that is rather strange.

   CB Is your liberalism today of the same kind?

AW   No. Let me take an example. You see, when my mother died the people who had most influence on me were very rich, well pretty rich, left-wing people, or rather, professedly left wing. They were business people and they were cultivated people. In those days I was very much drawn towards E.M. Forster. It's in my rejection of those surrogate parents rather than my own parents, in my rejection of the rich left-wing parents, that in a way I think I have rejected Forster's work. It is my absolute horror of the degree to which, in his apparent embracing of his concern for those who are weak, those who don't have, those who are underprivileged and so on, that I find he can be so totally rejectful of human beings. Forster has been a very important point for me. I can swallow, now, *A Passage to India* but *Howard's End* is my idea of the book I really almost detest most. There are certain passages in that which I can't bear: for example the daughter-in-law of the Wilcoxes, Olly Wilcox, a foolish woman no doubt, but he says about her, 'she was a stupid little thing and she knew it'. Now the concept that somebody can go round and be quite happy, that they can go round all their life and he didn't think that you should take them seriously, that he could accept that someone wouldn't be desperately unhappy if that was so, disturbs me. And then there's another passage in which he is talking about that clerk, Leonard, when he says that he had once had a marvellous experience which was when a Cambridge undergraduate spoke to him in a train!

What I think happened to me, after I had started writing but in the last twenty years, has been the rejection of all my parents. It was beginning, after all, with *Darling Dodos* and with other stories in the first books of short stories, a total rejection of the absolute underlying unconscious tenets of the cultivated liberals of this country. This is perhaps why I felt able to write about Kipling and why I was excited and interested by Kipling, and the thing that I fear, and it hasn't happened with me, is any movement from there into some kind of right-wing radicalism. What has happened is that coming to live in the country, perhaps, old age, I would think, probably being abroad a lot and therefore getting used to being with different groups of people and involved with groups of people, becoming intensely interested in architecture and painting, becoming a gardener and subsequently extremely interested in wildlife, I think I am very much less attracted by human beings than I used to be. I like meeting new people, people that I won't have to see very often. There are just a few people that I am very very fond of and with those I have deep ties, but that kind of humanism which typified me when I was between thirty and fifty, I would say, when I really did feel the only thing I cared about was making relationships with human beings, finding out about them, what they were doing, what they were and so on, has gone. I'm browned off with that enormously and this is one of the reasons why my books have been more concerned with form than they used to be because form has become more important in many ways than people.

CB But at the same time, several of your early stories and your novels offer a critique of liberalism.

AW Yes, indeed they do, such as *Darling Dodos* and others.

CB What seems to you really to have been liberalism's worst failure?

AW Patronage.

CB Patronage?

AW Intellectual and spiritual patronage, I think.

CB Does that include the desire which a number of your characters had to set things in order, both for themselves and usually, of course, for other people?

AW Yes, they are the inheritors of the old evangelical busybodying nineteenth-century world and I've got that side to me, but I think that when I was like that, or when I was involved with that, I didn't realize quite what it implied in terms of other human beings. I was often described in those early days when I wrote as being a do-gooder; I certainly agree with J.B. Priestley when we were talking about this, that this is better than being a do-badder, but it is the sublime lack of realization of what you are up to that accompanies this. I suppose from the very beginning my books have been about introspection and self-enquiry and they have usually, as you know, taken the form of somebody looking back and saying 'How did I get to be like this?' The inner conscience and so on. As I went deeper and deeper into this, not just with myself (because not too many of those characters come straight out of myself, very few of my characters) but with various human beings (always bringing it back to yourself as you must do when you are writing about a principal character), as I began to do that more, I became less and less satisfied with what I felt to be the easily established tenets of the liberal humanistic code of behaviour towards other people. I don't know whether I have been unfair to Forster, it is hard for me to say (he came here once to see me and I have met him many times and he was always very nice) but all the things that I am ever told about him do suggest a kind of opting out and a kind of patronage. And indeed the whole of that homosexual business with the working classes which is so typical of his generation. To me there is something deeply disturbing about this. A man who could go and live in King's all his life. It seems to belong to that kind of patronizing squire thing.

CB   But are you also worried that liberalism implies a degree of detachment which can actually be dangerous? *The Old Men at the Zoo* seems to suggest as much.

AW   Every kind of political attitude gets a blow in *The Old Men at the Zoo,* but certainly you are right about Simon in that. Yes, it is detachment, of course. The Fabians are another example of this kind of thing. I am revolted now by the Fabians. It is hard for me to quite get down to this because what comes in my mind now is how I always detested Bernard Shaw's attitude to human beings and always felt it was without any emotive capacity. I really thought him without any real emotive capacity, certainly without any possibility of identifying with other human beings and I used to hold Forster to be the opposite end, but as the years have gone by I have come to see them as being two opposite pictures of the same thing. And then, if this doesn't sound to be very contradictory, and it clearly is paradoxical, this realization, this feeling, this alienation from those people, because I feel that they are not sufficiently engaged with human beings, has grown upon me as I myself have found human beings rather more indifferent to me.

CB   You seem to me to judge those people who want to boast a conscience but don't want to push it to the point of action, but you are equally critical, particularly in something like *Hemlock and After,* of those who do push it to the point of action in that then they are tempted by power.

AW   Yes, indeed, yes indeed, I mean I detest it. This is probably why I am inclined towards abstraction, but of course I can't accept abstraction. I am much too deeply involved, I wouldn't be a novelist otherwise, much too deeply involved with people. And so you will see, for example in Hamo in *Magic,* a comic attack, I hope made with some kindness and feeling, upon a person who feels he can remain apart from human beings altogether, and who thinks that with sex, for example, it doesn't matter what he does because he pays for it. I could never accept this kind of standpoint, I couldn't accept it. I have not discovered, and I don't suppose I ever shall, the point where I feel that real human engagement takes place and how far it can take place with more than a limited number of people. I think again this has something to do with liberal humanism. Good God, I am thinking about the early nineteenth-century now, if you think of what people did to other people then, or indeed in Germany in the concentration camps, or Russia, yes, this very, very deep concern for one's treatment of other human beings is a vital thing. But I wonder how far a person who is an artist and a person who is writing novels which are to involve you deeply with human beings, how far you can establish a general principle because real involvement with human beings is not something which can be made into a general code. And the trouble about it being treated as a general code is that it may end, and I think it does end, with many of those liberals we are speaking about, by becoming only a general code and not a particular code.

CB Yes, in fact it seems to me that in your novels you very often associate liberalism with emotional myopia.

AW That's right, emotional anaemia, I would say, yes I would say so, very much so. On the other hand that doesn't mean to say that there isn't another very horrible kind of thing, which is the love of pushing people around. That can happen by the way also with Fabians and liberals. I mean I don't know whether you have read my play *The Mulberry Bush*, but one of the charges made against the old people there is that they push people around and patronize them. The things are not inseparable though. In fact, they may be closely connected. I suspect that to be Lord Godmanchester in *The Old Men at the Zoo* you have got to be about as dead to people as you would if you were going to be a do-gooder.

CB But that raises the question of whether humanism in the English novel doesn't become a kind of class prerogative, a middle-class stance.

AW It was in its day.

CB I mean your principal characters tend to be writers, artists, academics.

AW Yes, I write about the middle classes. In my new novel there are some people who are nearly into the aristocracy. I suppose I know a little bit more about that world. I began to meet people from the upper class, if you like to speak of such a thing, when I was in my late thirties and I have come to know a lot more since then, so I can take in a bit of that class and I can write about what are called working-class people, but primarily I really only know the middle classes and even that is a broad assumption and claim isn't it? I have never been someone whose novels have been unconnected with society. I see everything in societal terms but the fact remains that as I get older, I am less and less convinced that one can make any meaningful noise which goes farther than a very few people.

CB   But to take this point of class further, you are very sensitive in your novels about class.

AW   Well I was brought up in a deeply class-conscious world.

CB   I notice that very often when some of your middle-class characters want to soften a remark they tend to adopt a cockney accent. Do you think that paradoxically the British class sytem constitutes a kind of source of kinetic energy for the English novelist which isn't available to the American writer for example? Is it actually a resource that the writer can draw on in this country?

AW   Yes, I am sure it is. I was going to say is it any more? But I think that's not true. I think that despite popular journalism, despite television, despite all the general bourgeoisification of the populace at large, these class things do continue, but much less in younger people than in people of my generation. So whether it can remain for much longer a real kinetic force in the English novel is more dubious to me. I am interested to see, with someone like Malcolm Bradbury, that he finds his power and energy comes from seeing things within a section of the community in which these same things are reflected, but aren't any longer class relationships but various kinds of professional relationships. But the class relationship will remain for me enough, quite frankly, for the rest of my life. I wouldn't like to think it makes my later novels old fashioned, and indeed as you have seen in *Magic,* I felt very much the need to go outside England simply as a kind of cocking a snook at this. I don't know whether you saw that little speech I made which was very unpopular, when I gave the Booker prize. I abused novels that we had read in great number, and said they had all been deeply praised by the newspapers, and I thought this appalling because they were so narrow and seemed to consist entirely of NW3 and whether a husband, who was a television executive, had had it off with the au pair girl or not.

CB   This is the Hampstead novel?

AW   Yes, and I think that's the final dead end of the old class novel, and I think that's perhaps why I tried to go outside, further.

CB   Do you find that your books are read differently in America than they are in this country?

AW   Well, I can't answer that because I don't really know.

CB   But you have taught in America haven't you?

AW   Yes, I have never taught my own books. I have never taught my own books anywhere.

CB   So you have no sense actually of what an American reader perceives in these class terms?

AW   No, I don't know. I know about the American student faced with it in novels that I have taught, English novels. It isn't non-existent in the States, the whole class tension.

CB   It is just that the meaning for example of a middle-class person deliberately slipping into cockney must be difficult to perceive.

AW   But then I don't see America as being different to any foreign country in this way. I mean how is it translated and how does it produce an effect in France, or Italy, or Germany? I don't really like to answer that. What I think I would say is that the world which is summarized in *No Laughing Matter* (although it is altered a bit there because all the children succeed to some degree, they go up), the world of people going down, which is the world of my first stories, and the world I came out of, is the one phenomenon of English life (and it is a very important one in the English novel, the tradition of the gentleman or lady who has no longer got her position) that is unknown in America. In America if they lose their money they go. Talking to American people, I have always had to explain it; it's that part of my whole world that is really important which is unknown to them. I think it is very important because even though it is perhaps only in the first stories that it makes its appearance directly, it is the cause of the shape of my early novels, all my early novels, practically, not *The Old Men at the Zoo* but *Hemlock, Anglo-Saxon Attitudes, Mrs. Eliot* and *Late Call* are all about people who have lost something and that comes from this tremendous sense of the loss of caste in England and France. Half the novels are about old people that have seen better days. In America people disappear if they have seen better days, and if you were the daughter of a Senator and you haven't kept your money up, nobody has heard of you. This is not so, even today I think, in Europe. People can still reside on the gentility of their past, though nothing like what it was in my time.

CB   Can I ask you something else about your sense of the tradition of English writing? Your attachment to the nineteenth-century novel is very clear but what is it you find so compelling about it?

AW   I want to say very firmly that there are only two nineteenth-century novelists to whom I am deeply attached, and they are Dostoevsky and Dickens, and above all, Dickens.

CB   Not George Eliot.

AW   Oh no, no, no, no. I have as much doubts about George Eliot as I have about Forster.

CB   But is it the moral concern of Dosteovsky and Dickens, or what is it?

AW   No, you see this is why I have always thought the description of my novels as traditional was very odd. I remember when they first came out, when *Anglo-Saxon Attitudes* appeared in America, it was said it might not be appreciated by people who are not used to the old tradition of Dickens, as though Dickens was a tradition. He is a most extraordinary writer, unlike anybody else. The other writer for whom you know I have this enormous admiration is Richardson, but we needn't go into that, but he, too, was quite different to the rest of the eighteenth century. So the traditional English novel means nothing to me, if you mean by that George Eliot and Thackeray and Forster and Fielding, but Dickens was a person who I think was a fantastic, unconscious, experimentalist; I mean he found extraordinary forms and shapes to convey a nightmare and a dreamworld which was also a picture of the social world of his time and Dostoevsky has this to a great degree. Zola also. In my own work from the early days, the novels from *Hemlock* and certainly from *Anglo-Saxon Attitudes,* there is, I believe, something which is not at all traditional and which I don't find either in what is called the modern novel or the experimental novel, as it used to be called. It is the representation of the fact that in life we move along like this, which is called the narrative, and yet the whole of our life there are still other people existing, doing their thing, which is nothing to do with us, and which we are aware of, and which at certain moments we bang against. And that is what I call the ballet as opposed to the play of a novel, and this seems to be absolutely vital to great novels, the novels that I care for; *Bleak House* is a special example because it is where he wanted to point out that society was cruel and that people were disregarding it. All through that novel, despite the movement of the plot and what is happening to the central characters, there are these little people like Mrs Turveydrop and so on, doing their little ballets, round and round as though they were at the back of the stage.

Now to me, this was one of the great discoveries in novel writing that came to me. And from the earliest times I have tried to embody this in my writing. I don't think it is traditional, but it isn't experimental in the modernist sense at all, in the sense that modernism came to mean, which was Jamesian. I have never been really very influenced by James. I enjoy some of his work very much, but I have never been very influenced by him. It is this Dickensian, Dostoevskian thing which I have been excited by and it was the feeling that I had not got across that my work was in its own way quite revolutionary that led me to write *No Laughing Matter*, which was trying to do the same thing as I had always been doing, but doing it in a different form so that it should appear to be expressed. That is why I introduced those parodies and plays to express quite overtly what I felt I had always been doing, but that people just hadn't seemed to see. They seemed to think that I was writing a novel, as you say, like *Middlemarch* or something. As to the moral of the nineteenth-century novel, I detest the morality of *Middlemarch*. I teach *The Mill on the Floss* and, of course, I admire and respect her in many ways, and they are wonderful novels to read, but, oh no, I am a romantic, Chris, this is the first thing you must grasp about me, I think, I am essentially a romantic writer and am much more drawn to *Wuthering Heights* or *Jane Eyre* than I am to George Eliot.

CB It is curious you should say that because that is the next thing I wanted to ask you. Isn't there in fact, a romantic element in you. In your response to the natural world, and the intuitive spirit?

AW Yes, I am essentially a romantic writer I am quite certain. I am not an intellectual, never have been, and I am not a great moralist. I have at times been rather priggish in my life and there is an element of priggishness in some of my work, I am very well aware of it. *Hemlock and After,* for example, is a slightly priggish book. Mind you it was thought to be rather daring in its day; I am not now being nasty about myself, I mean it *was* daring. But on the other hand perhaps the kind of thing I feel now to be priggish is probably what I was unconsciously trying to get people to accept — what I was.

CB But I am surprised you are saying you are not a moral writer. I would have thought there was a very strong moral emphasis in your work, almost a desire to see some moral balance in your characters. You are worried about certain extremes; you are worried about quietism on the one hand, you are worried about total social commitment on the other hand, and to you the desirable area seems to lie in a sense of balance or continued tension or something of that kind.

AW Yes, how can I put this? They are being confronted with each other, these kinds of people, these different poles and I suppose that might suggest that I am asking people to find some sort of compromise.

CB It is the Jane Austen world I am thinking of.

AW You see the only book of Jane Austen's I really like is *Persuasion* because at the end it said she had married a sailor and so would know alarms. I don't mind *Mansfield Park*, I don't mind the fact that Fanny is a very priggish woman and so is Edmund. I mean they found happiness. What I can't bear is *Emma*. You haven't perhaps read the essay I have written about that, but it is all so terrible to me that this girl of wit and brilliance should be married off to this man, Mr Knightley, who is older than her and then in *Sense and Sensibility*, Marianne, who really is a wonderful person with tremendous passionate feeling, is married off to Colonel Brandon, who has white flannel waistcoats and so on. No, I can't bear it. No I am not at all a person of social stasis, I am a romantic person, a person of extreme temperament.

CB I didn't mean to imply social stasis, I meant a sense of moral balance.

AW I see, well my own emotional balance and nervous balance is very precarious, I have had one or two breakdowns though only one bad one, so it wouldn't be surprising if I seemed to be trying to find some such point, but let me be quite honest and say I have never found it in my life.

CB I suppose a case could be made for open endings as a characteristic of liberal novels, endings which imply new beginnings.

AW Yes.

CB But as a consequence isn't there inevitable doubt in the reader's mind as to whether whatever state of grace you have taken the individual characters to, whatever they have won through to, whether they will be able to carry that forward into the new life? I have had that doubt about *The Middle Age of Mrs. Eliot*. Clearly she makes the right decision, opting for an active life, but there is a kind of frenetic quality about that active life. She butterflies from one job to another in a manner which is rather reminiscent of the neurosis with which she started out.

AW Oh, you are quite right, I don't think she is a saved woman at all. That is a George Eliotish book in some ways. I am rather proud of it, but I think the scene where her brother David puts his hand back behind his chair to say goodnight to her and she has gone, is rather a sort of George Eliotish scene. You notice that I spoke about *Magic* having taken us abroad; it is notable that at the end of *Hemlock* Bernard's wife is flying, in the end of *Anglo-Saxon Attitudes* Gerald is just about to step into a plane to

Mexico, at the end of *Mrs. Eliot* Meg is with some Labour MP, she is on a plane she writes from. The other characters at the end of *No Laughing Matter* have all gone and settled in various places. They haven't found success; all I am saying is they must get away from *here*. They must get away. Don't settle down at Hartfield, get out, marry a sailor and know alarms. Why I think this is a step forward, in a way, in *Magic*, is that the characters go abroad early and Hamo dies and then Alexandra comes back to England and sees what she can do. She sees it is bloody little but she does come back. How awful it is at the end of *Middlemarch* that Lydgate is damned because he goes to London to become a doctor; it is not only awful but very silly because he probably had a much more interesting possibility of becoming a developed doctor in London than staying down in Middlemarch. The provincialism of the English novel, if that is any part of the liberal humane tradition, is absolutely awful to me.

CB But the irony at the end of *As If By Magic* is surely that her possibilities are created by money, that she is left money.

AW Yes they are, and there is a very limited amount she can do even then if she wants to what is called 'do good'.

CB She talks about herself as being a kind of deus ex machina.

AW Yes, she realizes that there is almost nothing, or very little she can do. In my present novel you will find they have become very rich. Well I won't go into that much, but once again it is going forward. I have left behind this business of going back and reflecting what has gone wrong.

CB Your characters, as you rightly stress, are always in a buzz of social activity, but at the heart of it all they are always intensely lonely people who are cut off from the world around them.

AW You see, I think I come back to the fact that, as the years have gone by, with the exception of a very few people, what I really care about are artifacts, and even more walking about in the countryside. There is this dilemma which has grown upon me and which first appears, I suppose, in *The Old Men at the Zoo*.

CB Yes, I want to come on to your attitude toward nature a little bit later. It seems to me you take your characters to the very edge of absurdity and even into self-parody.

AW And insanity too.

CB Right, and yet they are still battling on.

AW Oh yes, I believe in keeping going. Remember, and I have to say this, that despite all the awful part of my genteel upbringing, when we were about to be turned out of the hotel for not paying the bills and that kind of thing, or the deliveries from the tradesmen would be cut off, about every other month in my life, my grandmother would say 'but we had to carry on. We are Johnson Wilsons. What our class does matters.' Its deeply imbedded in me. I don't mean it nastily, I mean that was the one good thing about them, my God they did carry on.

CB But is the absurdity actually the path to grace?

AW It is part of it, but I think you have to be extremely careful. My brothers of the next generation, had a terrible upbringing and they had sad lives, never fulfilling themselves. They were very clever people. They never fulfilled themselves and they kept themselves going with a very witty mockery of life, and that comes out in *No Laughing Matter*. Absurdity is part of salvation but it is not enough.

CB I want to ask you about humour. Your books are very often extremely funny and your characters rely on humour as a way of dealing with things, dealing with pain and anguish.

AW Yes, that applies in my own life. These awful people you meet everywhere, they are all right really, but I do forget how awful they all are because they are so funny and that really does give me some capacity. You know me enough, Chris, to see that, confronted with any situation, if I suddenly see or hear someone say something absurd that can transform it for me. It is all right now because it is so funny.

CB On the other hand, we have got used, haven't we, in the last few decades, to humour being used in an ironic and reductive way?

AW Yes, I hope my books are not reductive. I was talking about this at the Sorbonne. The reason I turned from the short story and perhaps the pressing reason why I took that very great step of leaving the British Museum so that I could write longer novels, because I had written *Hemlock* and it seemed to me too tight, was a feeling that in those books, in those stories and everything, almost inevitably the mockery of life would come out and none of the depth of feeling. I think that the only other thing I could have done if I had gone on writing like that is that I could have pushed through the mockery into some kind of sentimental-ity. I think short stories are a bit like that. If you look at Katherine Mansfield you will see that she is a very clever person but her stories so often turn out either sentimental or purely mocking. And I felt it as a limitation. All my work has been an attempt to get away from all this. It has meant a great decrease in sales because I had already been typed that way. I was always regarded as this man with a serpent's tongue and all that kind of thing, and this isn't what I wanted. I was very pleased at the books' success, but I wanted to express more of myself than that. So a great deal of my work has been saying, yes, absurdity is part of the salvation of people, but to be able to see absurdity is not an adequate way of seeing human beings.

CB   And yet that raises the question of how you regard those writers who do seem to do that. I noticed, reading something you had written, that you regard Beckett as a humanist.

AW   Yes, I think I do.

CB   Is that simply because he cares enough about people to write about them or do you see him identifying qualities that are desirable or admirable?

AW   He writes about human beings when they have been reduced almost to nothing, and the humanity of them still seems to matter to him enough for him to write about them. I believe he could write something that would make you feel, at least make me feel, moved about a ward of people who had become cabbages *because* they were human beings. And that is a very remarkable thing. That is why I described him as a humanist. If you take another person who is a brilliant writer full of ridicule, Evelyn Waugh, his humanity is shown in a slightly different way. It is shown sometimes by the depth of his sense of unhappiness, and sometimes by the depth of his savagery towards people. I am not a wholly savage person, far from it, so it has been quite a battle. I don't think I have ever expressed in my novels the compassion that I think I can feel. And that perhaps is in part because it is difficult for me. I can write the comic side of Dickens but I am frightened of letting myself go in a way which might produce the really rather terrible sentimental side of Dickens. The only book that has that quality, and it did get criticized in that way by some people, is *Late Call*. There is an element there, the treatment of Sylvia, which comes near to some kind of Victorian sentimental approach to human beings.

CB   I suppose it is a risk that when you set up personal relationships, love between people, as being something which can neutralize power in other things you are constantly on the edge of a sentimentality.

AW   I think so, there is a danger there.

CB   And yet that is the resource that you would put forward isn't it?

AW   Yes, so far. I hope my new book* will be different. It has a very, very deep love between two brothers which is vital to the book. If that doesn't come off, the book won't come off. So far I feel I haven't really successfully suggested the importance of love between human beings, though I think I did succeed, and I am proud of it, in *Late Call* which is about a very simple person and not falsely simple. I mean I haven't made her into a sort of illiterate or something, I made her into a typical simple person of our time. And I don't think many writers in the twentieth century, who are clever, and I suppose I am what is called a clever writer, have been able to write about simple people.

CB   In the *Paris Review* interview, two decades ago, you expressed surprise when Frank O'Connor described you as an experimental writer, because then you were saying you were getting back to the Dickens tradition. I think you thought of Dickens in a rather different way probably at that time did you not?

AW   Well, yes I did in that sense. I'll tell you what made me amazed with Frank O'Connor. I used what seemed to me such a simple device, namely that business where Gerald 'thinks back', where a simple remark at a Christmas party carries him back to some event in his life. It was a pretty cumbrous device. I am not all that proud of that book. But he said, 'Why can't Mr Wilson tell his stories in a straightforward way, why does he have to use his experiments?' So I think my surprise was not so much that he should have called me an experimental writer but that he should have thought that was an experiment. If the man had read Joyce how could he think that that was an experiment? I couldn't quite understand it.

CB   On the other hand, I think anyone writing about you now would say that you were an experimental novelist, or that there was that very strong strain of experimentalism.

AW   Yes, I think both the last two novels, not the one I have just written which is perhaps less so, though we shall see, but certainly *No Laughing Matter* and *Magic* have strongly experimental things in. I let myself go first in doing something different in *The Old Men at the Zoo* and that was badly received, very badly received. That has been my difficulty, as far as establishing a public goes, because each novel has been so very different. They had just come to think that I was the person who understood middle-aged women and their dilemmas and so on, and so why the

Setting the World on Fire (1980).

hell is this man writing this awful science fiction thing. This would be the kind of thing people who liked *Mrs. Eliot* said. So I think that is the difficulty. And equally, on the other hand, people that liked the experiment of *The Old Men at the Zoo* were surprised at such a traditional novel as *Late Call* which came next. Although, then again, I can remember John Bowen, who is not a silly man, writing a review of that and saying 'it is strange that Angus Wilson should think it necessary to have this prologue. He doesn't seem to see that we are living in the twentieth century. He writes as though it was the eighteenth century. He even has a heading "The Old Woman's Tale." ' I knew what I was doing; I wasn't mad. So this business about experiment has been very difficult for me to understand and this is to do with Lubbock and James.

I think that for lots and lots of people, especially those who have coined or used the word 'modern' or 'modernist', the tendency is to suppose that experiment can only be identified post-Jamesian and is in some way connected with the Jamesian view about the narrator and so on. There are certain experimental novels which are absolutely vital for me. I suppose closer to me than any other novels in the twentieth century are *The Waves* and *Mrs Dalloway*, and they could be called experimental novels. But they do have this same thing that I am concerned with; they tie on to the kind of novel I like to write. I don't know, it is awfully difficult for me to understand why O'Connor said that about *Anglo-Saxon Attitudes*. I mean my objection to that book now would be that it seems to me cumbrous, I think it is rather good, some of it, but it seems to me cumbrous, especially in the telling, the rather obvious ways of going back into the past. I like to think I'd find something which flowed more easily than that now. With *Hemlock,* for example, it is quite a different thing, and that is sad because I think it is a very good novel in its way, but you see I hadn't been a novelist, I hadn't been a novelist at all, I had only written some short stories and I didn't really know anything. I wasn't conscious of what a creative artist was like, so that it seems to me that that is a good novel but that the hero, who is said to be a novelist, is really a headmaster of a school or something. There is no evidence of his being a creative writer at all in the book.

CB By the time you get to *No Laughing Matter,* though, you are playing very intricate games.

AW Yes, and I think that Margaret there is a real creative person. That's drawn out of my own experience. I think the parody there is very important.

CB   Why? Was that supposed to underline the fact that they were self-dramatizing characters?

AW   Yes, that very much is to do with the fact they are trying to make everything into a laughing matter but it can't be done that way. So these plays, these witty little plays, were a consequence of the fact that they were a theatrical kind of family, and so I wrote parodies of the plays of the period. They were, perhaps, a bit over subtle, especially the Chekhov one, and I am a bit worried about it. The Chekhov one, for example, is not so much a parody of Chekhov, as of English popular Chekhov of the thirties, as it was played by John Gielgud. I am pleased with that novel, I still think in a way that is my best, but I became a little worried that I had played a bit too many games just as I think that people who said, 'I did enjoy your *Anglo-Saxon Attitudes,* it is really a good English novel of the kind that we ought to see come back', that used to drive me mad. Equally, when I had done *No Laughing Matter* it annoyed me a bit when people said, 'Oh, I am fascinated, you have at last begun to really *write* haven't you?' It is a bit annoying.

CB   There is of course a novelist in there, in fact the family are all basically artists, writers, novelists or whatever.

AW   The old father, if you remember, always thought he imagined Arnold Bennett writing to him and saying he was one of the finest writers of our time.

CB   That's right. But the description of the kind of novel that the woman writes, the Carmichael novel, seems actually not very far away from the kind of novel you write as well.

AW   And also my short stories especially. She is very close to me, very, very close to me, Margaret.

CB   So is the book partly about the process of fictionalizing? Not only as artists but to the degree that all of them are constantly fictionalizing?

AW   And it is also about how that doesn't finally solve it.

CB   Is that why the heroine of *As if by Magic* actually wanted to turn her back on that process at the end of that book?

AW   Absolutely, yes. As you know, my central figure in my new book is a theatrical producer, but his brother is a lawyer. And I will just tell you this, it is an imaginary house built by Pratt and finished by Vanbrugh with a vast dome, which is a house which still survives near Westminster Abbey, and the dome is painted with the fall of Phaethon. We begin with the two boys, the elder one, who becomes the theatrical producer, is transported from the age of 8. When he first comes there, he wants to be Phaethon, he wants to go and drive those chariots. He thinks it's wonderful even if you go down. And the other boy believes that this world will crumble and tremble and collapse, that this man will bring the whole world down on us. They are absolutely devoted throughout their lives and the book ends in their late twenties. One becomes a theatrical producer and inherits the house, and the other is a lawyer, and it is called *Setting the World on Fire* which is deliberately ambiguous.

But so you see, here again I have got this, you are right to say Jane Austen, tension between order on the one hand, this tremendous sense of the need for order, and the need for freedom. And even my theatrical producer one, who wants to be Phaethon, he ends by saying yes, but we can't have Vanbrugh unless it is on the foundation of a properly constructed Pratt. I do believe in order and shape for books. I don't believe in happenings and Edward Bondism and all that. But on the other hand I do believe that great art is the symbol of what is worth doing. So it is always there that tension, which is in Jane Austen, even though she seems always to come down on the side of order, and that is why I love that book where she says 'marry a sailor and face alarms', because you must, I think. To me the only thing you can ever do is to say this is wonderful and that is the most exciting experience I have ever had, and my God it may last only one second longer. But on the other hand when you are in terror and anxiety, and the whole world seems to be cracking beneath your feet, it is still lifted up by this feeling that it might turn into exultation, so these two things go together with me deeply. A romantic trying to make shapes because he realizes that the romantic temperament is liable to go off the edge of the precipice. And if I tell you that I myself adore wandering about in the jungle but can't very easily go over bridges because I think they may collapse under me, you have the two things.

CB Do you in fact think of character, of individual character, as a real self buried underneath pretence and self deception, or as a series of roles. What is your model of character?

AW You mean a character in real life?

CB In real life and in your work.

AW I think that it is both. I think that the surface thing is the role playing, and some people never do more than live the surface role, playing life. But I think that anybody who has lived seriously is aware at certain moments that when they put off their role and they are left on their own, they are still faced with what lies inside themselves. So there is this double thing. Character is both a series of role playings, in the social sense, and the fact that somewhere inside the real person is the mystery that we are more than one real person.

CB   You talked about *The Middle Age of Mrs. Eliot* as being your most existential novel. Did you mean by that the fact that she reconstructs her identity, she remakes herself?

AW   She is, more than anybody else, finding her own existence. But of course I hadn't then written *Late Call*, and that is the same thing.

CB   But what kind of freedom do you actually see the individual as having, because that process requires a notion of freedom doesn't it?

AW   What it is, is being able to bear the acceptance of what you have to.

CB   That is the extent of the freedom.

AW   That's the freedom. Once you really can bear it then you are free.

CB   Can I come on to something you raised earlier, that is the question of the natural world? You talk in *The Old Men at the Zoo* of the need to nourish yourself through contact with the natural world and one of the things about Simon Carter is that he fails to do that for most of the novel; he has unplugged himself. So that the way the individuals in all your novels respond to that world is a way of finding out what their moral worth is. But we are living in a world now in which the predominant reality is an urban one, so does that mean that that image is a source of pessimism to you, that we are moving away from that contact which is so precious?

AW   Yes, it is. And the only substitute I can find is art and artifacts, especially architecture and this is why you will find that the two wicked things (well there are many wicked things) done in *Magic,* represent these two things. The one is that those small boys pelt the dugong with stones and bricks and the other is that Sir James is going to pull down decent looking houses and build ones which he knows are bloody bad and doesn't mind because they are prestige buildings. Now they represent the two dreadful things you can do. And it seems to me that if you can kill thoughtlessly, for fun, defenceless creatures, like dugongs, which are essentially something which is a dying species, and can pull down comely buildings (I won't give them even more than that, comely buildings) and put up things which you know are bloody awful for the sake of business prestige, then you can do anything to any human beings. And so although I am treating animals and see it in terms of animals and buildings, it is really a statement about human values.

CB   I see that, but couldn't you argue that there is something rather sentimental, escapist about that, in that the natural world is a way of getting away from the complexities of human relationships. The natural world is also strongly deterministic and really a rather violent world.

AW   Of course it is. There are other creatures that will destroy the dugong. But I have never been able to be satisfied that this Darwinian statement about the natural world is a good enough excuse for saying that I should destroy them as well. I find them a beauty, and I find the natural world of intense beauty; it is a hard word to define, but I am happy, I am filled with happiness in the natural scene, and I am filled with happiness when I see lovely buildings.

CB   But isn't that associated with what you describe as a kind of growing misanthropy?

AW   Yes it is, but I can only say that since that is so, I must learn to respect the natural world and the world of artifacts and hope that the respect that I have for those will work in relation to human beings insofar as I am involved with them. I think most people could do with a good deal more to balance against the social scene in the form of a feeling for artifacts or for natural scenery, but maybe they get it in the form of sports or something of this kind, but some kind of balance is required. What I do not believe is that you can become a person who is more humane or a better person towards other people by becoming what is called gregarious. I have seen too much of it and it is there in my early books; I lived in that way. That is to say, 'What I like is to meet lots of people and to be about with them.' But then you find yourself just being spiteful because you hate it so much. I can't see the force of that. But I do have to add that I am sure that my own work is in danger of, and may have already suffered from, a certain lack of the sharpness and fierceness, which perhaps I had when I first started writing. I went to every literary party there was and so on. I don't know how I survived. But there is a certain give and take of human experience, especially if you sit on committees or anything like that (I used to do quite a lot of that, and I don't want to do it any more, I know about it) and I think it may be that not doing that could freeze one's work a little bit, it could take a bit of life out of it. That is a danger, and in seeking to get away from sheer bitchery, which is what I feel is so present in a lot of my early work, and which is something I find so awful in human intercourse, in seeking to get away from that, I could have lost a bit of life.

CB   You use this natural world in another way. In *The Old Men at the Zoo* bear-bating becomes a kind of correlative of the social evil that you identify. Do you actually believe in evil as such or isn't that a kind of sentimentality. I am thinking particularly of Mrs Curry in *Hemlock and After*.

AW   Well, I do greatly love and admire *Clarissa,* almost more than any other novel, but I don't think that any of us, any writer, even before Jane Austen, could really think that they have any real belief in evil, in the sense that Richardson really did believe in evil and in good. It is no longer possible to write characters like Clarissa.

CB   Well, except that I was struck by something that Arthur Miller said once and that is that he regretted not having made Judge Danforth in *The Crucible* more evil because as a result of the war he had come to believe that evil actually did exist.

AW   Well of course it does exist, I agree, but it is all relative still to some extent; absolute evil, as was understood by Richardson, I think is no longer there. But real evil, yes I do believe in that. The other great crisis for the people of my generation was the revelation of the concentration camps, that what I had regarded as something which was to be found in Renaissance Italy was going on at my own time. I think people accept it now because it has been going on since then, and it always had been going on, as really one knows, but we didn't think so. Certainly people thought that somewhere from about 1850 things had changed, and they hadn't. So yes, I think I did believe, not in absolute evil, because that does mean some kind of positive religious belief which I just haven't got, but the existence of evil. Yes I am pretty sure of that. I am not quite sure that I would so easily identify it now. I think it is a simplistic thing that I so much identified it in my early works with a kind of sentimentality and sweetness. But I do think over-sweetness and over-sentimentality are very suspicious to me and I do think that going on in a sort of sweet childish way is likely to mean that underneath is some sort of moronic cruelty.

CB   You have said that all fiction is a kind of confidence trick in that you are trying to make people believe something is true that isn't. Do you see that as a moral question? Certain writers (Coover or Fowles come to mind) deal with that question by constantly reminding they readers that in fact it is trickery.

AW I have done that more in my last works perhaps because I felt able to. I think when I first started writing I didn't feel the confidence to do that, but it is also true that I do. I am not convinced that this is really a genuine way of avoiding tricking the reader; I think it is what might be called a double confidence trick. It is a well known thing that confidence tricksters frequently get away with it by simply saying that 'I'm a confidence trickster, ha, ha, ha.' So that I think what one wants, if you write a novel, is for your readers emotionally to accept your book.

CB But that makes you a manipulator and you are suspicious in your books of manipulators.

AW Yes. All one can then say is two things which I suppose confidence tricksters might say. One thing certainly they might say is 'I do hope you have a good time', and the other one I suppose is, 'Well you must remember that what I have told you has been awfully good for you hasn't it?' I am a little more worried about that, that comes nearer to the kind of patronizing liberal humanist I don't like. So that if you ask me for the justification for writing, it is that I just enjoy novels enormously myself and when I start to write them they seem to me very exciting, and I can only hope I shall convey it to other people. And a better thing than that, a very much better thing than that, is that I think a vast number of people just don't think what life is for or why or what they are doing, or even think about it very much and when they read novels they find themselves thinking about it and that is a very good thing.

CB John Fowles has said he feels there to be a gravitational pull towards realism in the novel and that he has felt it more and more strongly as the years have gone by. Do you recognize that?

AW I don't know. I mean yes, when one is writing one tries to make it as real as possible. I have just been writing today and I think I'll just read over what I wrote yesterday, and I'll say to myself, 'Yes but look here, would he have said this, I'll just alter that, this word would have been slightly different, he wouldn't have used that expression.' But I don't want the total thing to be something that people would feel to be like a photograph.

CB I don't think that is what Fowles means actually by realism.

AW Does he mean social realism? No.

CB No, I don't think he means social realism. I think it is a commitment to the real, a commitment to the real which may be expressed through a number of approaches.

AW Well, in that case I am on his side entirely.

CB   Not a hermetic, not a self-referential world.

AW   I can't do that. I think that some writers who are seen to be very traditional are really hermetic in just that way. But there are others like Firbank, for example, who, at his best, would seem to be like that, but is really immensely real in the sense that he is really writing about what he really cares about, and what he wants to write about. One uses games playing because it involves the reader, but I can't imagine writing any novel myself in which I just sat down and thought, let's have a bit of fun. To that extent I am a serious writer.

CB   In recent years, and I think that is reflected in your work, boundaries of various kinds have been broken down. Class boundaries, age boundaries, and to some degree sexual boundaries have got blurred over the last few years. In a way that may be a minor concern of *As If By Magic*. Is that actually a growing concern of yours, is it something that engages you, the collapse of old orders? Now you are writing about the aristocracy, maybe it isn't.

AW   No, anyway there are other people in that, although it finally is about the wealthy more than the aristocracy. They have had their money since the mid-eighteenth century but they have inherited a house which was from a family of the sixteenth century. I don't think I regret any of it insofar as it is too late for me to adapt and therefore I feel a bit left out. You know the young people in *Magic,* for example, they come from the younger generation that I knew, my great nephews and their friends and the hippy people that I met in India and so on. I liked them very much and if I feel any resentment against them it is that I can't easily fit in. That is an old man's resentment of life changing.

CB   But there is a negative side of that as well and that is that the collapse of these old systems of order leads to a kind of viscosity and people move rather uncertainly.

AW   Yes, of course they do, but so they have done, haven't they, always. I mean orders were breaking down enormously in my life time and they were breaking down in the 1830s.

CB   But Alexandra in *As If By Magic* tries to replace those kinds of orders by other kinds of magics which she invokes.

AW   Indeed, and I have suggested that, along with science, none of these magics work. But I hope it is clear that she is my favourite of all my heroines and my heroines are my favourite characters. Mostly I don't like the men in my books very much; the heroes seem to me somewhat dead, whereas the three women,

Meg Eliot, Sylvia and Alexandra, do seem to me to be living people and of those I am most fond of her really. I very much like women, not necessarily this self-consciousness of Women's Lib now, but I very much like women who have guts and courage. You see all the time I say that about Women's Lib, that shows you what I mean. I have always been regarded as a person who was on the side of women, but a lot of Women's Libism now I don't feel in touch with at all. I have been one of the first people to write about gay life but there are aspects of Gay Lib and so on which leave me quite cold. I think I may be quite justified in not caring for them but I think it is only that as you get older the world changes and you really see that at 65 you won't have time to catch up with this and perhaps it is just a resentment of the fact that the world is going to go on when you have gone. I must say this, with all my love of artifacts and of natural life, I would love to live for another 200 years just to know what people are going to be and whether they will be as funny as they have been in my day and so on.

CB As you just said, a number of your novels have had homosexual characters. In the early books that took place against a background in which homosexuality was actually illegal and consequently, I think, invested with a kind of mystery as far as a large percentage of the population was concerned. It was an unknown world. Now that world has actually gone, does that mean that in a sense its power as an image and as a fact has diminished? Do you have a sense of dealing with it differently now?

AW Well I haven't had many gay characters who belong to the modern gay world and Hamo is very much of the closet world.

CB Except that he lives in the new world.

AW Yes, but he is very much of the closet world, that is the nature of him, and it is a tragic world. I mean any outlawed world is a tragic world. Even Alexandra, in that book, is still fighting a woman's battle but not in a way that now is being fought by Women's Lib people. I think all my characters do belong to a world where people were fighting to get through the barriers. Now those barriers, as you say, have been broken down to a great degree. You may be right in thinking that there is a resentment somewhere there or a dislike of the viscosity of it. I certainly do like shape in life so it could well be that now these barriers have gone I feel a lack of shape. But I come back to the fact that my suspicion is that the reason I don't like it is that I can't participate in it.

CB To ask something about the way in which you write, why do you favour so strongly the third-person narrative?

AW　I have only written one book in the first person. I often wonder about that. I think it is that first of all I very much want to go inside the consciousness of more than one person within a book, I usually do. In this present book I have tried to keep it to two people. But I do dislike the first person very much. I don't know why I used it in *The Old Men at the Zoo*. When I open a book, even *David Copperfield* and *Great Expectations* as opposed to other books by Dickens, it puts me off a little because I feel this. I, as a reader, have this resistance as soon as I open a book saying 'I'. I have an absolute resistance to 'I' as used by Conrad, where it's a narrator. I like some of Conrad's books but from the moment that Marlow starts to talk I think, this is a bloody bore, and I shut my mind. But even when people are narrating their own story, I think, well that's enough of that, you have told us enough about yourself, and so I don't easily write in that way because I know I resist it as a reader.

CB　There are lots of kinds of ironies, however, which you can play with when you are using a narrator figure.

AW　Yes, of course you can, but I don't really want to write a book which is like that. There is a short story I have written which is of the kind you are speaking, it is called 'More Friend than Lodger', and it is about a publisher's wife who gives herself away as being a proper bitch and a bit dotty at that. But I wouldn't want to write a whole novel which at the end you think, 'Ha ha! I see, so she didn't know.' It doesn't seem quite worthwhile.

CB　Is there such a thing as a literary community in England?

AW　Well yes, I am sure there is, but not in the sense that there is on the Continent, nor as there is in New York. But there is a literary life in London, I think. I am not one to speak to very much about it because I don't spend much of my time in it. When I went to Stephen Spender's seventieth birthday party, there were a whole mixture of people there, academic and literary people, all sorts. Yes, there is, I think; if you look at the *New Review* you get that feeling. May I just tell you a story about a French reporter coming here. It was when the EEC negotiations had broken down and the French papers decided to say what English writers thought about this. Can you imagine English papers asking a lot of writers? This Frenchman arrived here and he had been to Evelyn Waugh in Somerset and to Iris in Oxford and he said 'Mais pourquoi vous n'êtes pas à Londres?' And he couldn't understand it. It was incredible to him that he couldn't find the literary world within a narrrow compass.

CB   Yet there is an irony in a solitary individual sitting there eight hours a day writing about the need for human contact.

AW   Yes it is. It is a big paradox of a writer's life. I had to write a lecture about being a writer and I say that as a child I lived in these hotels and I was like an only child, and I was the only child in the hotel and part of the time was spent in the sitting room, drawing room as it was called, with people chatting their heads off, grown-up people, and I didn't know what they were talking about. Then I would go up to my room and I would make games up such as you get in my children's stories. And sometimes I would think how wonderful to be on my own up in that room and sometimes when I was up there I would think, why can't I go down. And I would creep down and they wouldn't say anything, and I would stand there while there were masses of old colonels and divorced ladies screaming their heads off and I would just stand there. And so I think that a writer's life is an enormous conflict. Just as you want lots of human contact because you feel you lack material for writing you reach a moment when you have your belly full of people and you want to sit down and start the book. It is a very strange profession, very, very, strange, more strange I think than a painter because a painter has the model. Or maybe not. I suppose it must be a bit odd when people are evoking life, like the impressionists were, when they have finished their original sketches and then shut themselves up in the studio to bring life alive on the canvas. But the only thing like this, isn't it, is drama writing, and even drama writing, as I know when I wrote for the theatre or the television theatre, is much easier because there comes a point when you do actually come into contact with people and the whole thing is brought alive by people with you being involved. But this thing is, as you say, solitary confinement, and God knows what the other is but involving yourself with as much of life as you can. And if I have implied that I cut myself off altogether that would not be true; all it means is that I no longer mix so much with a particular group. I spend my time going to all sorts of other places but being involved with people, it is a paradox. I think it is what makes all writers rather tiresome.